The Memoirs of Victor Hugo

The Memoirs of Victor Hugo

Victor Hugo

MINT EDITIONS

The Memoirs of Victor Hugo was first published in 1899.

This edition published by Mint Editions 2021.

ISBN 9781513291352 | E-ISBN 9781513294209

Published by Mint Editions®

MINT
EDITIONS

minteditionbooks.com

Publishing Director: Jennifer Newens
Design & Production: Rachel Lopez Metzger
Project Manager: Micaela Clark
Translated by: John William Harding
Typesetting: Westchester Publishing Services

Contents

Preface

This volume of memoirs has a double character—historical and intimate. The life of a period, the XIX Century, is bound up in the life of a man, VICTOR HUGO. As we follow the events set forth we get the impression they made upon the mind of the extraordinary man who recounts them; and of all the personages he brings before us he himself is assuredly not the least interesting. In portraits from the brushes of Rembrandts there are always two portraits, that of the model and that of the painter.

This is not a diary of events arranged in chronological order, nor is it a continuous autobiography. It is less and it is more, or rather, it is better than these. It is a sort of haphazard *chronique* in which only striking incidents and occurrences are brought out, and lengthy and wearisome details are avoided. VICTOR HUGO's long and chequered life was filled with experiences of the most diverse character—literature and politics, the court and the street, parliament and the theatre, labour, struggles, disappointments, exile and triumphs. Hence we get a series of pictures of infinite variety.

Let us pass the gallery rapidly in review.

It opens in 1825, at Rheims, during the coronation of CHARLES X, with an amusing *causerie* on the manners and customs of the Restoration. The splendour of this coronation ceremony was singularly spoiled by the pitiable taste of those who had charge of it. These worthies took upon themselves to mutilate the sculpture work on the marvellous façade and to "embellish" the austere cathedral with Gothic decorations of cardboard. The century, like the author, was young, and in some things both were incredibly ignorant; the masterpieces of literature were then unknown to the most learned *littérateurs*: CHARLES NODIER had never read the "Romancero", and VICTOR HUGO knew little or nothing about Shakespeare.

At the outset the poet dominates in VICTOR HUGO; he belongs wholly to his creative imagination and to his literary work. It is the theatre; it is his "Cid", and "Hernani", with its stormy performances; it is the group of his actors, Mlle. MARS, Mlle. GEORGES, FREDERICK LEMAITRE, the French KEAN, with more genius; it is the Academy, with its different kind of coteries.

About this time Victor Hugo questions, anxiously and not in vain, a passer-by who witnessed the execution of Louis XVI, and an officer who escorted Napoleon to Paris on his return from the Island of Elba.

Next, under the title, "Visions of the Real", come some sketches in the master's best style, of things seen "in the mind's eye," as Hamlet says. Among them "The Hovel" will attract attention. This sketch resembles a page from Edgar Poe, although it was written long before Poe's works were introduced into France.

With "Love in Prison" Victor Hugo deals with social questions, in which he was more interested than in political questions. And yet, in entering the Chamber of Peers he enters public life. His sphere is enlarged, he becomes one of the familiars of the Tuileries. Louis Philippe, verbose and full of recollections that he is fond of imparting to others, seeks the company and appreciation of this listener of note, and makes all sorts of confidences to him. The King with his very haughty bonhomie and his somewhat infatuated wisdom; the grave and sweet Duchess D'Orleans, the boisterous and amiable princes—the whole commonplace and home-like court—are depicted with kindliness but sincerity.

The horizon, however, grows dark, and from 1846 the new peer of France notes the gradual tottering of the edifice of royalty. The revolution of 1848 bursts out. Nothing could be more thrilling than the account, hour by hour, of the events of the three days of February. Victor Hugo is not merely a spectator of this great drama, he is an actor in it. He is in the streets, he makes speeches to the people, he seeks to restrain them; he believes, with too good reason, that the Republic is premature, and, in the Place de la Bastille, before the evolutionary Faubourg Saint Antoine, he dares to proclaim the Regency.

Four months later distress provokes the formidable insurrection of June, which is fatal to the Republic.

The year 1848 is the stormy year. The atmosphere is fiery, men are violent, events are tragical. Battles in the streets are followed by fierce debates in the Assembly. Victor Hugo takes part in the mêlée. We witness the scenes with him; he points out the chief actors to us. His "Sketches" made in the National Assembly are "sketched from life" in the fullest acceptation of the term. Twenty lines suffice. Odilon Barrot and Changarnier, Prudhon and Blanqui, Lamartine and "Monsieur Thiers" come, go, speak—veritable living figures.

The most curious of the figures is LOUIS BONAPARTE when he arrived in Paris and when he assumed the Presidency of the Republic. He is gauche, affected, somewhat ridiculous, distrusted by the Republicans, and scoffed at by the Royalists. Nothing could be more suggestive or more piquant than the inauguration dinner at the Elysee, at which VICTOR HUGO was one of the guests, and the first and courteous relations between the author of "Napoleon the Little" and the future Emperor who was to inflict twenty years of exile upon him.

But now we come to the year which VICTOR HUGO has designated "The Terrible Year," the war, and the siege of Paris. This part of the volume is made up of extracts from note-books, private and personal notes, dotted down from day to day. Which is to say that they do not constitute an account of the oft-related episodes of the siege, but tell something new, the little side of great events, the little incidents of everyday life, the number of shells fired into the city and what they cost, the degrees of cold, the price of provisions, what is being said, sung, and eaten, and at the same time give the psychology of the great city, its illusions, revolts, wrath, anguish, and also its gaiety; for during these long months Paris never gave up hope and preserved an heroic cheerfulness.

On the other hand a painful note runs through the diary kept during the meeting of the Assembly at Bordeaux. France is not only vanquished, she is mutilated. The conqueror demands a ransom of milliards—it is his right, the right of the strongest; but he tears from her two provinces, with their inhabitants devoted to France; it is a return towards barbarism. VICTOR HUGO withdraws indignantly from the Assembly which has agreed to endorse the Treaty of Frankfort. And three days after his resignation he sees CHARLES HUGO, his eldest son, die a victim to the privations of the siege. He is stricken at once in his love of country and in his paternal love, and one can say that in these painful pages, more than in any of the others, the book is history that has been lived.

PAUL MAURICE
Paris, Sept. 15, 1899

At Rheims, 1823–1838

It was at Rheims that I heard the name of Shakespeare for the first time. It was pronounced by Charles Nodier. That was in 1825, during the coronation of Charles X.

No one at that time spoke of Shakespeare quite seriously. Voltaire's ridicule of him was law. Mme. de Staël had adopted Germany, the great land of Kant, of Schiller, and of Beethoven. Ducis was at the height of his triumph; he and Delille were seated side by side in academic glory, which is not unlike theatrical glory. Ducis had succeeded in doing something with Shakespeare; he had made him possible; he had extracted some "tragedies" from him; Ducis impressed one as being a man who could chisel an Apollo out of Moloch. It was the time when Iago was called Pezare; Horatio, Norceste; and Desdemona, Hedelmone. A charming and very witty woman, the Duchess de Duras, used to say: "Desdemona, what an ugly name! Fie!" Talma, Prince of Denmark, in a tunic of lilac satin trimmed with fur, used to exclaim: "Avaunt! Dread spectre!" The poor spectre, in fact, was only tolerated behind the scenes. If it had ventured to put in the slightest appearance M. Evariste Dumoulin would have given it a severe talking to. Some Génin or other would have hurled at it the first cobble-stone he could lay his hand on—a line from Boileau: *L'esprit n'est point ému de ce qu'il ne croit pas.* It was replaced on the stage by an "urn" that Talma carried under his arm. A spectre is ridiculous; "ashes," that's the style! Are not the "ashes" of Napoleon still spoken of? Is not the translation of the coffin from St. Helena to the Invalides alluded to as "the return of the ashes"? As to the witches of Macbeth, they were rigorously barred. The hall-porter of the Théâtre-Français had his orders. They would have been received with their own brooms.

I am mistaken, however, in saying that I did not know Shakespeare. I knew him as everybody else did, not having read him, and having treated him with ridicule. My childhood began, as everybody's childhood begins, with prejudices. Man finds prejudices beside his cradle, puts them from him a little in the course of his career, and often, alas! takes to them again in his old age.

During this journey in 1825 Charles Nodier and I passed our time recounting to each other the Gothic tales and romances that have taken root in Rheims. Our memories and sometimes our imaginations, clubbed together. Each of us furnished his legend. Rheims is one of the most impossible towns in the geography of story. Pagan lords have lived there, one of whom gave as a dower to his daughter the strips of land in Borysthenes called the "race-courses of Achilles." The Duke de Guyenne, in the fabliaux, passes through Rheims on his way to besiege Babylon; Babylon, moreover, which is very worthy of Rheims, is the capital of the Admiral Gaudissius. It is at Rheims that the deputation sent by the Locri Ozolae to Apollonius of Tyana, "high priest of Bellona," "disembarks." While discussing this disembarkation we argued concerning the Locri Ozolae. These people, according to Nodier, were called the Fetidae because they were half monkeys; according to myself, because they inhabited the marshes of Phocis. We reconstructed on the spot the tradition of St. Remigius and his adventures with the fairy Mazelane. The Champagne country is rich in tales. Nearly all the old Gaulish fables had their origin in this province. Rheims is the land of chimeras. It is perhaps for this reason that kings were crowned there.

Legends are so natural to this place, are in such good soil, that they immediately began to germinate upon the coronation of Charles X itself. The Duke of Northumberland, the representative of England at the coronation ceremonies, was reputed fabulously wealthy. Wealthy and English, how could he be otherwise than *a la mode*? The English, at that period, were very popular in French society, although not among the people. They were liked in certain salons because of Waterloo, which was still fairly recent, and to Anglicize the French language was a recommendation in ultra-fashionable society. Lord Northumberland, therefore, long before his arrival, was popular and legendary in Rheims. A coronation was a godsend to Rheims. A flood of opulent people inundated the city. It was the Nile that was passing. Landlords rubbed their hands with glee.

There was in Rheims in those days, and there probably is today, at the corner of a street giving on to the square, a rather large house with a carriage-entrance and a balcony, built of stone in the royal style of Louis XIV, and facing the cathedral. About this house and Lord Northumberland the following was related:

In January, 1825, the balcony of the house bore the notice: "House for Sale." All at once the "Moniteur" announced that the coronation of Charles X would take place at Rheims in the spring. There was great rejoicing in the city. Notices of rooms to let were immediately hung out everywhere. The meanest room was to bring in at least sixty francs a day. One morning a man of irreproachable appearance, dressed in black, with a white cravat, an Englishman who spoke broken French, presented himself at the house in the square. He saw the proprietor, who eyed him attentively.

"You wish to sell your house?" queried the Englishman.

"How much?"

"Ten thousand francs."

"But I don't want to buy it."

"What do you want, then?"

"Only to hire it."

"That's different. For a year?"

"For six months?"

"No. I want to hire it for three days."

"How much will you charge?"

"Thirty thousand francs."

The gentleman was Lord Northumberland's steward, who was looking for a lodging for his master for the coronation ceremonies. The proprietor had smelled the Englishman and guessed the steward. The house was satisfactory, and the proprietor held out for his price; the Englishman, being only a Norman, gave way to the Champenois; the duke paid the 30,000 francs, and spent three days in the house, at the rate of 400 francs an hour.

Nodier and I were two explorers. When we travelled together, as we occasionally did, we went on voyages of discovery, he in search of rare books, I in search of ruins. He would go into ecstasies over a *Cymbalum Mound* with margins, and I over a defaced portal. We had given each other a devil. He said to me: "You are possessed of the demon Ogive." "And you," I answered, "of the demon Elzevir."

At Soissons, while I was exploring Saint Jean-des-Vignes, he had discovered, in a suburb, a ragpicker. The ragpicker's basket is the hyphen between rags and paper, and the ragpicker is the hyphen between the beggar and the philosopher. Nodier who gave to the poor, and sometimes to philosophers, had entered the ragpicker's abode. The ragpicker turned out to be a book dealer. Among the books Nodier noticed a rather thick volume of six or eight hundred pages, printed in Spanish, two columns to a page, badly damaged by worms, and the binding missing from the back. The ragpicker, asked what he wanted for it, replied, trembling lest the price should be refused: "Five francs," which Nodier paid, also trembling, but with joy. This book was the *Romancero* complete. There are only three complete copies of this edition now in existence. One of these a few years ago sold for 7,500 francs. Moreover, worms are vying with each other in eating up these three remaining copies. The peoples, feeders of princes, have something else to do than spend their money to preserve for new editions the legacies of human intellect, and the *Romancero*, being merely an Iliad, has not been reprinted.

During the three days of the coronation there were great crowds in the streets of Rheims, at the Archbishop's palace, and on the promenades along the Vesdre, eager to catch a glimpse of Charles X. I said to Charles Nodier: "Let us go and see his majesty the cathedral."

Rheims is a proverb in Gothic Christian art. One speaks of the "nave of Amiens, the bell towers of Chartres, the façade of Rheims." A month before the coronation of Charles X a swarm of masons, perched on ladders and clinging to knotted ropes, spent a week smashing with hammers every bit of jutting sculpture on the façade, for fear a stone might become detached from one of these reliefs and fall on the King's head. The debris littered the pavement and was swept away. For a long time I had in my possession a head of Christ that fell in this way. It was stolen from me in 1851. This head was unfortunate; broken by a king, it was lost by an exile.

Nodier was an admirable antiquary, and we explored the cathedral from top to bottom, encumbered though it was with scaffolding, painted scenery, and stage side lights. The nave being only of stone, they had hidden it by an edifice of cardboard, doubtless because the latter bore a greater resemblance to the monarchy of that period. For the coronation of the King of France they had transformed a church into a theatres and it has since been related, with perfect accuracy, that on arriving at the entrance I asked of the bodyguard on duty: "Where is my box?"

This cathedral of Rheims is beautiful above all cathedrals. On the façade are kings; on the absis, people being put to the torture by executioners. Coronation of kings with an accompaniment of victims. The façade is one of the most magnificent symphonies ever sung by that music, architecture. One dreams for a long time before this oratorio. Looking up from the square you see at a giddy height, at the base of the two towers, a row of gigantic statues representing kings of France. In their hands they hold the sceptre, the sword, the hand of justice, and the globe, and on their heads are antique open crowns with bulging gems. It is superb and grim. You push open the bell-ringer's door, climb the winding staircase, "the screw of St. Giles," to the towers, to the high regions of prayer; you look down and the statues are below you. The row of kings is plunging into the abysm. You hear the whispering of the enormous bells, which vibrate at the kiss of vague zephyrs from the sky.

One day I gazed down from the top of the tower through an embrasure. The entire façade sheered straight below me. I perceived in the depth, on top of a long stone support that extended down the wall directly beneath me to the escarpment, so that its form was lost, a sort of round basin. Rain-water had collected there and formed a narrow mirror at the bottom; there were also a tuft of grass with flowers in it, and a swallow's nest. Thus in a space only two feet in diameter were a lake, a garden and a habitation—a birds' paradise. As I gazed the swallow was giving water to her brood. Round the upper edge of the basin were what looked like crenelles, and between these the swallow had built her nest. I examined these crenelles. They had the form of fleurs-de-lys. The support was a statue. This happy little world was the stone crown of an old king. And if God were asked: "Of what use was this Lothario, this Philip, this Charles, this Louis, this emperor, this king?" God peradventure would reply: "He had this statue made and lodged a swallow."

The coronation occurred. This is not the place to describe it. Besides my recollections of the ceremony of May 27, 1825, have been recounted elsewhere by another, more ably than I could set them forth.

Suffice it to say that it was a radiant day. God seemed to have given his assent to the fête. The long clear windows—for there are no more stained-glass windows at Rheims—let in bright daylight; all the light of May was in the church. The Archbishop was covered with gilding and the altar with rays. Marshal de Lauriston, Minister of the King's Household, rejoiced at the sunshine. He came and went, as busy as could be, and conversed in low tones with Lecointe and Hittorf, the architects. The fine morning afforded the occasion to say, "the sun of the coronation," as one used to say "the sun of Austerlitz." And in the resplendent light a profusion of lamps and tapers found means to beam.

At one moment Charles X, attired in a cherry-coloured simar striped with gold, lay at full length at the Archbishop's feet. The peers of France on the right, embroidered with gold, beplumed in the Henri IV style, and wearing long mantles of velvet and ermine, and the Deputies on the left, in dress-coats of blue cloth with silver fleurs-de-lys on the collars, looked on.

About all the forms of chance were represented there: the Papal benediction by the cardinals, some of whom had witnessed the coronation of Napoleon; victory by the marshals; heredity by the Duke d'Angoulême, dauphin; happiness by M. de Talleyrand, lame but able to get about; the rising and falling of stocks by M. de Villèle; joy by the birds that were released and flew away, and the knaves in a pack of playing-cards by the four heralds.

A vast carpet embroidered with fleurs-de-lys, made expressly for the occasion, and called the "coronation carpet," covered the old flagstones from one end of the cathedral to the other and concealed the tombstones in the pavement. Thick, luminous smoke of incense filled the nave. The birds that had been set at liberty flew wildly about in this cloud.

The King changed his costume six or seven times. The first prince of the blood, Louis Philippe, Duke d'Orleans, aided him. The Duke de Bordeaux, who was five years old, was in a gallery.

The pew in which Nodier and I were seated adjoined those of the Deputies. In the middle of the ceremony, just before the King prostrated himself at the feet of the Archbishop, a Deputy for the Doubs department, named M. Hémonin, turned towards Nodier, who was close to him, and with his finger on his lips, as a sign that he did not wish to disturb the Archbishop's orisons by speaking, slipped something into my friend's hand. This something was a book. Nodier took it and glanced over it.

"What is it?" I whispered.

"Nothing very precious," he replied. "An odd volume of Shakespeare, Glasgow edition."

One of the tapestries from the treasure of the church hanging exactly opposite to us represented a not very historical interview between John Lackland and Philip Augustus. Nodier turned over the leaves of the book for a few minutes, then pointed to the tapestry.

"You see that tapestry?"

"Yes."

"Do you know what it represents?"

"No."

"John Lackland."

"Well, what of it?"

"John Lackland is also in this book."

The volume, which was in sheep binding and worn at the corners, was indeed a copy of *King John*.

M. Hémonin turned to Nodier and said: "I paid six sous for it."

In the evening the Duke of Northumberland gave a ball. It was a magnificent, fairylike spectacle. This Arabian Nights ambassador brought one of these nights to Rheims. Every woman found a diamond in her bouquet.

I could not dance. Nodier had not danced since he was sixteen years of age, when a great aunt went into ecstasies over his terpsichorean efforts and congratulated him in the following terms: "*Tu est charmant, tu danses comme rim chou!*" We did not go to Lord Northumberland's ball.

"What shall we do tonight?" said I to Nodier. He held up his odd volume and answered:

"Let us read this."

We read.

That is to say, Nodier read. He knew English (without being able to speak it, I believe) enough to make it out. He read aloud, and translated as he read. At intervals, while he rested, I took the book bought from the ragpicker of Soissons, and read passages from the *Romancero*. Like Nodier, I translated as I read. We compared the English with the Castilian book; we confronted the dramatic with the epic. Nodier stood up for Shakespeare, whom he could read in English, and I for the *Romancero*, which I could read in Spanish. We brought face to face, he the bastard Faulconbridge, I the bastard Mudarra. And little by little in contradicting we convinced each other, and Nodier became filled with enthusiasm for the *Romancero*, and I with admiration for Shakespeare.

Listeners arrived. One passes the evening as best one can in a provincial town on a coronation day when one doesn't go to the ball. We formed quite a little club. There was an academician, M. Roger; a man of letters, M. d'Eckstein; M. de Marcellus, friend and country neighbour of my father, who poked fun at his royalism and mine; good old Marquis d'Herbouville, and M. Hémonin, donor of the book that cost six sous.

"It isn't worth the money!" exclaimed M. Roger.

The conversation developed into a debate. Judgment was passed upon *King John*. M. de Marcellus declared that the assassination of Arthur was an improbable incident. It was pointed out to him that it was a matter of history. It was with difficulty that he became reconciled to it. For kings to kill each other was impossible. To M. de Marcellus's mind the murdering of kings began on January 21. Regicide was synonymous with '93. To kill a king was an unheard-of thing that the "populace" alone were capable of doing. No king except Louis XVI had ever been violently put to death. He, however, reluctantly admitted the case of Charles I. In his death also he saw the hand of the populace. All the rest was demagogic lying and calumny.

Although as good a royalist as he, I ventured to insinuate that the sixteenth century had existed, and that it was the period when the Jesuits had clearly propounded the question of "bleeding the basilic vein," that is to say of cases in which the king ought to be slain; a question which, once brought forward, met with such success that it resulted in two kings, Henry III and Henry IV, being stabbed, and a Jesuit, Father Guignard, being hanged.

Then we passed to the details of the drama, situations, scenes, and personages. Nodier pointed out that Faulconbridge is the same person spoken of by Mathieu Paris as Falcasius de Trente, bastard of Richard Coeur de Lion. Baron d'Eckstein, in support of this, reminded his hearers that, according to Hollinshed, Faulconbridge, or Falcasius, slew the Viscount de Limoges to avenge his father Richard, who had been wounded unto death at the siege of Chaluz; and that this castle of Chaluz, being the property of the Viscount de Limoges, it was only right that the Viscount, although absent, should be made to answer with his head for the falling of an arrow or a stone from the castle upon the King. M. Roger laughed at the cry of "Austria Limoges" in the play and at Shakespeare's confounding the Viscount de Limoges with the Duke of Austria. M. Roger scored the success of the evening and his laughter settled the matter.

The discussion having taken this turn I said nothing further. This revelation of Shakespeare had moved me. His grandeur impressed me. *King John* is not a masterpiece, but certain scenes are lofty and powerful, and in the motherhood of Constance there are bursts of genius.

The two books, open and reversed, remained lying upon the table. The company had ceased to read in order to laugh. Nodier at length became silent like myself. We were beaten. The gathering broke up with a laugh, and our visitors went away. Nodier and I remained alone and pensive, thinking of the great works that are unappreciated, and amazed that the intellectual education of the civilized peoples, and even our own, his and mine, had advanced no further than this.

At last Nodier broke the silence. I can see his smile now as he said:

"They know nothing about the Romancero!"

I replied:

"And they deride Shakespeare!"

Thirteen years later chance took me to Rheims again.

It was on August 28, 1838. It will be seen further on why this date impressed itself on my memory.

I was returning from Vouziers, and seeing the two towers of Rheims in the distance, was seized with a desire to visit the cathedral again. I therefore went to Rheims.

On arriving in the cathedral square I saw a gun drawn up near the portal and beside it gunners with lighted fuses in their hands. As I had seen artillery there on May 27, 1825, I supposed it was customary to keep a cannon in the square, and paid little attention to it. I passed on and entered the church.

A beadle in violet sleeves, a sort of priest, took me in charge and conducted me all over the church. The stones were dark, the statues dismal, the altar mysterious. No lamps competed with the sun. The latter threw upon the sepulchral stones in the pavement the long white silhouettes of the windows, which through the melancholy obscurity of the rest of the church looked like phantoms lying upon these tombs. No one was in the church. Not a whisper, not a footfall could be heard.

This solitude saddened the heart and enraptured the soul. There were in it abandonment, neglect, oblivion, exile, and sublimity. Gone the whirl of 1825. The church had resumed its dignity and its calmness. Not a piece of finery, not a vestment, not anything. It was bare and beautiful. The lofty vault no longer supported a canopy. Ceremonies of the palace arc not suited to these severe places; a coronation ceremony is merely tolerated; these noble ruins are not made to be courtiers. To rid it of the throne and withdraw the king from the presence of God increases the majesty of a temple. Louis XIV hides Jehovah from sight.

Withdraw the priest as well. All that eclipsed it having been taken away, you will see the light of day direct. Orisons, rites, bibles, formulas, refract and decompose the sacred light. A dogma is a dark chamber. Through a religion you see the solar spectre of God, but not God. Desuetude and crumbling enhance the grandeur of a temple. As human religion retires from this mysterious and jealous edifice, divine religion enters it. Let solitude reign in it and you will feel heaven there. A sanctuary deserted and in ruins, like Jumièges, like St. Bertin, like Villers, like Holyrood, like Montrose Abbey, like the temple of Paestum, like the hypogeum of Thebes, becomes almost an element, and possesses the virginal and religious grandeur of a savannah or of a forest. There something of the real Presence is to be found.

Such places are truly holy; man has meditated and communed with himself therein. What they contained of truth has remained and become greater. The *à-peu-près* has no longer any voice. Extinct dogmas have not left their ashes; the prayer of the past has left its perfume. There is something of the absolute in prayer, and because of this, that which was a synagogue, that which was a mosque, that which was a pagoda, is venerable. A stone on which that great anxiety that is called prayer has left its impress is never treated with ridicule by the thinker. The trace left by those who have bowed down before the infinite is always imposing.

In strolling about the cathedral I had climbed to the triforium, then under the arched buttresses, then to the top of the edifice. The timber-work under the pointed roof is admirable; but less remarkable than the "forest" of Amiens. It is of chestnut-wood.

These cathedral attics are of grim appearance. One could almost lose one's self in the labyrinths of rafters, squares, traverse beams, superposed joists, traves, architraves, girders, madriers, and tangled lines and curves. One might imagine one's self to be in the skeleton of Babel. The place is as bare as a garret and as wild as a cavern. The wind whistles mournfully through it. Rats are at home there. The spiders, driven from the timber by the odour of chestnut, make their home in the stone of the basement where the church ends and the roof begins, and low down in the obscurity spin their webs in which you catch your face. One respires a mysterious dust, and the centuries seem to mingle with one's breath. The dust of churches is not like the dust of houses; it reminds one of the tomb, it is composed of ashes.

The flooring of these colossal garrets has crevices in it through which one can look down into the abysm, the church, below. In the corners that one cannot explore are pools of shadow, as it were. Birds of prey enter through one window and go out through the other. Lightning is also familiar with these high, mysterious regions. Sometimes it ventures too near, and then it causes the conflagration of Rouen, of Chartres, or of St. Paul's, London.

My guide the beadle preceded me. He looked at the dung on the floor, and tossed his head. He knew the bird by its manure, and growled between his teeth:

"This is a rook; this is a hawk; this is an owl."

"You ought to study the human heart," said I.

A frightened bat flew before us.

While walking almost at hazard, following this bat, looking at this manure of the birds, respiring this dust, in this obscurity among the cobwebs and scampering rats, we came to a dark corner in which, on a big wheelbarrow, I could just distinguish a long package tied with string and that looked like a piece of rolled up cloth.

"What is that?" I asked the beadle.

"That," said he, "is Charles X's coronation carpet."

I stood gazing at the thing, and as I did so—I am telling truthfully what occurred—there was a deafening report that sounded like a thunder-clap, only it came from below. It shook the timber-work and echoed and re-echoed through the church. It was succeeded by a second roar, then a third, at regular intervals. I recognised the thunder of the cannon, and remembered the gun I had seen in the square.

I turned to my guide:

"What is that noise?"

"The telegraph has been at work and the cannon has been fired."

"What does it mean?" I continued.

"It means," said the beadle, "that a grandson has just been born to Louis Philippe."

The cannon announced the birth of the Count de Paris.

These are my recollections of Rheims.

RECOUNTED BY EYE-WITNESSES

I. The Execution of Louis XVI
II. The Arrival of Napoleon I in Paris in 1815

I. The Execution of Louis XVI

THERE WERE CERTAIN CHARACTERISTIC DETAILS connected with the execution of Louis XVI that are not recorded in history. They were recounted to me by an eye-witness* and are here published for the first time.

The scaffold was not, as is generally believed, erected in the very centre of the Place, on the spot where the obelisk now stands, but on a spot which the decree of the Provisional Executive Council designates in these precise terms: "between the pied d'estal and the Champs-Elysées."

What was this pedestal? Present generations who have seen so many things happen, so many statues crumble and so many pedestals overthrown do not quite know what meaning to give to this very vague designation, and would be embarrassed to tell for what monument the mysterious stone which the Executive Council of the Revolution laconically calls the "pied d'estal" served as a base. This stone had borne the statue of Louis XV.

Let it be noted *en passant* that this strange Place which had been called successively the Place Louis XV, Place de la Revolution, Place de la Concorde, Place Louis XVI, Place du Garde-Meuble and Place des Champs-Elysées, and which could not retain any name, could not keep any monument either. It has had the statue of Louis XV, which disappeared; an expiatory fountain which was to have laved the bloody centre of the Place was projected, but not even the first stone was laid; a rough model of a monument to the Charter was made: we have never seen anything but the socle of this monument. Just when a bronze figure representing the Charter of 1814 was about to be erected, the Revolution of July arrived with the Charter of 1830. The pedestal of Louis XVIII vanished, as fell the pedestal of Louis XV Now on this

---

* This eye witness was one Leboucher, who arrived in Paris from Bourges in December, 1792, and was present at the execution of Louis XVI. In 1840 he recounted to Victor Hugo most of these details which, as can easily be imagined, had impressed themselves deeply upon his mind.

same spot we have placed the obelisk of Sesostris. It required thirty centuries for the great Desert to engulf half of it; how many years will the Place de la Revolution require to swallow it up altogether?

In the Year II of the Republic, what the Executive Council called the "pied d'estal" was nought but a shapeless and hideous block. It was a sort of sinister symbol of the royalty itself. Its ornaments of marble and bronze had been wrenched off, the bare stone was everywhere split and cracked. On the four sides were large square gaps showing the places where the destroyed bas reliefs had been. Scarcely could a remnant of the entablature still be distinguished at the summit of the pedestal, and beneath the cornice a string of ovolos, defaced and worn, was surmounted by what architects call a "chaplet of paternosters." On the table of the pedestal one could perceive a heap of debris of all kinds, in which tufts of grass were growing here and there. This pile of nameless things had replaced the royal statue.

The scaffold was raised a few steps distant from this ruin, a little in rear of it. It was covered with long planks, laid transversely, that masked the framework. A ladder without banisters or balustrade was at the back, and what they venture to call the head of this horrible construction was turned towards the Garde-Meuble. A basket of cylindrical shape, covered with leather, was placed at the spot where the head of the King was to fall, to receive it; and at one of the angles of the entablature, to the right of the ladder, could be discerned a long wicker basket prepared for the body, and on which one of the executioners, while waiting for the King, had laid his hat.

Imagine, now, in the middle of the Place, these two lugubrious things, a few paces from each other: the pedestal of Louis XV and the scaffold of Louis XVI; that is to say, the ruins of royalty dead and the martyrdom of royalty living; around these two things four formidable lines of armed men, preserving a great empty square in the midst of an immense crowd; to the left of the scaffold, the Champs-Elysees, to the right the Tuileries, which, neglected and left at the mercy of the public had become an unsightly waste of dirt heaps and trenches; and over these melancholy edifices, over these black, leafless trees, over this gloomy multitude, the bleak, sombre sky of a winter morning, and one will have an idea of the aspect which the Place de la Revolution presented at the moment when Louis XVI, in the carriage of the Mayor of Paris, dressed in white, the Book of Psalms clasped in his hands, arrived there to die at a few minutes after ten o'clock on January 21, 1793.

Strange excess of abasement and misery: the son of so many kings, bound and sacred like the kings of Egypt, was to be consumed between two layers of quicklime, and to this French royalty, which at Versailles had had a throne of gold and at St. Denis sixty sarcophagi of granite, there remained but a platform of pine and a wicker coffin.

Here are some unknown details. The executioners numbered four; two only performed the execution; the third stayed at the foot of the ladder, and the fourth was on the waggon which was to convey the King's body to the Madeleine Cemetery and which was waiting a few feet from the scaffold.

The executioners wore breeches, coats in the French style as the Revolution had modified it, and three-cornered hats with enormous tri-colour cockades.

They executed the King with their hats on, and it was without taking his hat off that Samson, seizing by the hair the severed head of Louis XVI, showed it to the people, and for a few moments let the blood from it trickle upon the scaffold.

At the same time his valet or assistant undid what were called "les sangles" (straps); and, while the crowd gazed alternately upon the King's body, dressed entirely in white, as I have said, and still attached, with the hands bound behind the back, to the swing board, and upon that head whose kind and gentle profile stood out against the misty, sombre trees of the Tuileries, two priests, commissaries of the Commune, instructed to be present, as Municipal officials, at the execution of the King, sat in the Mayor's carriage, laughing and conversing in loud tones. One of them, Jacques Roux, derisively drew the other's attention to Capet's fat calves and abdomen.

The armed men who surrounded the scaffold had only swords and pikes; there were very few muskets. Most of them wore large round hats or red caps. A few platoons of mounted dragoons in uniform were mingled with these troops at intervals. A whole squadron of dragoons was ranged in battle array beneath the terraces of the Tuileries. What was called the Battalion of Marseilles formed one of the sides of the square.

The guillotine—it is always with repugnance that one writes this hideous word—would appear to the craftsmen of today to be very badly constructed. The knife was simply suspended to a pulley fixed in the centre of the upper beam. This pulley and a rope the thickness of a man's thumb constituted the whole apparatus. The knife, which was not very heavily weighted, was of small dimensions and had a curved edge, which gave it the form of a reversed Phrygian cap. No hood was placed to shelter the King's head and at the same time to hide and circumscribe its fall. All that crowd could see the head of Louis XVI drop, and it was thanks to chance, thanks perhaps to the smallness of the knife which diminished the violence of the shock, that it did not bound beyond the basket to the pavement. Terrible incident, which often occurred at executions during the Terror. Nowadays assassins and poisoners are decapitated more decently. Many improvements in the guillotine have been made.

At the spot where the King's head fell, a long rivulet of blood streamed down the planks of the scaffold to the pavement. When the execution was over, Samson threw to the people the King's coat, which was of white molleton, and in an instant it disappeared, torn by a thousand hands.

At the moment when the head of Louis XVI fell, the Abbé Edgeworth was still near the King. The blood spirted upon him. He hastily donned a brown overcoat, descended from the scaffold and was lost in the crowd. The first row of spectators opened before him with a sort of wonder mingled with respect; but after he had gone a few steps, the attention of everybody was still so concentrated upon the centre of the Place where the event had just been accomplished, that nobody took any further notice of Abbé Edgeworth.

The poor priest, enveloped in his thick coat which concealed the blood with which he was covered, fled in bewilderment, walking as one in a dream and scarcely knowing where he was going. However, with that sort of instinct which preserves somnambulists he crossed the river, took the Rue du Bac, then the Rue du Regard and thus managed to reach the house of Mme. de Lézardière, near the Barrière du Maine.

Arrived there he divested himself of his soiled clothing and remained for several hours, in a state of collapse, without being able to collect a thought or utter a word.

Some Royalists who rejoined him, and who had witnessed the execution, surrounded the Abbé Edgeworth and reminded him of the adieu he had addressed to the King: "Son of St. Louis, ascend to heaven!" These words, however, memorable though they were, had left no trace on the mind of him who had uttered them. "We heard them," said the witnesses of the catastrophe, still moved and thrilled. "It is possible," he replied, "but I do not remember having said such a thing."

Abbé Edgeworth lived a long life without ever being able to remember whether he really did pronounce these words.

Mme. de Lézardière, who had been seriously ill for more than a month, was unable to support the shock of the death of Louis XVI. She died on the very night of January 21.

II. Arrival of Napoleon in Paris

March 20, 1815

History and contemporaneous memoirs have truncated, or badly related, or even omitted altogether, certain details of the arrival of the Emperor in Paris on March 20, 1815. But living witnesses are to be met with who saw them and who rectify or complete them.

During the night of the 19th, the Emperor left Sens. He arrived at three o'clock in the morning at Fontainebleau. Towards five o'clock, as day was breaking, he reviewed the few troops he had taken with him and those who had rallied to him at Fontainebleau itself. They were of every corps, of every regiment, of all arms, a little of the Grand Army, a little of the Guard. At six o'clock, the review being over, one hundred and twenty lancers mounted their horses and went on ahead to wait for him at Essonnes. These lancers were commanded by Colonel Galbois, now lieutenant general, and who has recently distinguished himself at Constantine.

They had been at Essonnes scarcely three-quarters of an hour, resting their horses, when the carriage of the Emperor arrived. The escort of lancers were in their saddles in the twinkling of an eye and surrounded the carriage, which immediately started off again without having changed horses. The Emperor stopped on the way at the large villages to receive petitions from the inhabitants and the submission of the authorities, and sometimes to listen to harangues. He was on the rear seat of the carriage, with General Bertrand in full uniform seated on his left. Colonel Galbois galloped beside the door on the Emperor's side; the door on Bertrand's side was guarded by a quartermaster of lancers named Ferrès, today a wineshop keeper at Puteaux, a former and very brave hussar whom the Emperor knew personally and addressed by name. No one on the road approached the Emperor. Everything that was intended for him passed through General Bertrand's hands.

Three or four leagues beyond Essonnes the imperial cortege found the road suddenly barred by General Colbert, at the head of two squadrons and three regiments echelonned towards Paris.

General Colbert had been the colonel of the regiment of lancers from which the detachment that escorted the Emperor had been drawn. He recognised his lancers and his lancers recognised him. They cried: "General, come over to us!" The General answered: "My children, do your duty, I am doing mine." Then he turned rein and went off to the right across country with a few mounted men who followed him. He could not have resisted; the regiments behind him were shouting: "Long live the Emperor!"

This meeting only delayed Napoleon a few minutes. He continued on his way. The Emperor, surrounded only by his one hundred and twenty lancers, thus reached Paris. He entered by the Barrière de Fontainebleau, took the large avenue of trees which is on the left, the Boulevard dim Mont-Parnasse, the other boulevards to the Invalides, then the Pont do la Concorde, the quay along the river and the gate of the Louvre.

At a quarter past eight o'clock in the evening he was at the Tuileries.

Visions of the Real

I. The Hovel

You want a description of this hovel? I hesitated to inflict it upon you. But you want it. I' faith, here it is! You will only have yourself to blame, it is your fault.

"Pshaw!" you say, "I know what it is. A bleared, bandy ruin. Some old house!"

In the first place it is not an old house, it is very much worse, it is a new house.

Really, now, an old house! You counted upon an old house and turned up your nose at it in advance. Ah! yes, old houses; don't you wish you may get them! A dilapidated, tumble-down cottage! Why, don't you know that a dilapidated, tumble-down cottage is simply charming, a thing of beauty? The wall is of beautiful, warm and strong colour, with moth holes, birds' nests, old nails on which the spider hangs his rose-window web, a thousand amusing things that break its evenness. The window is only a dormer, but from it protrude long poles on which all sorts of clothing, of all sorts of colours, hang and dry in the wind—white tatters, red rags, flags of poverty that give to the hut an air of gaiety and are resplendent in the sunshine. The door is cracked and black, but approach and examine it; you will without doubt find upon it a bit of antique ironwork of the time of Louis XIII, cut out like a piece of guipure. The roof is full of crevices, but in each crevice there is a convolvulus that will blossom in the spring, or a daisy that will bloom in the autumn. The tiles are patched with thatch. Of course they are, I should say so! It affords the occasion to have on one's roof a colony of pink dragon flowers and wild marsh-mallow. A fine green grass carpets the foot of this decrepit wall, the ivy climbs joyously up it and cloaks its bareness—its wounds and its leprosy mayhap; moss covers with green velvet the stone seat at the door. All nature takes pity upon this degraded and charming thing that you call a hovel, and welcomes it. 0 hovel! honest and peaceful old dwelling, sweet and good to see! rejuvenated every year by April and May! perfumed by the wallflower and inhabited by the swallow!

No, it is not of this that I write, it is not, I repeat, of an old house, it is of a new house,—of a new hovel, if you will.

This thing has not been built longer than two years. The wall has that hideous and glacial whiteness of fresh plaster. The whole is wretched, mean, high, triangular, and has the shape of a piece of Gruyère cheese cut for a miser a dessert. There are new doors that do not shut properly, window frames with white panes that are already spangled here and there with paper stars. These stars are cut coquettishly and pasted on with care. There is a frightful bogus sumptuousness about the place that causes a painful impression—balconies of hollow iron badly fixed to the wall; trumpery locks, already rotten round the fastenings, upon which vacillate, on three nails, horrible ornaments of embossed brass that are becoming covered with verdigris; shutters painted grey that are getting out of joint, not because they are worm-eaten, but because they were made of green wood by a thieving cabinet maker.

A chilly feeling comes over you as you look at the house. On entering it you shiver. A greenish humidity leaks at the foot of the wall. This building of yesterday is already a ruin; it is more than a ruin, it is a disaster; one feels that the proprietor is bankrupt and that the contractor has fled.

In rear of the house, a wall white and new like the rest, encloses a space in which a drum major could not lie at full length. This is called the garden. Issuing shiveringly from the earth is a little tree, long, spare and sickly, which seems always to be in winter, for it has not a single leaf. This broom is called a poplar. The remainder of the garden is strewn with old potsherds and bottoms of bottles. Among them one notices two or three list slippers. In a corner on top of a heap of oyster shells is an old tin watering can, painted green, dented, rusty and cracked, inhabited by slugs which silver it with their trails of slime.

Let us enter the hovel. In the other you will find perhaps a ladder "rickety," as Regnier says, "from the top to the bottom." Here you will find a staircase.

This staircase, "ornamented" with brass-knobbed banisters, has fifteen or twenty wooden steps, high, narrow, with sharp angles, which rise perpendicularly to the first floor and turn upon themselves in a spiral of about eighteen inches in diameter. Would you not be inclined to ask for a ladder?

At the top of these stairs, if you get there, is the room.

To give an idea of this room is difficult. It is the "new hovel" in all its abominable reality. Wretchedness is everywhere; a new wretchedness, which has no past, no future, and which cannot take root anywhere. One divines that the lodger moved in yesterday and will move out tomorrow. That he arrived without saying whence he came, and that he will put the key under the door when he goes away.

The wall is "ornamented" with dark blue paper with yellow flowers, the window is "ornamented" with a curtain of red calico in which holes take the place of flowers. There is in front of the window a rush-bottom chair with the bottom worn out; near the chair a stove; on the stove a stewpot; near the stewpot a flowerpot turned upside down with a tallow candle stuck in the hole; near the flowerpot a basketful of coal which evokes thoughts of suicide and asphyxiation; above the basket a shelf encumbered with nameless objects, distinguishable among which are a worn broom and an old toy representing a green rider on a crimson horse. The mantelpiece, mean and narrow, is of blackish marble with a thousand little white blotches. It is covered with broken glasses and unwashed cups. Into one of these cups a pair of tin rimmed spectacles is plunging. A nail lies on the floor. In the fireplace a dishcloth is hanging on one of the fire-iron holders. No fire either in the fireplace or in the stove. A heap of frightful sweepings replaces the heaps of cinders. No looking glass on the mantelpiece, but a picture of varnished canvas representing a nude negro at the knees of a white woman in a decolletée ball dress in an arbour. Opposite the mantelpiece, a man's cap and a woman's bonnet hang from nails on either side of a cracked mirror.

At the end of the room is a bed. That is to say, a mattress laid on two planks that rest upon a couple of trestles. Over the bed, other boards, with openings between them, support an undesirable heap of linen, clothes and rags. An imitation cashmere, called "French cashmere," protrudes between the boards and hangs over the pallet.

Mingled with the hideous litter of all these things are dirtiness, a disgusting odour, spots of oil and tallow, and dust everywhere. In the corner near the bed stands an enormous sack of shavings, and on a chair beside the sack lies an old newspaper. I am moved by curiosity to look at the title and the date. It is the "Constitutionnel" of April 25, 1843.

And now what can I add? I have not told the most horrible thing about the place. The house is odious, the room is abominable, the pallet is hideous; but all that is nothing.

When I entered a woman was sleeping on the bed—a woman old, short, thickset, red, bloated, oily, tumefied, fat, dreadful, enormous. Her frightful bonnet, which was awry, disclosed the side of her head, which was grizzled, pink and bald.

She was fully dressed. She wore a yellowish fichu, a brown skirt, a jacket, all this on her monstrous abdomen; and a vast soiled apron like the linen trousers of a convict.

At the noise I made in entering she moved, sat up, showed her fat legs, that were covered with unqualifiable blue stockings, and with a yawn stretched her brawny arms, which terminated with fists that resembled those of a butcher.

I perceived that the old woman was robust and formidable.

She turned towards me and opened her eyes. I could not see them.

"Monsieur," she said, in a very gentle voice, "what do you want?"

When about to speak to this being I experienced the sensation one would feel in presence of a sow to which it behoved one to say: "Madam."

I did not quite know what to reply, and thought for a moment. Just then my gaze, wandering towards the window, fell upon a sort of picture that hung outside like a sign. It was a sign, as a matter of fact, a picture of a young and pretty woman, decolletée, wearing an enormous beplumed hat and carrying an infant in her arms; the whole in the style of the chimney boards of the time of Louis XVIII. Above the picture stood out this inscription in big letters:

Mme. BECOEUR
Midwife
BLEEDS AND VACCINATES

"Madam," said I, "I want to see Mme. Bécoeur."
The sow metamorphosed into a woman replied with an amiable smile: "I am Mme. Bécoeur, Monsieur."

II. Pillage. The Revolt in Santo Domingo

I THOUGHT THAT I MUST be dreaming. None who did not witness the sight could form any idea of it. I will, however, endeavour to depict something of it. I will simply recount what I saw with my own eyes. This small portion of a great scene minutely reproduced will enable you to form some notion as to the general aspect of the town during the three days of pillage. Multiply these details *ad libitum* and you will get the ensemble.

I had taken refuge by the gate of the town, a puny barrier made of long laths painted yellow, nailed to cross laths and sharpened at the top. Near by was a kind of shed in which some hapless colonists, who had been driven from their homes, had sought shelter. They were silent and seemed to be petrified in all the attitudes of despair. Just outside of the shed an old man, weeping, was seated on the trunk of a mahogany tree which was lying on the ground and looked like the shaft of a column. Another vainly sought to restrain a white woman who, wild with fright, was trying to flee, without knowing where she was going, through the crowd of furious, ragged, howling negroes.

The negroes, however, free, victorious, drunk, mad, paid not the slightest attention to this miserable, forlorn group of whites. A short distance from us two of them, with their knives between their teeth, were slaughtering an ox, upon which they were kneeling with their feet in its blood. A little further on two hideous negresses, dressed as marchionesses, covered with ribbons and pompons, their breasts bare, and their heads encumbered with feathers and laces, were quarrelling over a magnificent dress of Chinese satin, which one of them had grasped with her nails while the other hung on to it with her teeth. At their feet a number of little blacks were ransacking a broken trunk from which the dress had been taken.

The rest was incredible to see and impossible to describe. It was a crowd, a mob, a masquerade, a revel, a hell, a terrible buffoonery. Negroes, negresses and mulattoes, in every posture, in all manner of disguises, displayed all sorts of costumes, and what was worse, their nudity.

Here was a pot-bellied, ugly mulatto, of furious mien, attired like the planters, in a waistcoat and trousers of white material, but with a bishop's mitre on his head and a crosier in his hand. Elsewhere three or four negroes with three-cornered hats stuck on their heads and wearing red or blue military coats with the shoulder belts crossed upon their black skin, were harassing an unfortunate militiaman they had captured, and who, with his hands tied behind his back, was being dragged through the town. With loud bursts of laughter they slapped his powdered hair and pulled his long pigtail. Now and then they would stop and force the prisoner to kneel and by signs give him to understand that they were going to shoot him there. Then prodding him with the butts of their rifles they would make him get up again, and go through the same performance further on.

A number of old mulattresses had formed a ring and were skipping round in the midst of the mob. They were dressed in the nattiest costumes of our youngest and prettiest white women, and in dancing raised their skirts so as to show their lean, shrivelled legs and yellow thighs. Nothing queerer could be imagined than all these charming fashions and finery of the frivolous century of Louis XV, these Watteau shepherdess costumes, furbelows, plumes and laces, upon these black, ugly-faced, flat-nosed, woolly-headed, frightful people. Thus decked out they were no longer even negroes and negresses; they were apes and monkeys.

Add to all this a deafening uproar. Every mouth that was not making a contortion was emitting yells.

I have not finished; you must accept the picture complete to its minutest detail.

Twenty paces from me was an inn, a frightful hovel, whose sign was a wreath of dried herbs hung upon a pickaxe. Nothing but a roof window and three-legged tables. A low ale-house, rickety tables. Negroes and mulattoes were drinking there, intoxicating and besotting themselves, and fraternising. One has to have seen these things to depict them. In front of the tables of the drunkards a fairly young negress was displaying herself. She was dressed in a man's waistcoat, unbuttoned, and a woman's skirt loosely attached. She wore no chemise and her abdomen was bare. On her head was a magistrate's wig. On one shoulder she carried a parasol, and on the other a rifle with bayonet fixed.

A few whites, stark naked, ran about miserably in the midst of this pandemonium. On a litter was being borne the nude body of a stout man, in whose breast a dagger was sticking as a cross is stuck in the ground.

On every hand were gnomes bronze-coloured, red, black, kneeling, sitting, squatting, heaped together, opening trunks, forcing locks, trying on bracelets, clasping necklaces about their necks, donning coats or dresses, breaking, ripping, tearing. Two blacks were trying to get into the same coat; each had got an arm on, and they were belabouring each other with their disengaged fists. It was the second stage of a sacked town. Robbery and joy had succeeded rage. In a few corners some were still engaged in killing, but the great majority were pillaging. All were carrying off their booty, some in their arms, some in baskets on their backs, some in wheelbarrows.

The strangest thing about it all was that in the midst of the incredible, tumultuous mob, an interminable file of pillagers who were rich and fortunate enough to possess horses and vehicles, marched and deployed, in order and with the solemn gravity of a procession. This was quite a different kind of a medley!

Imagine carts of all kinds with loads of every description: a four-horse carriage full of broken crockery and kitchen utensils, with two or three dressed-up and beplumed negroes on each horse; a big wagon drawn by oxen and loaded with bales carefully corded and packed, damask armchairs, frying pans and pitchforks, and on top of this pyramid a negress wearing a necklace and with a feather stuck in her hair; an old country coach drawn by a single mule and with a load of ten trunks and, ten negroes, three of whom were upon the animal's back. Mingle with all this bath chairs, litters and sedan chairs piled high with loot of all kinds, precious articles of furniture with the most sordid objects. It was the hut and the drawing-room pitched together pell-mell into a cart, an immense removal by madmen defiling through the town.

What was incomprehensible was the equanimity with which the petty robbers regarded the wholesale robbers. The pillagers afoot stepped aside to let the pillagers in carriages pass.

There were, it is true, a few patrols, if a squad of five or six monkeys disguised as soldiers and each beating at his own sweet will on a drum can be called a patrol.

Near the gate of the town, through which this immense stream of vehicles was issuing, pranced a mulatto, a tall, lean, yellow rascal, rigged out in a judge's gown and white tie, with his sleeves rolled up, a sword in his hand, and his legs bare. He was digging his heels into a fat-bellied horse that pawed about in the crowd. He was the magistrate charged with the duty of preserving order at the gate.

A little further on galloped another group. A negro in a red coat with a blue sash, a general's epaulettes and an immense hat surcharged with tri-colour feathers, was forcing his way through the rabble. He was preceded by a horrible, helmetted negro boy beating upon a drum, and followed by two mulattoes, one in a colonel's coat, the other dressed as a Turk with a hideous Mardi Gras turban on his ugly Chinese-like head.

Out on the plain I could see battalions of ragged soldiers drawn up round a big house, on which was a crowded balcony draped with a tricolour flag. It had all the appearance of a balcony from which a speech was being delivered.

Beyond these battalions, this balcony, this flag and this speech was a calm, magnificent prospect-trees green and charming, mountains of superb shape, a cloudless sky, the ocean without a ripple.

Strange and sad it is to see the grimace of man made with such effrontery in presence of the face of God!

III. A Dream

September 6, 1847

Last night I dreamed this—we had been talking all the evening about riots, a propos of the troubles in the Rue Saint Honoré:

I entered an obscure passage way. Men passed and elbowed me in the shadow. I issued from the passage. I was in a large square, which was longer than it was wide, and surrounded by a sort of vast wall, or high edifice that resembled a wall, which enclosed it on all four sides. There were neither doors nor windows in this wall; just a few holes here and there. At certain spots it appeared to have been riddled with shot; at others it was cracked and hanging over as though it had been shaken by an earthquake. It had the bare, crumbling and desolate aspect of places in Oriental cities.

No one was in sight. Day was breaking. The stone was grey, the sky also. At the extremity of the place I perceived four obscure objects that looked liked cannon levelled ready for firing.

A great crowd of ragged men and children rushed by me with gestures of terror.

"Save us!" cried one of them. "The grape shot is coming!"

"Where are we?" I asked. "What is this place?"

"What! do you not belong to Paris?" responded the man. "This is the Palais-Royal."

I gazed about me and, in effect, recognised in this frightful, devastated square in ruins a sort of spectre of the Palais-Royal.

The fleeing men had vanished, I knew not whither.

I also would have fled. I could not. In the twilight I saw a light moving about the cannon.

The square was deserted. I could hear cries of: "Run! they are going to shoot!" but I could not see those who uttered them.

A woman passed by. She was in tatters and carried a child on her back. She did not run. She walked slowly. She was young, cold, pale, terrible.

As she passed me she said: "It is hard lines! Bread is at thirty-four sous, and even at that the cheating bakers do not give full weight."

I saw the light at the end of the square flare up and heard the roar of the cannon. I awoke.

Somebody had just slammed the front door.

IV. The Panel with the Coat of Arms

THE PANEL WHICH WAS OPPOSITE the bed had been so blackened by time and effaced by dust that at first he could distinguish only confused lines and undecipherable contours; but the while he was thinking of other things his eyes continually wandered back to it with that mysterious and mechanical persistence which the gaze sometimes has. Singular details began to detach themselves from the confused and obscure whole. His curiosity was roused. When the attention becomes fixed it is like a light; and the tapestry growing gradually less cloudy finally appeared to him in its entirety, and stood out distinctly against the sombre wall, as though vaguely illumined.

It was only a panel with a coat of arms upon it, the blazon, no doubt, of former owners of the château; but this blazon was a strange one.

The escutcheon was at the foot of the panel, and it was not this that first attracted attention. It was of the bizarre shape of German escutcheons of the fifteenth century. It was perpendicular and rested, although rounded at the base, upon a worn, moss covered stone. Of the two upper angles, one bent to the left and curled back upon itself like the turned down corner of a page of an old book; the other, which curled upward, bore at its extremity an immense and magnificent morion in profile, the chinpiece of which protruded further than the visor, making the helm look like a horrible head of a fish. The crest was formed of two great spreading wings of an eagle, one black, the other red, and amid the feathers of these wings were the membranous, twisted and almost living branches of a huge seaweed which bore more resemblance to a polypus than to a plume. From the middle of the plume rose a buckled strap, which reached to the angle of a rough wooden pitchfork, the handle of which was stuck in the ground, and from there descended to a hand, which held it.

To the left of the escutcheon was the figure of a woman, standing. It was an enchanting vision. She was tall and slim, and wore a robe of brocade which fell in ample folds about her feet, a ruff of many pleats and a necklace of large gems. On her head was an enormous and superb turban of blond hair on which rested a crown of filigree that was not round, and that followed all the undulations of the hair. The face, although somewhat too round and large, was exquisite. The eyes were those of an angel, the mouth was that of a virgin; but in those heavenly eyes there was a terrestrial look and on that virginal mouth was the smile of a woman. In that place, at that hour, on that tapestry, this mingling of divine ecstasy and human voluptuousness had something at once charming and awful about it.

Behind the woman, bending towards her as though whispering in her ear, appeared a man.

Was he a man? All that could be seen of his body—legs, arms and chest—was as hairy as the skin of an ape; his hands and feet were crooked, like the claws of a tiger. As to his visage, nothing more fantastic and frightful could be imagined. Amid a thick, bristling beard, a nose like an owl's beak and a mouth whose corners were drawn by a wild-beast-like rictus were just discernible. The eyes were half hidden by his thick, bushy, curly hair. Each curl ended in a spiral, pointed and twisted like a gimlet, and on peering at them closely it could be seen that each of these gimlets was a little viper.

The man was smiling at the woman. It was disquieting and sinister, the contact of these two equally chimerical beings, the one almost an angel, the other almost a monster; a revolting clash of the two extremes of the ideal. The man held the pitchfork, the woman grasped the strap with her delicate pink fingers.

As to the escutcheon itself, it was sable, that is to say, black, and in the middle of it appeared, with the vague whiteness of silver, a fleshless, deformed thing, which, like the rest, at length became distinct. It was a death's head. The nose was lacking, the orbits of the eyes were hollow and deep, the cavity of the ear could be seen on the right side, all the seams of the cranium could be traced, and there only remained two teeth in the jaws.

But this black escutcheon, this livid death's head, designed with such minuteness of detail that it seemed to stand out from the tapestry, was less lugubrious than the two personages who held up the hideous blazon and who seemed to be whispering to each other in the shadow.

At the bottom of the panel in a corner was the date: 1503.

V. The Easter Daisy

May 29, 1841

A few days ago I was passing along the Rue de Chartres.* A palisade of boards, which linked two islands of high six-story houses, attracted my attention. It threw upon the pavement a shadow which the sunshine, penetrating between the badly joined boards, striped with beautiful parallel streaks of gold, such as one sees on the fine black satins of the Renaissance. I strolled over to it and peered through the cracks.

This palisade encloses the site on which was built the Vaudeville Theatre, that was destroyed by fire two years ago, in June, 1839.

It was two o'clock in the afternoon, the sun shone hotly, the street was deserted.

A sort of house door, painted grey, still ornamented with rococo carving and which a hundred years ago probably was the entrance to the boudoir of some little mistress, had been adjusted to the palisade. There was only a latch to raise, and I entered the enclosure.

Nothing could be sadder or more desolate. A chalky soil. Here and there blocks of stone that the masons had begun to work upon, but had abandoned, and which were at once white as the stones of sepulchres and mouldy as the stones of ruins. No one in the enclosure. On the walls of the neighbouring houses traces of flame and smoke still visible.

However, since the catastrophe two successive springtides had softened the ground, and in a corner of the trapezium, behind an enormous stone that was becoming tinted with the green of moss, and beneath which were haunts of woodlice, millepeds, and other insects, a little patch of grass had grown in the shadow.

I sat on the stone and bent over the grass.

Oh! my goodness! there was the prettiest little Easter daisy in the world, and flitting about it was a charming microscopical gnat.

This flower of the fields was growing peaceably and in accordance with the sweet law of nature, in the open, in the centre of Paris, between a couple of streets, two paces from the Palais-Royal, four paces from the Carrousel, amid passers-by, omnibuses and the King's carriages.

---

* The little Rue de Chartres was situated on the site now occupied by the Pavilion de Rohan. It extended from the open ground of the Carrousel to the Place du Palais-Royal. The old Vaudeville Theatre was situated in it.

This wild flower, neighbour of the pavement, opened up a wide field of thought. Who could have foreseen, two years ago, that a daisy would be growing on this spot! If, as on the ground adjoining, there had never been anything but houses, that is to say, proprietors, tenants, and hall porters, careful residents extinguishing candle and fire at night before going to sleep, never would there have been a wild flower here.

How many things, how many plays that failed or were applauded, how many ruined families, how many incidents, how many adventures, how many catastrophes were summed up in this flower! To all those who lived upon the crowd that was nightly summoned here, what a spectre this flower would have been had it appeared to them two years ago! What a labyrinth is destiny and what mysterious combinations there were that led up to the advent of this enchanting little yellow sun with its white rays. It required a theatre and a conflagration, which are the gaiety and the terror of a city, one of the most joyous inventions of man and one of the most terrible visitations of God, bursts of laughter for thirty years and whirlwinds of flame for thirty horn's to produce this Easter daisy, the delight of a gnat.

Theatre

I. Joanny

March 7, 1830, Midnight

They have been playing "Hernani" at the Théâtre-Français since February 25. The receipts for each performance have been five thousand francs. The public every night hisses all the verses. It is a rare uproar. The parterre hoots, the boxes burst with laughter. The actors are abashed and hostile; most of them ridicule what they have to say. The press has been practically unanimous every morning in making fun of the piece and the author. If I enter a reading room I cannot pick up a paper without seeing: "Absurd as 'Hernani'; silly, false, bombastic, pretentious, extravagant and nonsensical as 'Hernani'." If I venture into the corridors of the theatre while the performance is in progress I see spectators issue from their boxes and slam the doors indignantly. Mlle. Mars plays her part honestly and faithfully, but laughs at it, even in my presence. Michelot plays his resignedly and laughs at it behind my back. There is not a scene shifter, not a super, not a lamp lighter but points his finger at me.

Today I dined with Joanny, who had invited me. Joanny plays Ruy Gomez. He lives at No. 1 Rue du Jardinet, with a young seminarist, his nephew. The dinner party was sober and cordial. There were some journalists there, among others M. Merle, the husband of Mme. Dorval. After dinner, Joanny, who has the most beautiful white hair in the world, rose, filled his glass, turned towards me. I was on his right hand. Here literally is what he said to me; I have just returned home and I write his words:

"Monsieur Victor Hugo, the old man, now unknown, who two hundred years ago filled the role of Don Diègue in 'Le Cid' was not more penetrated with respect and admiration in presence of the great

Corneille than the old man who plays Don Buy Gomez is today in your presence."

II. Mademoiselle Mars

IN HER LAST ILLNESS MLLE. MARS was often delirious. One evening the doctor arrived. She was in the throes of a high fever, and her mind was wandering. She prattled about the theatre, her mother, her daughter, her niece Georgina, about all that she held dear; she laughed, wept, screamed, sighed deeply.

The doctor approached her bed and said to her: "Dear lady, calm yourself, it is I." She did not recognise him and her mind continued to wander. He went on: "Come, show me your tongue, open your mouth." Mlle. Mars gazed at him, opened her mouth and said: "Here, look. Oh! all my teeth are my very own!"

Célimène still lived.

III. Frédérick Lemaitre

FRÉDÉRICK LEMAITRE IS CROSS, MOROSE and kind. He lives in retirement with his children and his mistress, who at present is Mlle. Clarisse Miroy.

Frédérick likes the table. He never invites anybody to dinner except Porcher, the chief of the claque.* Frédérick and Porcher "thee-thou" each other. Porcher has common sense, good manners, and plenty of money, which he lends gallantly to authors whose rent is due. Porcher is the man of whom Harel said: "He likes, protects and disdains Literary men."

Frédérick has never less than fifteen dishes at his table. When the servant brings them in he looks at them and judges them without tasting them. Often he says:

"That is bad."

"Have you eaten of it?"

"No, God forbid!"

"But taste it."

---

* A band of men and boys who are paid to applaud a piece or a certain actor or actress at a given signal. The applause contractor, or *chef de claque*, is an important factor in French theatrical affairs.

"It is detestable."

"I will taste it," says Clarisse.

"It is execrable. I forbid you to do so."

"But let me try it."

"Take that dish away! It is filthy!" And he sends for his cook and rates her soundly.

He is greatly feared by all his household. His domestics live in a state of terror. At table, if he does not speak, no one utters a word. Who would dare to break the silence when he is mute? One would think it was a dinner of dumb people, or a supper of Trappists, except for the good cheer. He likes to wind up the repast with fish. If there is turbot he has it served after the creams. He drinks, when dining, a bottle and a half of Bordeaux wine. Then, after dinner, he lights his cigar, and while smoking drinks two other bottles of wine.

For all that he is a comedian of genius and a very good fellow. He is easily moved to tears, which start to his eyes at a word said to him angrily or reproachfully.

This dates back to 1840. Mlle. Atala Beaudouin (the actress who under the name of Louise Beaudouin created the role of the Queen in Ruy Bias) had left Frédérick Lemaître, the great and marvellous comedian. Frédérick adored her and was inconsolable.

Mlle. Atala's mother had strongly advised her daughter on this occasion. Frédérick was occasionally violent, notwithstanding that he was very amorous; and, besides, a Russian prince had presented himself. In short, Mlle. Atala persisted in her determination and positively refused to see Frederick.

Frederick made frightful threats, especially against the mother. One morning there was a violent ringing at Mlle. Atala's bell. Her mother opened the door and recoiled in terror. It was Frédérick. He entered, dropped into the chair that was handiest to him, and said to the old woman:

"Don't be afraid, I haven't come to kick your—, I have come to weep."

IV. The Comiques

September, 1846

Potier, having grown old, played at the Porte Saint Martin towards the close of his life. He was the same in the street as he was on the stage. Little boys would follow him, saying: "There is Potier!" He had a small cottage near Paris and used to come to rehearsals mounted on a small horse, his long thin legs dangling nearly to the ground.

Tiercelin was a Hellenist. Odry is a connoisseur of chinaware. The elephantine Lepeintre junior runs into debt and lives the life of a *coquin de neuveu*.

Alcide Tousez, Sainville and Ravel carry on in the green room just as they do on the stage, inventing cock-and-bull yarns and cracking jokes.

Arnal composes classic verse, admires Samson, waxes wrath because the cross has not been conferred upon him. And, in the green room, with rouge on his nose and cheeks and a wig on his head, talks, between two slaps in the face given or received, about Guizot's last speech, free trade and Sir Robert Peel; he interrupts himself, makes his entry upon the stage, plays his part, returns and gravely resumes: "I was saying that Robert Peel—"

Poor Arnal recently was driven almost insane. He had a mistress whom he adored. This woman fleeced him. Having become rich enough she said to him: "Our position is an immoral one and an end must be put to it. An honest man has offered me his name and I am going to get married." Arnal was disconsolate. "I give you the preference," said the belle, "marry me." Arnal is married. The woman left him and has become a bourgeoise. Arnal nearly lost his reason through grief. This does not prevent him from playing his pasquinades every night at the Vaudeville. He makes fun of his ugliness, of his age, of the fact that he is pitted with small-pox—laughs at all those things that prevented him from pleasing the woman he loved, and makes the public laugh—and his heart is broken. Poor red queue! What eternal and incurable sorrows there be in the gaiety of a buffoon! What a lugubrious business is that of laughter!

V. Mademoiselle Georges

October, 23, 1867

Mlle. George came to see me today. She was sad, and elegantly dressed in a blue dress with white stripes. She said: "I am weary and disgusted. I asked for Mars' reversion. They granted me a pension of two thousand francs which they do not pay. Just a mouthful of bread, and even that I do not get a chance to eat! They wanted to engage me at the Historique (at the Théâtre Historique). I refused. What could I do there among those transparencies! A stout woman like me! Besides, where are the authors? Where are the pieces? Where are the roles? As to the provinces, I tried touring last year, but it is impossible without Harel.* I don't know how to manage actors. How do you think I can get on with these evil doers? I was to have finished the 24th. I paid them on the 20th, and fled. I returned to Paris to visit poor Harel's tomb. It is frightful, a tomb! It is horrible to see his name there on the stone! Yet I did not weep. I was dry-eyed and cold. What a strange thing is life! To think that this man who was so clever, so witty, should die an idiot! He passed his days doing like this with his fingers. Not a spark of reason remained. It is all over. I shall have Rachel at my benefit; I shall play with her that chestnut "Iphigênie". We shall make money, but I don't care. Besides, I'm sure she wouldn't play Rodogune! I will also play, if you will permit me, an act of "Lucrèce Borgia". You see, I am for Rachel; she is an artful one, if you like. See how she checkmates those rascally French actors! She renews her engagements, assures for herself pyrotechnics, vacations, heaps of gold. When the contract is signed she says: "By the bye, I forgot to tell you that I have been enceinte for four months; it will be five months before I am able to play." She does well. If I had done the same thing I shouldn't have to die like a dog on a litter of straw. Tragedians, you see, are comedians after all. That poor Dorval, what has become of her, do you know? There is one to be pitied, if you like! She is playing I know not where, at Toulouse, at Carpentras, in barns, to earn her living! She is reduced like me to showing her bald head and dragging her poor old carcass on badly planed boards behind footlights of four tallow candles, among strolling actors who have been to the galleys, or who ought to be there! Ah! Monsieur Hugo, all this is nothing to you who are in good health and well off, but we are poor miserable creatures!"

VI. Tableaux Vivants

IN THE YEAR 1846 THERE was a spectacle that caused a furore in Paris. It was that afforded by women attired only in pink tights and

---

* M. Harel was manager of the Porte St. Martin Theatre. Mlle. Georges lived with him.

a gauze skirt executing poses that were called *tableaux vivants*, with a few men to complete the groups. This show was given at the Porte Saint Martin and at the Cirque. I had the curiosity one night to go and see the women behind the scenes. I went to the Porte Saint Martin, where, I may add in parentheses, they were going to revive "Lucrêce Borgia". Villemot, the stage manager, who was of poor appearance but intelligent, said: "I will take you into the gynecium."

A score of men were there—authors, actors, firemen, lamp lighters, scene shifters—who came, went, worked or looked on, and in the midst of them seven or eight women, practically nude, walked about with an air of the most naïve tranquillity. The pink tights that covered them from the feet to the neck were so thin and transparent that one could see not only the toes, the navel, and the breasts, but also the veins and the colour of the least mark on the skin on all parts of their bodies. Towards the abdomen, however, the tights became thicker and only the form was distinguishable. The men who assisted them were similarly arranged. All these people were English.

At intervals of five minutes the curtain parted and they executed a *tableau*. For this they were posed in immobile attitudes upon a large wooden disc which revolved upon a pivot. It was worked by a child of fourteen who reclined on a mattress beneath it. Men and women were dressed up in chiffons of gauze or merino that were very ugly at a distance and very ignoble *de près*. They were pink statues. When the disc had revolved once and shown the statues on every side to the public crowded in the darkened theatre, the curtain closed again, another tableau was arranged, and the performance recommenced a moment later.

Two of these women were very pretty. One resembled Mme. Rey, who played the Queen in "Ruy Blas" in 1840; it was this one who represented Venus. She was admirably shaped. Another was more than pretty: she was handsome and superb. Nothing more magnificent could be seen than her black, sad eyes, her disdainful mouth, her smile at once bewitching and haughty. She was called Maria, I believe. In a tableau which represented "A Slave Market," she displayed the imperial despair and the stoical dejection of a nude queen offered for sale to the first bidder. Her tights, which were torn at the hip, disclosed her firm white flesh. They were, however only poor girls of London. All had dirty finger nails.

When they returned to the green room they laughed as freely with the scene shifters as with the authors, and talked broken French while they adjusted all kinds of frightful rags upon their charming visages. Their smile was the calm smile of perfect innocence or of complete corruption.

At the Academy

CHARLES NODIER: The Academy, yielding to custom, has suppressed universally the double consonant in verbs where this consonant supplanted euphoniously the *d* of the radical *ad*.

MYSELF: I avow my profound ignorance. I had no idea that custom had effected this suppression and that the Academy had sanctioned it. Thus one should no longer write *atteindre, approuver, appeler, apprehender*, etc., but *ateindre, aprouver, apeler, apréhender*?

M. VICTOR COUSIN: I desire to point out to M. Hugo that the alterations of which he complains come from the movement of the language, which is nothing else than decadence.

MYSELF: M. Cousin having addressed a personal observation to me, I beg to point out to him in turn that his opinion is, in my estimation, merely an opinion and nothing more. I may add that, as I view it, "movement of the language" and decadence have nothing in common. Nothing could be more distinct than these two things. Movement in no way proves decadence. The language has been moving since the first day of its formation; can it be said to be deteriorating? Movement is life; decadence is death.

M. COUSIN: The decadence of the French language began in 1789.

MYSELF: At what hour, if you please?

October 8, 1844

This is what was told to me at today's session:

Salvandy recently dined with Villemain. The repast over, they adjourned to the drawing-room, and conversed. As the clock struck eight Villemain's three little daughters entered to kiss their father good night. The youngest is named Lucette; her birth cost her mother her reason; she is a sweet and charming child of five years.

"Well, Lucette, dear child," said her father, "won't you recite one of Lafontaine's fables before you go to bed?"

"Here," observed M. de Salvandy, "is a little person who today recites fables and who one of these days will inspire romances."

Lucette did not understand. She merely gazed with her big wondering eyes at Salvandy who was lolling in his chair with an air of benevolent condescension.

"Well, Lucette." he went on, "will you not recite a fable for us?"

The child required no urging, and began in her naïve little voice, her fine, frank, sweet eyes still fixed upon Salvandy:

One easily believes one's self to be somebody in France.

1845

During the run of M. Ponsard's "Lucrece", I had the following dialogue with M. Viennet at a meeting of the Academy:

M. Viennet: Have you seen the "Lucrece" that is being played at the Odéon?

Myself: No.

M. Viennet: It is very good.

Myself: Really, is it good?

M. Viennet: It is more than good, it is fine.

Myself: Really, is it fine?

M. Viennet: It is more than fine, it is magnificent.

Myself: Really, now, magnificent?

M. Viennet: Oh! magnificent!

Myself: Come, now, is it as good as "Zaire"?

M. Viennet: Oh! no! Oh! you are going too far, you know. Gracious! "Zaire"! No, it is not as good as "Zaire".

Myself: Well, you see, "Zaire" is a very poor piece indeed!

An Election Session

Thirty-one Academicians present. Sixteen votes are necessary.

First ballot.

Emile Deschamps	2 votes.
Victor Leclerc	14 "
Empis	15 "

Lamartine and M. Ballanche arrive at the end of the first ballot. M. Thiers arrives at the commencement of the second; which makes 34.

The director asks M. Thiers whether he has promised his vote. He laughingly replies: "No," and adds: "I have offered it." (Laughter.)

M. Cousin, to M. Lebrun, director: "You did not employ the sacramental expression. One does not ask an Academician whether he has *promised* his vote, but whether he has *pledged* it."

Second ballot.

Emile Deschamps	2 votes.
Empis	18 "
Victor Leclerc	14 "

M. Empis is elected. The election was decided by Lamartine and M. Ballanche.

On my way out I meet Leon Gozlan, who says to me: "Well?"

I reply: "There has been an election. It is Empis."

"How do you look at it?" he asks.

"In both ways."

"Empis?—"

"And *tant pis*!"

March 16, 1847

At the Academy today, while listening to the poems, bad to the point of grotesqueness, that have been sent for the competition of 1847, M. de Barante remarked: "Really, in these times, we no longer know how to make mediocre verses."

Great praise of the poetical and literary excellence of these times, although M. de Barante was not conscious of it.

April 22, 1847

Election of M. Ampere. This is an improvement upon the last. A slow improvement. But Academies, like old people, go slowly.

During the session and after the election Lamartine sent to me by an usher the following lines:

> *C'est un état peu prospere*
> *D'aller d'Empis en Ampere.*

I replied to him by the same usher:

> *Toutefois ce serait pis*
> *D'aller d'Ampere en Empis.*

October 4, 1847

I have just heard M. Viennet say: "I think in bronze."

December 29, 1848. Friday

Yesterday, Thursday, I had two duties to attend to at one and the same time, the Assembly and the Academy; the salt question on the one hand, on the other the much smaller question of two vacant seats. Yet I gave the preference to the latter. This is why: At the Palais Bourbon the Cavaignac party had to be prevented from killing the new Cabinet; at the Palais Mazarin the Academy had to be prevented from offending the memory of Chateaubriand. There are cases in which the dead count for more than the living; I went to the Academy.

The Academy last Thursday had suddenly decided, at the opening of the session, at a time when nobody had yet put in an appearance, when there were only four or five round the green table, that on January 11 (that is to say, in three weeks) it would fill the two seats left vacant by MM. de Chateaubriand and Vatout. This strange alliance, I do not say of names, but of words,—"replace MM. de Chateaubriand and Vatout,"—did not stop it for one minute. The Academy is thus made; its wit and that wisdom which produces so many follies, are composed of extreme lightness combined with extreme heaviness. Hence a good deal of foolishness and a good many foolish acts.

Beneath this lightness, however, there was an intention. This giddiness was fraught with deep meaning. The brave party that leads the Academy, for there are parties everywhere, even at the Academy, hoped, public attention being directed elsewhere, politics absorbing everything, to juggle the seat of Chateaubriand pell-mell with the seat of M. Vatout; two peas in the same goblet. In this way the astonished public would turn round one fine morning and simply see M. de Noailles in Chateaubriand's seat: a small matter, a great lord in the place of a great writer!

Then, after a roar of laughter, everybody would go about his business again, distractions would speedily come, thanks to the veering of politics, and, as to the Academy, oh! a duke and peer the more in it, a little more ridicule upon it, what would that matter? It would go on just the same!

Besides, M. de Noailles is a considerable personage. Bearing a great name, being lofty of manner, enjoying an immense fortune, of certain political weight under Louis Philippe, accepted by the Conservatives although, or because, a Legitimist, reading speeches that were listened to, he occupied an important place in the Chamber of Peers; which proves that the Chamber of Peers occupied an unimportant place in the country.

Chateaubriand, who hated all that could replace him and smiled at all that could make him regretted, had had the kindness to tell him sometimes, by Mme. Récamier's fireside, "that he hoped he would be his successor;" which prompted M. de Noailles to dash off a big book in two volumes about Mme. de Maintenon, at the commencement of which, on the first page of the preface, I was stopped by a lordly breach of grammar.

This was the state of things when I concluded to go to the Academy.

The session which was announced to begin at two o'clock, as usual, opened, as usual, at a quarter past three. And at half past three—

At half past three the candidacy of Monsieur the Duke do Noailles, *replacing* Chateaubriand, was irresistibly acclaimed.

Decidedly, I ought to have gone to the Assembly.

March 26, 1850. Tuesday

I had arrived early, at noon.

I was warming myself, for it is very cold, and the ground is covered with snow, which is not good for the apricot trees. M. Guizot, leaning against the mantelpiece, was saying to me:

"As a member of the dramatic prize committee, I read yesterday, in a single day, mind you, no fewer than six plays!"

"That," I responded, "was to punish you for not having seen one acted in eighteen years."

At this moment M. Thiers came up and the two men exchanged greetings. This is how they did it:

M. THIERS: Good afternoon, Guizot.

M. GUIZOT: Good afternoon, Monsieur.

March 28, 1850

M. Guizot presided. At the roll call, when M. Pasquier's name was reached he said: "Monsieur the Chancellor—" When he got to that of M. Dupin, President of the National Assembly, he called: "Monsieur Dupin."

First ballot.

Alfred de Musset	5 votes.
M. Nisard	23 "
M. Nisard is elected.	

Today, September 12, the Academy worked at the dictionary. A propos of the word "increase," this example, taken from the works of Mme. de Staël, was proposed:

"Poverty increases ignorance, and ignorance poverty."

Three objections were immediately raised:

1. Antithesis.
2. Contemporary writer.
3. Dangerous thing to say.

The Academy rejected the example.

Love in Prison

I

BESIDES MISDEEDS, ROBBERIES, THE DIVISION of spoils after an ambuscade, and the twilight exploitation of the barriers of Paris, footpads, burglars, and gaol-birds generally have another industry: they have ideal loves.

This requires explanation.

The trade in negro slaves moves us, and with good reason; we examine this social sore, and we do well. But let us also learn to lay bare another ulcer, which is more painful, perhaps: the traffic in white women.

Here is one of the singular things connected with and characteristic of this poignant disorder of our civilization:

Every gaol contains a prisoner who is known as the "artist."

All kinds of trades and professions peculiar to prisons develop behind the bars. There is the vendor of liquorice-water, the vendor of scarfs, the writer, the advocate, the usurer, the hut-maker, and the barker. The artist takes rank among these local and peculiar professions between the writer and the advocate.

To be an artist is it necessary to know how to draw? By no means. A bit of a bench to sit upon, a wall to lean against, a lead pencil, a bit of pasteboard, a needle stuck in a handle made out of a piece of wood, a little Indian ink or sepia, a little Prussian blue, and a little vermilion in three cracked beechwood spoons,—this is all that is requisite; a knowledge of drawing is superfluous. Thieves are as fond of colouring as children are, and as fond of tattooing as are savages. The artist by means of his three spoons satisfies the first of these needs, and by means of his needle the second. His remuneration is a "nip" of wine.

The result is this:

Some prisoners, say, lack everything, or are simply desirous of living more comfortably. They combine, wait upon the artist, offer him their glasses of wine or their bowls of soup, hand him a sheet of paper and order of him a bouquet. In the bouquet there must be as many flowers as there are prisoners in the group. If there be three prisoners, there must be three flowers. Each flower bears a figure, or, if preferred, a number, which number is that of the prisoner.

The bouquet when painted is sent, through the mysterious means of communication between the various prisons that the police are powerless to prevent, to Saint Lazare. Saint Lazare is the women's prison, and where there are women there also is pity. The bouquet circulates from hand to hand among the unfortunate creatures that the police detain administratively at Saint Lazare; and in a few days the infallible secret post apprises those who sent the bouquet that Palmyre has chosen the tuberose, that Fanny prefers the azalea, and that Seraphine has adopted the geranium. Never is this lugubrious handkerchief thrown into the seraglio without being picked up.

Thenceforward the three bandits have three servants whose names are Palmyre, Fanny, and Seraphine. Administrative detentions are relatively of short duration. These women are released from prison before the men. And what do they do? They support them. In elegant phraseology they are providences; in plain language they are milch-cows.

Pity has been transformed into love. The heart of woman is susceptible of such sombre graftings. These women say:

"I am married." They are married indeed. By whom? By the flower. With whom? With the abyss. They are fiancées of the unknown. Enraptured and enthusiastic fiancées. Pale Sulamites of fancy and fog. When the known is so odious, how can they help loving the unknown?

In these nocturnal regions and with the winds of dispersion that blow, meetings are almost impossible. The lovers see each other in dreams. In all probability the woman will never set eyes on the man. Is he young? Is he old? Is he handsome? Is he ugly? She does not know; she knows nothing about him. She adores him. And it is because she does not know him that she loves him. Idolatry is born of mystery.

This woman, drifting aimlessly on life's tide, yearns for something to cling to, a tie to bind her, a duty to perform. The pit from amid its scum throws it to her; she accepts it and devotes herself to it. This mysterious bandit, transformed into heliotrope or iris, becomes a religion to her. She espouses him in the presence of night. She has a thousand little wifely attentions for him; poor for herself, she is rich for him; she whelms this manure with her delicate solicitude. She is faithful to him with all the fidelity of which she is still capable; the incorruptible emanates from the corruptible. Never does this woman betray her love. It is an immaterial, pure, ethereal love, subtile as the breath of spring, solid as brass.

A flower has done all this. What a well is the human heart, and how giddy it makes one to peer into it! Lo! the cloaca. Of what is it thinking? Of perfume. A prostitute loves a thief through a lily. What plunger into human thought could reach the bottom of this? Who shall fathom this immense yearning for flowers that springs from mud? In the secret self of these hapless women is a strange equilibrium that consoles and reassures them. A rose counterbalances an act of shame.

Hence these amours based on and sustained by illusion. This thief is idolized by this girl. She has not seen his face, she does not know his name; she sees him in visions induced by the perfume of jessamine or of pinks. Henceforward flower-gardens, the May sunshine, the birds in their nests, exquisite tints, radiant blossoms, boxes of orange trees and daphne odora, velvet petals upon which golden bees alight, the sacred odours of spring-tide, balms, incense, purling brooks, and soft green grass are associated with this bandit. The divine smile of nature penetrates and illumines him.

This desperate aspiring to paradise lost, this deformed dream of the beautiful, is not less tenacious on the part of the man. He turns towards the woman; and this preoccupation, become insensate, persists even when the dreadful shadow of the two red posts of the guillotine is thrown upon the window of his cell. The day before his execution Delaporte, chief of the Trappes band, who was wearing the strait-jacket, asked of the convict Cogniard, whom, through the grating in the door of the condemned cell, he saw passing by: "Are there any pretty women in the visitors' parlor this morning?" Another condemned man, Avril (what a name!), in this same cell, bequeathed all that he possessed—five francs—to a female prisoner whom he had seen at a distance in the women's yard, "in order that she may buy herself a fichu a la mode."

Between the male and female wretch dreams build a Bridge of Sighs, as it were. The mire of the gutter dallies with the door of a prison cell. The Aspasia of the street-corner aspires and respires with the heart of the Alcibiades who waylays the passer-by at the corner of a wood.

You laugh? You should not. It is a terrible thing.

II

THE MURDERER IS A FLOWER for the courtesan. The prostitute is the Clytia of the assassin sun. The eye of the woman damned languourously seeks Satan among the myrtles.

What is this phenomenon? It is the need of the ideal. A sublime and awful need.

A terrible thing, I say.

Is it a disease? Is it a remedy? Both. This noble yearning is at the same time and for the same beings a chastisement and a reward; a voluptuousness full of expiation; a chastisement for faults committed, a recompense for sorrows borne! None may escape it. It is a hunger of angels felt by demons. Saint Theresa experiences it, Messalina also. This need of the immaterial is the most deeply rooted of all needs. One must have bread; but before bread, one must have the ideal. One is a thief, one is a street-walker—all the more reason. The more one drinks of the darkness of night the more is one thirsty for the light of dawn. Schinderhannes becomes a cornflower, Poulailler a violet. Hence these sinisterly ideal weddings.

And then, what happens?

What I have just said.

Cloaca, but abyss. Here the human heart opens partly, disclosing unimaginable depths. Astarte becomes platonic. The miracle of the transformation of monsters by love is being accomplished. Hell is being gilded. The vulture is being metamorphosed into a bluebird. Horror ends in the pastoral. You think you are at Vouglans's and Parent-Duchâtelet's; you are at Longus's. Another step and you will stumble into Berquin's. Strange indeed is it to encounter Daphnis and Chloe in the Forest of Bondy!

The dark Saint Martin Canal, into which the footpad pushes the passer-by with his elbow as he snatches his victim's watch, traverses the Tender and empties itself into the Lignon. Poulmann begs a ribbon bow; one is tempted to present a shepherdess's crook to Papavoine. Through the straw of the sabot one sees gossamer wings appearing on horrible heels. The miracle of the roses is performed for Goton. All fatalities combined have for result a flower. A vague Rambouillet Palace is superposed upon the forbidding silhouette of the Salpêtrière. The leprous wall of evil, suddenly covered with blossoms, affords a pendant to the wreath of Juliet. The sonnets of Petrarch, that flight of the ideal which soars in the shadow of souls, venture through the twilight towards this abjection and suffering, attracted by one knows not what obscure affinity, even as a swarm of bees is sometimes seen humming over a dungheap from which arises, perceptible to the bees alone and mingling with the miasms, the perfume of a hidden flower. The gemoniae are Elysian. The chimerical thread of celestial unions floats 'neath the darkest vault of the human Erebus and binds despairing hearts to hearts that are monstrous. Manon through the infinite sends to Cartouche a smile ineffable as that with which Everallin entranced Fingal. From one pole of misery to the other, from one gehenna to another, from the galleys to the brothel, tenebrous mouths wildly exchange the kiss of azure.

It is night. The monstrous ditch of Clamart opens. From it arises a miasm, a phosphorescent glow. It shines and flickers in two separate tarts; it takes shape, the head rejoins the body, it is a phantom; the phantom gazes into the darkness with wild, baleful eyes, rises, grows bigger and blue, hovers for an instant and then speeds away to the zenith to open the door of the palace of the sun where butterflies flit from flower to flower and angels flit from star to star.

In all these strange, concordant phenomena appears the inadmissibility of the principle that is all of man. The mysterious marriage which we have just related, marriage of servitude with captivity, exaggerates the ideal from the very fact that it is weighed down by all the most hideous burdens of destiny. A frightful combination! It is the From it rises a miasm, a phosphorescent glow. It shines meeting of these two redoubtable words in which human existence is summed up: enjoy and suffer.

Alas! And how can we prevent this cry from escaping us? For these hapless ones, enjoy, laugh, sing, please, and love exist, persist; but there is a death-rattle in sing, a grating sound in laugh, putrefaction in enjoy, there are ashes in please, there is night in love. All these joys are attached to their destiny by coffin-nails.

What does that matter? They thirst for these lugubrious, chimerical glimpses of light that are full of dreams.

What is tobacco, that is so precious and so dear to the prisoner? It is a dream. "Put me in the dungeon," said a convict, "but give me some tobacco." In other words: "Throw me into a pit, but give me a palace." Press the prostitute and the bandit, mix Tartarus and Avernus, stir the fatal vat of social mire, pile all the deformities of matter together, and what issues therefrom? The immaterial.

The ideal is the Greek fire of the gutter. It burns there. Its brightness in the impure water dazzles the thinker and touches his heart. Nini Lassive stirs and brightens with Fiesehi's bilets-doux that sombre lamp of Vesta which is in the heart of every woman, and which is as inextinguishable in that of the courtesan as in that of the Carmelite. This is what explains the word "virgin," accorded by the Bible equally to the foolish virgin and to the wise virgin.

That was so yesterday, it is so today. Here again the surface has changed, the bottom remains the same. The frank harshness of the Middle Ages has been somewhat softened in our times. Ribald is pronounced light o' love; Toinon answers to the name of Olympia or Imperia; Thomasse-la-Maraude is called Mme. de Saint Alphonse. The caterpillar was real, the butterfly is false; that is the only change. Clout has become chiffon.

Regnier used to say "sows"; we say "fillies."

Other fashions; same manners.

The foolish virgin is lugubriously immutable.

III

Whosoever witnesses this kind of anguish witnesses the extreme of human misfortune.

Dark zones are these. Baleful night bursts and spreads o'er them. Evil accumulated dissolves in misfortune upon them, they are swept with blasts of despair by the tempest of fatalities, there a downpour of trials and sorrows streams upon dishevelled heads in the darkness; squalls, hail, a hurricane of distress, swirl and whirl back and forth athwart them; it rains, rains without cease: it rains horror, it rains vice, it rains crime, it rains the blackness of night; yet we must explore this obscurity, and in the sombre storm the mind essays a difficult flight, the flight of a wet bird, as it were.

There is always a vague, spectral dread in these low regions where hell penetrates; they are so little in the human order and so disproportionate that they create phantoms. It is hardly surprising, therefore, that a legend should be connected with this sinister bouquet offered by Bicêtre to La Salpêtrière or by La Force to Saint Lazare; it is related at night in the cells and wards after the keepers have gone their rounds.

It was shortly after the murder of the money-changer Joseph. A bouquet was sent from La Force to a woman's prison, Saint Lazare or the Madelonnettes. In this bouquet was a sprig of white lilac which one of the women prisoners selected.

A month or two elapsed; the woman was released from prison. She was extremely enamoured, through the white lilac, of the unknown master she had given to herself. She began to perform for him her strange function of sister, mother, and mystic spouse, ignorant of his name, knowing only his prison number. All her miserable savings, religiously deposited with the clerk of the prison, went to this man. In order the better to affiance herself to him, she took advantage of the advent of spring to cull a sprig of real lilac in the fields. This sprig of lilac, attached by a piece of sky-blue ribbon to the head of his bed, formed a pendant to a sprig of consecrated box, an ornament which these poor desolate alcoves never lack. The lilac withered thus.

This woman, like all Paris, had heard of the affair of the Palais-Royal and of the two Italians, Malagutti and Ratta, arrested for the murder of the money-changer.

She thought little about the tragedy, which did not concern her, and lived only in her white lilac. This lilac was all in all to her; she thought only of doing her "duty" to it.

One bright, sunny day she was seated in her room, sewing some garment or other for her sorry evening toilet. Now and then she looked up from her work at the lilac that hung at the head of the bed. At one of these moments while her gaze was fixed upon the sprig of faded flower the clock struck four.

Then she fancied she saw an extraordinary thing.

A sort of crimson pearl oozed from the extremity of the stalk of the flower, grew larger, and dripped on to the white sheet of the bed.

It was a spot of blood.

That day, at that very hour, Ratta and Malagutti were executed.

It was evident that the white lilac was one of these two. But which one?

The hapless girl became insane and had to be confined in La Salpêtrière. She died there. From morn to night, and from night to morn, she would gibber: "I am Mme. Ratta-Malagutti."

Thus are these sombre hearts.

IV

PROSTITUTION IS AN ISIS WHOSE final veil none has raised. There is a sphinx in this gloomy odalisk of the frightful Sultan Everybody. None has solved its enigma. It is Nakedness masked. A terrible spectacle!

Alas! in all that we have just recounted man is abominable, woman is touching.

How many hapless ones have been driven to their fall!

The abyss is the friend of dreams. Fallen, as we have said, their lamentable hearts have no other resource than to dream.

What caused their ruin was another dream, the dreadful dream of riches; nightmare of glory, of azure, and ecstasy which weighs upon the chest of the poor; flourish of trumpets heard in the gehenna, with the triumph of the fortunate appearing resplendent in the immense night; prodigious overture full of dawn! Carriages roll, gold falls in showers, laces rustle.

Why should I not have this, too? Formidable thought!

This gleam from the sinister vent-hole dazzled them; this puff of the sombre vapour inebriated them, and they were lost, and they were rich.

Wealth is a fatal distant light; woman flies frantically towards it. This mirror catches this lark.

Wherefore they have been rich. They, too, have had their day of enchantment, their minute of fête, their sparkle.

They have had that fever which is fatal to modesty. They have drained the sonorous cup that is full of nothingness. They have drunk of the madness of forgetfulness. What a flattering hope! What temptation! To do nothing and have everything; alas! and also to have nothing, not even one's own self. To be slave-flesh, to be beauty for sale, a woman fallen to a thing! They have dreamed and they have had—which is the same thing, complete possession being but a dream—mansions, carriages, servants in livery, suppers joyous with laughter, the house of gold, silk, velvet, diamonds, pearls, life giddy with voluptuousness— every pleasure.

Oh! how much better is the innocence of those poor little barefooted ones on the shore of the sea, who hear at nightfall the tinkling of the cracked bells of the goats on the cliffs!

There was a disastrous morrow to these brief, perfidious joys that they had savoured. The word love signified hatred. The invisible doubles the visible, and it is lugubrious. Those who shared their raptures, those to whom they gave all, received all and accepted nothing. They—the fallen ones—sowed their seed in ashes. They were deserted even as they were being embraced. Abandonment sniggered behind the mask of the kiss.

And now, what are they to do? They must perforce continue to love.

V

OH! IF THEY COULD, THE unhappy creatures, if they could put from them their hearts, their dreams, harden themselves with a hardness that could not be softened, be forever cold and passionless, tear out their entrails, and, since they are filth, become monsters! If they could no longer think! If they could ignore the flower, efface the star, stop up the mouth of the pit, close heaven! They would at least no longer suffer. But no. They have a right to marriage, they have a right to the heart, they have a right to torture, they have a right to the ideal. No chilling of their hearts can put out the internal fire. However cold they may be they burn. This, we have said, is at once their misery and their crown. This sublimeness combines with their abjection to overwhelm them and raise them up. Whether they will or not, the inextinguishable does not become extinguished. Illusion is untamable. Nothing is more invincible than dreams, and man is almost made up of dreams. Nature will not agree to be insolvable. One must contemplate, aspire, love. If need be marble will set the example. The statue becomes a woman rather than the woman a statue.

The sewer is a sanctuary in spite of itself. It is unhealthy, there is vitiated air in it, but the irresistible phenomenon is none the less accomplished; all the holy generosities bloom livid in this cave. Cynicism and the secret despair of pity are driven back by ecstasy, the magnificences of kindness shine through infamy; this orphan creature feels herself to be wife, sister, mother; and this fraternity which has no family, and this maternity which has no children, and this adoration which has no altar, she casts into the outer darkness. Some one marries her. Who? The man in the gloom. She sees on her finger the ring made of the mysterious gold of dreams. And she sobs. Torrents of tears well from her eyes. Sombre delights!

And at the same time, let us repeat it, she suffers unheard-of tortures. She does not belong to him to whom she has given herself. Everybody takes her away again. The brutal public hand holds the wretched creature and will not let her go. She fain would flee. Flee whither? From whom? From you, herself, above all from him whom she loves, the funereal ideal man. She cannot.

Thus, and these are extreme afflictions, this hapless wight expiates, and her expiation is brought upon her by her grandeur. Whatever she may do, she has to love. She is condemned to the light. She has to condole, she has to succour, she has to devote herself, she has to be kind. A woman who has lost her modesty, fain would know love no more; impossible. The refluxes of the heart are as inevitable as those of the sea; the lights of the heart are as fixed as those of the night.

There is within us that which we can never lose. Abnegation, sacrifice, tenderness, enthusiasm, all these rays turn against the woman within her inmost self and attack and burn her. All these virtues remain to avenge themselves upon her. When she would have been a wife, she is a slave. Hers is the hopeless, thankless task of lulling a brigand in the blue nebulousness of her illusions and of decking Mandrin with a starry rag. She is the sister of charity of crime. She loves, alas! She endures her inadmissible divinity; she is magnanimous and thrills at so being. She is happy with a horrible happiness. She enters backwards into indignant Eden.

We do not sufficiently reflect upon this that is within us and cannot be lost.

Prostitution, vice, crime, what matters!

Night may become as black as it likes, the spark is still there. However low you go there is light. Light in the vagabond, light in the mendicant, light in the thief, light in the street-walker. The deeper you go the more the miraculous light persists in showing itself.

Every heart has its pearl, which is the same for the heart gutter and the heart ocean—love.

No mire can dissolve this particle of God.

Wherefore, there, at the extreme of gloom, of despondency, of chill-heartedness and abandonment; in this obscurity, in this putrefaction, in these gaols, in these dark paths, in this shipwreck; beneath the lowest layer of the heap of miseries, under the bog of public disdain which is ice and night; behind the eddying of those frightful snowflakes the judges, the gendarmes, the warders and the executioners for the bandit, the passers-by for the prostitute, which cross each other, innumerable, in the dull grey mist that for these wretches replace the sun; beneath these pitiless fatalities; beneath this bewildering maze of vaults, some of granite, the others of hatred; at the deepest depths of horror; in the midst of asphyxiation; at the bottom of the chaos of all possible blacknesses; under the frightful thickness of a deluge composed of expectorations, there where all is extinct, where all is dead, something moves and shines. What is it? A flame.

And what flame?

The soul.

O adorable prodigy!

Love, the ideal, is found even in the Pit.

At the Tuileries, 1844–1848

I. The King*

June, 28, 1844

The King told me that Talleyrand said to him one day:

"You will never be able to do anything with Thiers, although he would make an excellent tool. He is one of those men one cannot make use of unless one is able to satisfy them. Now, he never will be satisfied. It is unfortunate for him, as for you, that in our times, he cannot be made a cardinal."

A propos of the fortifications of Paris, the King told me how the Emperor Napoleon learned the news of the taking of Paris by the allies.

The Emperor was marching upon Paris at the head of his guard. Near Juvisy, at a place in the Forest of Fontainebleau where there is an obelisk ("that I never see without feeling heavy at heart," remarked the King), a courier on his way to meet Napoleon brought him the news of the capitulation of Paris. Paris had been taken. The enemy had entered it. The Emperor turned pale. He hid his face in his hands and remained thus, motionless, for a quarter of an hour. Then, without saying a word, he turned about and took the road back to Fontainebleau.

General Athalin witnessed this scene and recounted it to the King.

July, 1844

A few days ago the King said to Marshal Soult (in presence of others):

"Marshal, do you remember the siege of Cadiz?"

"Rather, sire, I should think so. I swore enough before that cursed Cadiz. I invested the place and was forced to go away as I had come."

"Marshal, while you were before it, I was inside it."

"I know, sire."

"The Cortes and the English Cabinet offered me the command of the Spanish army."

---

* Louis Philippe.

"I remember it."

"The offer was a grave one. I hesitated long. Bear arms against France! For my family, it is possible; but against my country! I was greatly perplexed. At this juncture you asked me, through a trusty person, for a secret interview in a little house situated on the Cortadura, between the city and your camp. Do you remember the fact, Monsieur the Marshal?"

"Perfectly, sire; the day was fixed and the interview arranged."

"And I did not turn up."

"That is so."

"Do you know why?"

"I never knew."

"I will tell you. As I was preparing to go to meet you, the commander of the English squadron, apprised of the matter, I know not how, dropped upon me brusquely and warned me that I was about to fall into a trap; that Cadiz being impregnable, they despaired of seizing me, but that at the Cortadura I should be arrested by you; that the Emperor wished to make of the Duke d'Orleans a second volume of the Duke d'Enghien, and that you would have me shot immediately. There, really," added the King with a smile, "your hand on your conscience, were you going to shoot me?"

The Marshal remained silent for a moment, then replied, with a smile not less inexpressible than that of the King:

"No, sire; I wanted to compromise you."

The subject of conversation was changed. A few minutes later the Marshal took leave of the King, and the King, as he watched him go, said with a smile to the person who heard this conversation:

"Compromise! compromise! Today it is called compromise. In reality, he would have shot me!"

August 4, 1844

Yesterday the King said to me:

"One of my embarrassments at present, in all this affair of the University and the clergy, is M. Affre."*

"Then why, sire," said I, "did you appoint him?"

"I made a mistake, I admit. I had at first appointed to the archbishopric of Paris the Cardinal of Arras, M. de la Tour d'Auvergne."

"It was a good choice," I observed.

---

* Archbishop Affre was shot and killed in the Faubourg Saint Antoine on September 25, 1848, while trying to stop the fighting between the troops and insurgents.

VICTOR HUGO

"Yes, good. He is insignificant. An honest old man of no account. An easy-going fellow. He was much sought after by the Carlists. Greatly imposed upon. His whole family hated me. He was induced to refuse. Not knowing what to do, and being in haste, I named M. Affre. I ought to have been suspicious of him. His countenance is neither open nor frank. I took his underhand air for a priestly air; I did wrong. And then, you know, it was in 1840. Thiers proposed him to me, and urged me to appoint him. Thiers is no judge of archbishops. I did it without sufficient reflection. I ought to have remembered what Talleyrand said to me one day: 'The Archbishop of Paris must always be an old man. The see is quieter and becomes vacant more frequently.' I appointed M. Affre, who is young; it was a mistake. However, I will re-establish the chapter of St. Denis and appoint as primate of it the Cardinal de la Tour d'Auvergne. The Papal Nuncio, to whom I spoke of my project just now, laughed heartily at it, and said: 'The Abbé Affre will commit some folly. Should he go to Rome the Pope will receive him very badly. He has acted pusillanimously and blunderingly on all occasions since he has been an archbishop. An archbishop of Paris who has any wit ought always to be on good terms with the King here and the Pope yonder.'"

August, 1844

A month or two ago the King went to Dreux. It was the anniversary of the death of the Duke d'Orleans. The King had chosen this day to put the coffins of his relatives in the family vault in order.

Among the number was a coffin that contained all the bones of the princes of the House of Orleans that the Duchess d'Orleans, mother of the King, had been able to collect after the Revolution, when the sepulchre was violated and they were dispersed. The coffin, placed in a separate vault, had recently been smashed in by the fall of an arch. The debris of the arch, stones and plaster, had become mingled with the bones.

The King had the coffin brought and opened before him. He was alone in the vault with the chaplain and two aides-de-camp. Another coffin, larger and stronger, had been prepared. The King himself, with his own hands, took, one after the other, the bones of his ancestors from the broken coffin and arranged them carefully in the new one. He would not permit any one else to touch them. From time to time he counted the skulls and said: "This is Monsieur the Duke de Penthièvre. This is

Monsieur the Count de Beaujolais." Then to the best of his ability and as far as he was able to he completed each group of bones.

This ceremony lasted from nine o'clock in the morning until seven o'clock in the evening without the King taking either rest or nourishment.

August, 1844

Yesterday, the 15th, after having dined at M. Villemain's, who lives in a country house near Neuilly, I called upon the King.

The King was not in the salon, where there were only the Queen, Madame Adelaide and a few ladies, among them Mme. Firmin-Rogier, who is charming. There were many visitors, among others the Duke de Brogue and M. Rossi, who were of the dinner party at which I had been present, M. de Lesseps, who lately distinguished himself as consul at Barcelona, M. Firmin-Rogier and the Count d'Agout.

I bowed to the Queen, who spoke to me at length about the Princess de Joinvile, who was delivered the day before yesterday, and whose baby arrived on the very day the news of the bombardment of Tangier by its father was received. It is a little girl. The Princess de Joinvile passes the whole day kissing her and saying: "How pretty she is!" with that sweet southern accent which the raillery of her brothers-in-law has not yet caused her to lose.

While I was talking to the Queen, the Duchess d'Orleans, dressed in black, came in and sat beside Madame Adelaide, who said to her: "Good evening, dear Helene."

A moment afterwards, M. Guizot, in black, wearing a chain of decorations, with a red ribbon in his buttonhole and the badge of the Legion of Honour on his coat, and looking pale and grave, crossed the salon. I grasped his hand as he passed and he said:

"I have sought you vainly during the past few days. Come and spend a day with me in the country. We have a lot to talk about. I am at Auteuil, No. 4, Place d'Agueneau."

"Will the King come tonight?" I asked.

"I do not think so," he replied. "He is with Admiral de Mackau. There is serious news. He will be occupied all the evening."

Then M. Guizot went away.

It was nearly ten o'clock, and I also was about to take my departure when one of Madame Adelaide's ladies of honour, sent by the Princess, came and told me that the King desired to speak with me and requested that I would remain. I returned to the salon, which had become almost empty.

A moment later, as ten o'clock was striking, the King came in. He wore no decorations and had a preoccupied air. As he passed by he said to me:

"Wait until I have gone my round; we shall have a little more time when everybody has left. There are only four persons here now and I have only four words to say to them."

In truth, he only tarried a moment with the Prussian Ambassador and M. de Lesseps, who had to communicate to him a letter from Alexandria relative to the strange abdication of the Pacha of Egypt.

Everybody took leave, and then the King came to me, thrust his arm in mine and led me into the large anteroom where he seated himself, and bade me be seated, upon a red lounge which is between two doors opposite the fireplace. Then he began to talk rapidly, energetically, as though a weight were being lifted from his mind:

"Monsieur Hugo, I am pleased to see you. What do you think of it all? All this is grave, yet it appears graver than it really is. But in politics, I know, one has sometimes to take as much into account that which appears grave as that which is grave. We made a mistake in taking this confounded protectorate.* We thought we were doing something popular for France, and we have done something embarrassing for the world. The popular effect was mediocre; the embarrassing effect is enormous. What did we want to hamper ourselves with Tahiti (the King pronounced it Taëte) for? What to us was this pinch of tobacco seeds in the middle of the ocean? What is the use of lodging our honour four thousand leagues away in the box of a sentry insulted by a savage and a madman? Upon the whole there is something laughable about it. When all is said and done it is a small matter and nothing big will come of it. Sir Robert Peel has spoken thoughtlessly. He has acted with schoolboy foolishness. He has diminished his consideration in Europe. He is a serious man, but capable of committing thoughtless acts. Then he does not know any languages. Unless he be a genius there are perforce gaps in the ideas of a man who is not a linguist. Now, Sir Robert has no genius. Would you believe it? He does not know French. Consequently he does not understand anything about France. French ideas pass before him like shadows. He is not malevolent, no; he is not

---

* The protectorate of Tahiti.

open, that is all. He has spoken without reflection. I judged him to be what he is forty years ago. It was, too, forty years ago that I saw him for the first time. He was then a young man and secretary of the Earl of—(I did not quite catch the name. The King spoke quickly). I often visited that house. I was then in England. When I saw young Peel I felt sure that he would go a long way, but that he would stop. Was I mistaken? There are Englishmen, and of the highest rank, who do not understand Frenchmen a bit. Like that poor Duke of Clarence, who afterwards was William IV. He was but a sailor. One must beware of the sailor mind, as I often say to my son Joinville. He who is only a sailor is nothing on land. Well, this Duke of Clarence used to say to me: 'Duke d'Orleans, a war between France and England is necessary every twenty years. History shows it.' I would reply: 'My dear duke, of what use are people of intelligence if they allow mankind to do the same foolish things over and over again?' The Duke of Clarence, like Peel, did not know a word of French.

"What a difference between these men and Huskisson! You know, Huskisson who was killed on a railway. He was a masterly man, if you like. He knew French and liked France. He had been my comrade at the Jacobins' Club. I do not say this in bad part. He understood everything. If there were in England now a man like him, he and I would ensure the peace of the world.—Monsieur Hugo, we will do it without him. I will do it alone. Sir Robert Peel will reconsider what he has said. Egad! he said that! Does he even know why or how?

"Have you seen the English Parliament? You speak from your place, standing, in the midst of your own party; you are carried away; you say more often than not what others think instead of what you think yourself. There is a magnetic communication. You are subjected to it. You rise (here the King rose and imitated the gesture of an orator speaking in Parliament). The assembly ferments all round and close to you; you let yourself go. On this side somebody says: 'England has suffered a gross insult;' and on that side: 'with gross indignity.' It is simply applause that is sought on both sides. Nothing more. But this is bad. It is dangerous. It is baleful. In France our tribune which isolates the orator has many advantages.

"Of all the English statesmen, I have known only one who was able to withstand this influence of assemblies. He was M. Pitt. M. Pitt was a clever man, although he was very tall. He had an air of awkwardness and spoke hesitatingly. His lower jaw weighed a hundredweight. Hence a certain slowness which forcibly brought prudence into his speeches. Besides, what a statesman this Pitt was! They will render justice to him one of these days, even in France. Pitt and Coburg are still being harped upon. But it is a childish foolishness that will pass. M. Pitt knew French. To carry on politics properly we must have Englishmen who know French and Frenchmen who know English.

"Look here, I am going to England next month. I shall be very well received: I speak English. And then, Englishmen appreciate the fact that I have studied them closely enough not to detest them. For one always begins by detesting the English. This is an effect of the surface. I esteem them, and pride myself upon the fact. Between ourselves, there is one thing I apprehend in going to England, and that is, a too warm welcome. I shall have to elude an ovation. Popularity there would render me unpopular here. But I must not get myself badly received either. Badly received there, taunted here. Oh! it is not easy to move when one is Louis Philippe, is it, Monsieur Hugo?

"However, I will endeavour to manage it better than that big stupid the Emperor of Russia, who went riding full gallop in search of a fall. There is an addle-pate for you. What a simpleton! He is nothing but a Russian corporal, occupied with a boot-heel and a gaiter button. What an idea to arrive in London on the eve of the Polish ball! Do you think I would go to England on the eve of the anniversary of Waterloo? What is the use of running deliberately into trouble? Nations do not derange their ideas for us princes.

"Monsieur Hugo! Monsieur Hugo! intelligent princes are very rare. Look at this Pacha of Egypt, who had a bright mind and who abdicates, like Charles V, who, although he was not without genius, committed the same foolish action. Look at this idiotic King of Morocco! What a job to govern amid this mob of bewildered Kings. They won't force me into committing the great mistake of going to war. I am being pushed, but they won't push me over. Listen to this and remember it: the secret of maintaining peace is to look at everything from the good side and at nothing from the bad point of view. Oh! Sir Robert Peel is a singular man to speak so wildly. He does not know all our strength. He does not reflect!

"The Prince of Prussia made a very true remark to my daughter at Brussels last winter: 'What we envy France, is Algeria. Not on account of the territory, but on account of the war. It is a great and rare good fortune for France to have at her doors a war that does not trouble Europe and which is making an army for her. We as yet have only review and parade soldiers. When a collision occurs we shall only have soldiers who have been made by peace. France, thanks to Algiers, will have soldiers made by war.' This is what the Prince of Prussia said, and it was true.

"Meanwhile, we are making children, too. Last month it was my daughter of Nemours, this month it is my daughter of Joinville. She has given me a princess. I would have preferred a prince. But, pish! in view of the fact that they are trying to isolate my house among the royal houses of Europe future alliances must be thought of. Well, my grandchildren will marry among themselves. This little one who was born yesterday will not lack cousins, nor, consequently, a husband."

Here the King laughed, and I rose. He had spoken almost without interruption for an hour and a quarter. I had only said a few words here and there. During this sort of long monologue Madame Adelaide passed as she retired to her apartments. The King said to her: "I will join you directly," and he continued his conversation with me. It was nearly half-past eleven when I quitted the King.

It was during this conversation that the King said to me:

"Have you ever been to England?"

"No, sire."

"Well, when you do go—for you will go—you will see how strange it is. It resembles France in nothing. Over there are order, arrangement, symmetry, cleanliness, wellmown lawns, and profound silence in the streets. The passers-by are as serious and mute as spectres. When, being French and alive, you speak in the street, these spectres look back at you and murmur with an inexpressible mixture of gravity and disdain: 'French people!' When I was in London I was walking arm-in-arm with my wife and sister. We were conversing, not in a too loud tone of voice, for we are well-bred persons, you know; yet all the passers-by, bourgeois and men of the people, turned to gaze at us and we could hear them growling behind us: 'French people! French people!'"

September 5, 1844

The King rose, paced to and fro for a few moments, as though violently agitated, then came and sat beside me and said:

"Look here, you made a remark to Villemain that he repeated to me. You said to him:

"'The trouble between France and England a propos of Tahiti and Pritchard reminds me of a quarrel in a café between a couple of sub-lieutenants, one of whom has looked at the other in a way the latter does not like. A duel to the death is the result. But two great nations ought not to act like a couple of musketeers. Besides, in a duel to the death between two nations like England and France, it is civilization that would be slain.'

"This is really what you said, is it not?"

"Yes, Sire."

"I was greatly struck by your observation, and this very evening I reproduced it in a letter to a crowned head, for I frequently write all night long. I pass many a night doing over again what others have undone. I do not say anything about it. So far from being grateful to me they would only abuse me for it. Oh! yes, mine is hard work indeed. At my age, with my seventy-one years, I do not get an instant of real repose either by day or by night. I am always unquiet, and how can it be otherwise when I feel that I am the pivot upon which Europe revolves?"

September 6, 1844

The King said to me yesterday:

"What makes the maintenance of peace so difficult is that there are two things in Europe that Europe detests, France and myself—myself even more than France. I am talking to you in all frankness. They hate me because I am Orleans; they hate me because I am myself. As for France, they dislike her, but would tolerate her in other hands. Napoleon was a burden to them; they overthrew him by egging him on to war of which he was so fond. I am a burden to them; they would like to throw me down by forcing me to break that peace which I love."

Then he covered his eyes with his hands, and leaning his head back upon the cushions of the sofa, remained thus for a space pensive, and as though crushed.

September 6, 1844

"I only met Robespierre in society once," said the King to me. "It was at a place called Mignot, near Poissy, which still exists. It belonged to a wealthy cloth manufacturer of Louviers, named M. Decréteau. It was in ninety-one or two. M. Decréteau one day invited me to dinner at Mignot. I went. When the time came we took our places at table. The other guests were Robespierre and Pétion, but I had never before seen Robespierre. Mirabeau aptly traced his portrait in a word when he said that his face was suggestive of that of 'a cat drinking vinegar.' He was very gloomy, and hardly spoke. When he did let drop a word from time to time, it was uttered sourly and with reluctance. He seemed to be vexed at having come, and because I was there.

"In the middle of the dinner, Pétion, addressing M. Decréteau, exclaimed: 'My dear host, you must get this buck married!' He pointed to Robespierre.

"'What do you mean, Pétion?' retorted Robespierre.

"'Mean,' said Pétion, 'why, that you must get married. I insist upon marrying you. You are full of sourness, hypochondria, gall, bad humour, biliousness and atrabiliousness I am fearful of all this on our account. What you want is a woman to sweeten this sourness and transform you into an easy-going old fogey.'

"Robespierre tossed his head and tried to smile, but only succeeded in making a grimace. It was the only time," repeated the King, "that I met Robespierre in society. After that I saw him in the tribune of the Convention. He was wearisome to a supreme degree, spoke slowly, heavily and at length, and was more sour, more gloomy, more bitter than ever. It was easy to see that Pétion had not married him."

September 7, 1844

Said the King to me last Thursday:

"M. Guizot has great qualities and immense defects. (Queerly enough, M. Guizot on Tuesday had made precisely the same remark to me about the King, beginning with the defects.) M. Guizot has in the highest degree, and I esteem him for it profoundly, the courage of his unpopularity among his adversaries; among his friends he lacks it. He does not know how to quarrel momentarily with his partisans, which was Pitt's great art. In the affair of Tahiti, as in that of the right of search, M. Guizot is not afraid of the Opposition, nor of the press, nor of the Radicals, nor of the Carlists, nor of the Legitimists, nor of the hundred thousand howlers in the hundred thousand public squares of France; he is afraid of Jacques Lefebvre. What will Jacques Lefebvre say? And Jacques Lefebvre is afraid of the Twelfth Arrondissement.* What will the Twelfth Arrondissement say? The Twelfth Arrondissement does not like the English: we must stand firm against the English; but it does not like war: we must give way to the English. Stand firm and give way. Reconcile that. The Twelfth Arrondissement governs Jacques Lefebvre,

---

* Twelfth District of Paris.

Jacques Lefebvre governs Guizot; a little more and the Twelfth Arrondissement will govern France. I say to Guizot: 'What are you afraid of? Have a little pluck. Have an opinion.' But there they all stand, pale and motionless and make no reply. Oh! fear! Monsieur Hugo, it is a strange thing, this fear of the hubbub that will be raised outside! It seizes upon this one, then that one, then that one, and it goes the round of the table. I am not a Minister, but if I were, it seems to me that I should not be afraid. I should see the right and go straight towards it. And what greater aim could there be than civilization through peace?"

The Duke d'Orleans, a few years ago, recounted to me that during the period which followed immediately upon the revolution of July, the King gave him a seat at his council table. The young Prince took part in the deliberations of the Ministers. One day M. Merilhou, who was Minister of Justice, fell asleep while the King was speaking.

"Chartres," said the King to his son, "wake up Monsieur the Keeper of the Seals."

The Duke d'Orleans obeyed. He was seated next to M. Merilhou, and nudged him gently with his elbow. The Minister was sleeping soundly; the Prince recommenced, but the Minister slept on. Finally the Prince laid his hand upon M. Merilhou's knee. The Minister awoke with a start and exclaimed:

"Leave off, Sophie, you are tickling me!"

This is how the word "subject" came to be eliminated from the preamble of laws and ordinances.

M. Dupont de l'Eure, in 1830, was Minister of Justice. On August 7, the very day the Duke d'Orleans took the oath as King, M. Dupont de l'Eure laid before him a law to sign. The preamble read: "Be it known and decreed to all our subjects," etc. The clerk who was instructed to copy the law, a hot-headed young fellow, objected to the word "subjects," and did not copy it.

The Minister of Justice arrived. The young man was employed in his office.

"Well," said the Minister, "is the copy ready to be taken to the King for signature?"

"No, Monsieur the Minister," replied the clerk.

Explanations. M. Dupont de l'Eure listened, then pinching the young man's ear said, half smilingly, half angrily:

"Nonsense, Monsieur the Republican, you just copy it at once."

The clerk hung his head, like a clerk that he was, and copied it.

M. Dupont, however, laughingly told the King about it. The King did not laugh. Everything appeared to be a serious matter at that time. M. Dupin senior, Minister without a portfolio, had entered the council chamber. He avoided the use of the word and got round the obstacle. He proposed this wording, which was agreed to and has always been used since: "Be it known and decreed to all."

1847

The State carriage of Louis Philippe was a big blue coach drawn by eight horses. The interior was of gold coloured damask. On the doors was the King's monogram surmounted by a crown, and on the panels were royal crowns. The roof was bordered by eight little silver crowns. There was a gigantic coachman on the box and three lackeys behind. All wore silk stockings and the tri-colour livery of the d'Orleans.

The King would enter the carriage first and seat himself in the right hand corner. Then the Duke de Nemours would take his place beside the King. The three other princes would follow and seat themselves, M. de Joinville opposite the King, M. de Montpensier opposite M. de Nemours, and M. d'Aumale in the middle.

The day the King attended Parliament, the grand deputations from both Houses, twelve peers and twenty-five deputies chosen by lot, awaited him on the grand staircase of the Palais Bourbon. As the sessions were nearly always held in winter, it was very cold on the stairs, a biting wind made all these old men shiver, and there are old generals of the Empire who did not die as the result of having been at Austerlitz, at Friedland, at the cemetery at Eylau, at the storming of the grand redoubt at Moskowa and under the fire of the Scottish squares at Waterloo, but of having waited in the cold upon these stairs.

The peers stood to the right and the deputies to the left, leaving the middle of the stairs clear. The staircase was partitioned off with hangings of white drill with blue stripes, which was a poor protection against draughts. Where are the good and magnificent tapestries of Louis XIV. They were indeed royal; wherefore they were taken down. Drill is a common material and more pleasing to the deputies. It charms and it freezes them.

The Queen arrived first with the princesses, but without the Duchess d'Orleans, who came separately with the Count de Paris. These ladies walked quickly upstairs, bowing to right and left, without speaking, but graciously, followed by a swarm of aides-de-camp and grim turbaned old women whom M. de Joinville called "the Queen's Turks"—Mmes. de Dolokieu, de Chanaleilles, etc.

At the royal session of 1847, the Queen gave her arm to the Duchess de Montpensier. The princess was muffled up on account of the cold. I could see only a big red nose. The three other princesses walked behind, chatting and laughing. M. Anatole de Montesquiou came next in the much worn uniform of a major-general.

The King arrived about five minutes after the Queen; he walked upstairs even more quickly than she had done, followed by the princes running like schoolboys, and bowed to the peers on the right and the deputies on the left. He tarried a moment in the throne-room and exchanged a few greetings with the members of the two deputations. Then he entered the large hall.

The speech from the throne was written on parchment, on both sides of the sheet, and usually filled four pages. The King read it in a firm, well modulated voice.

Marshal Soult was present, resplendent with decorations, sashes, and gold lace, and complaining of his rheumatism. M. Pasquier, the Chancellor, did not put in an appearance. He had excused himself on the plea of the cold and of his eighty years. He had been present the year before. It was the last time.

In 1847 I was a member of the grand deputation. While I strolled about the waiting room, conversing with M. Villemain about Cracow, the Vienna treaties and the frontier of the Rhine, I could hear the buzzing of the groups around me, and scraps of conversation reached my ears.

Count de Lagrange: Ah! here comes the Marshal (Soult).

Baron Pedre Lacaze: He is getting old.

Viscount Cavaignac: Sixty-nine years!

Marquis Dr. Raigecourt: Who is the dean of the Chamber of Peers at present?

Duke de Trevise: M. de Pontecoulant, is he not?

Marquis de Laplace: No, President Boyer. He is ninety-two.

President Barthe: He is older than that.

Baron d'Oberlin: He no longer comes to the Chamber.

M. Viennet: They say that M. Rossi is returning from Rome.

DUKE DE FESENZAC: Well, I pity him for quitting Rome. It is the finest and most amiable city in the world. I hope to end my days there.

COUNT DE MONTALEMBERT: And Naples!

BARON THENARD: I prefer Naples.

M. FULCHIRON: Yes, Naples, that's the place. By the by, I was there when poor Nourrit killed himself. I was staying in the house next to his.

BARON CHARLES DUPIN: He took his life? It was not an accident?

M. FULCHIRON: Oh! it was a case of suicide, sure enough. He had been hissed the previous day. He could not stand that. It was in an opera composed expressly for him—"Polyceucte." He threw himself from a height of sixty feet. His voice did not please that particular public. Nourrit was too much accustomed to sing Glück and Mozart. The Neapolitans said of him: "Vecchico canto."

BARON DUPIN: Poor Nourrit! why did he not wait! Duprez has lost his voice. Eleven years ago Duprez demolished Nourrit; today Nourrit would demolish Duprez.

MARQUIS DE BOISSY: How cold it is on this staircase.

COUNT PHILIPPE DE SEGUR: It was even colder at the Academy the other day. That poor Dupaty is a good man, but he made a bad speech.

BARON FEUTRIER: I am trying to warm myself. What a frightful draught! It is enough to drive one away.

BARON CHARLES DUPIN: M. Français de Nantes had conceived this expedient to rid himself of those who came to solicit favours and abridge their solicitations: he was given to receiving people between two doors.

M. Thiers at this time had a veritable court of deputies about him. After the session he walked out in front of me. A gigantic deputy, whose back only I could see, stepped aside, saying: "Make way for historical men!" And the big man let the little man pass.

Historical? May be. In what way?

II. The Duchess d'Orleans

MADAME THE DUCHESS D'ORLEANS IS a rare woman, of great wit and common sense. I do not think that she is fully appreciated at the Tuileries. The King, though, holds her in high esteem and often engages in long conversations with her. Frequently he gives her his arm to escort her from the family drawing-room to her apartments. The royal daughters-in-law do not always appear to act as kindly towards her.

February 26, 1844

Yesterday the Duchess d'Orleans said to me:

"My son is not what one would call an amiable child. He is not one of those pretty little prodigies who are an honour to their mothers, and of whom people say: 'What a clever child! What wit! What grace!' He has a kind heart, I know; he has wit, I believe; but nobody knows and believes this save myself. He is timid, wild, uncommunicative, easily scared. What will he become? I have no idea. Often at his age a child in his position understands that he must make himself agreeable, and, little as he is, sets himself to play his role. Mine hides himself in his mother's skirt and lowers his eyes. But I love him, just as he is. I even prefer him this way. I like a savage better than a comedian."

August, 1844

The Count de Paris has signed the birth certificate of the Princess Françoise de Joinville. It was the first time that the little prince had signed his name. He did not know what was wanted of him, and when the King handed him the certificate and said "Paris, sign your name," the child refused. The Duchess d'Orleans took him on her knee and whispered something to him. Then the child took the pen, and at the dictation of his grandfather wrote upon the certificate L. P. d. O. He made the O much too large and wrote the other letters awkwardly, and was very much embarrassed and shy.

He is charming, though, and adores his mother, but he hardly knows that his name is Louis Philippe d'Orleans. He writes to his comrades, to his tutor, and to his mother, but he signs his little missives "Paris." It is the only name he knows himself by.

This evening the King sent for M. Regnier, the prince's tutor, and gave him orders to teach the Count de Paris to sign his name.

1847

The Count de Paris is of a grave and sweet disposition; he learns well. He is imbued with a natural tenderness, and is kind to those who suffer.

His young cousin of Wurtemberg, who is two months older, is jealous of him; as his mother, the Princess Marie, was jealous of the mother of the Count de Paris. During the lifetime of the Duke d'Orleans little Wurtemberg was long the object of the Queen's preferences, and, in the little court of the corridors and bedchambers, it was the custom to flatter the Queen by comparisons between the one and the other that were always favourable to Wurtemberg. Today that inequality has ceased. The Queen, by a touching sentiment, inclined towards little Wurtemberg because he had lost his mother; now there is no reason why she should not lean towards the Count de Paris, seeing that he has lost his father.

Little Michel Ney plays with the two princes every Sunday. He is eleven years old, and the son of the Duke d'Elchingen. The other day he said to his mother:

"Wurtemberg is an ambitious fellow. When we play he always wants to be the leader. Besides, he insists upon being called Monseigneur. I don't mind calling him Monseigneur, but I won't let him be leader. One day I invented a game, and I said to him: 'No, Monseigneur, you are not going to be the leader. I will be leader, for I invented the game, and Chabannes will be my lieutenant. You and the Count de Paris will be soldiers.' Paris was willing, but Wurtemberg walked away. He is an ambitious fellow."

Of these young mothers of the Château, apart from the Duchess d'Orleans, Mme. de Joinville is the only one who does not spoil her children. At the Tuileries, everybody, even the King himself, calls her little daughter "Chiquette." The Prince of Joinville calls his wife "Chicarde" since the pierrots' ball, hence "Chiquette." At this pierrots' ball the King exclaimed: "How Chicarde is amusing herself!" The Prince de Joinville danced all the risquée dances. Mme. de Montpensier and Mme. Liadères were the only ones who were not decolletees. "It is not in good taste," said the Queen. "But it is pretty," observed the King.

III. The Princes

1847

At the Tuileries the Prince de Joinville passes his time doing all sorts of wild things. One day he turned on all the taps and flooded the apartments. Another day he cut all the bell ropes. A sign that he is bored and does not know what to do with himself.

And what bores these poor princes most is to receive and talk to people ceremoniously. This is almost a daily obligation. They call it—for princes have their slang—"performing the function." The Duke de Montpensier is the only one who performs it gracefully. One day the Duchess d'Orleans asked him the reason. He replied: "It amuses me."

He is twenty years old, he is beginning.

When the marriage of M. de Montpensier with the Infanta was published, the King of the Belgians was sulky with the Tuileries. He is an Orleans, but he is a Coburg. It was as though his left hand had smitten his right cheek.

The wedding over, while the young couple were making their way from Madrid to Paris, King Leopold arrived at Saint Cloud, where King Louis Philippe was staying. The King of the Belgians wore an air of coldness and severity. Louis Philippe, after dinner, took him aside into a recess of the Queen's drawing-room, and they conversed for fully an hour. Leopold's face preserved its thoughtful and *English* expression. However at the conclusion of the conversation, Louis Philippe said to him:

"See Guizot."

"He is precisely the man I do not want to see."

"See him," urged the King. "We will resume this conversation when you have done so."

The next day M. Guizot waited upon King Leopold. He had with him an enormous portfolio filled with papers. The King received him. His manner was cold in the extreme. Both were reserved. It is probable that M. Guizot communicated to the King of the Belgians all the documents relative to the marriage and all the diplomatic papers. No one knows what passed between them. What is certain is that when M. Guizot left the King's room Leopold's air was gracious, though sad, and that he was heard to say to the Minister as he took leave of him: "I came here greatly dissatisfied with you. I shall go away satisfied. You have, in fact, in this affair acquired a new title to my esteem and to our gratitude. I intended to scold you; I thank you."

These were the King's own words.

The Prince de Joinville's deafness increases. Sometimes it saddens him, sometimes he makes light of it. One day he said to me: "Speak louder, I am as deaf as a post." On another occasion he bent towards me and said with a laugh:

"*J'abaisse le pavillion de l'oreille.*"

"It is the only one your highness will ever lower," I replied.

M. de Joinville is of somewhat queer disposition. Now he is joyous to the point of folly, anon gloomy as a hypochondriac. He is silent for three days at a time, or his bursts of laughter are heard in the very attics of the Tuileries. When he is on a voyage he rises at four o'clock in the morning, wakes everybody up and performs his duties as a sailor conscientiously. It is as though he were to win his epaulettes afterwards.

He loves France and feels all that touches her. This explains his fits of moodiness. Since he cannot talk as he wants to, he keeps his thoughts to himself, and this sours him, He has spoken more than once, however, and bravely. He was not listened to and he was not heeded. "They needn't talk about me," he said to me one day, "it is they who are deaf!"

Unlike the late Duke d'Orleans, he has no princely coquettishness, which is such a victorious grace, and has no desire to appear agreeable. He rarely seeks to please individuals. He loves the nation, the country, his profession, the sea. His manner is frank, he has a taste for noisy pleasures, a fine appearance, a handsome face, with a kind heart, and a few feats of arms to his credit that have been exaggerated; he is popular.

M. de Nemours is just the contrary. At court they say: "There is something unlucky about the Duke de Nemours."

M. de Montpensier has the good sense to love, to esteem and to honour profoundly the Duchess d'Orleans.

The other day there was a masked and costumed ball, but only for the family and the intimate court circle—the princesses and ladies of honour. M. de Joinville appeared all in rags, in complete Chicard costume. He was extravagantly gay and danced a thousand unheard-of dances. These capers, prohibited elsewhere, rendered the Queen thoughtful. "Wherever did he learn all this?" she asked, and added: "What naughty dances! Fie!" Then she murmured: "How graceful he is!"

Mme. de Joinville was dressed as a bargee and affected the manner of a street gamin. She likes to go to those places that the court detests the most, *the theatres and concerts of the boulevards*.

The other day she greatly shocked Mme. de Hall, the wife of an admiral, who is a Protestant and Puritan, by asking her: "Madame, have you seen the "Closerie des Genêts"?"

The Prince de Joinville had imagined a nuisance that exasperated the Queen. He procured an old barrel organ somewhere, and would enter her apartments playing it and singing in a hoarse, grating voice. The Queen laughed at first. But it lasted a quarter of an hour, half an hour. "Joinville, stop it!" He continued to grind away. "Joinville, go away!" The prince, driven out of one door, entered by another with his organ, his songs and his hoarseness. Finally the Queen fled to the King's apartments.

The Duchess d'Aumale did not speak French very fluently; but as soon as she began to speak Italian, the Italian of Naples, she thrilled like a fish that falls back into the water, and gesticulated with Neapolitan verve. "Put your hands in your pockets," the Duke d'Aumale would say to her. "I shall have to have your hands tied. Why do you gesticulate like that?"

"I didn't notice it," the princess would reply.

"That is true, she doesn't notice it," said the Prince to me one day. "You wouldn't believe it, but my mother, who is so dignified, so cold, so reserved when she is speaking French, begins gesticulating like Punchinello when by chance she speaks Neapolitan."

The Duke de Montpensier salutes passers-by graciously and gaily. The Duke d'Aumale does not salute more often than he is compelled to; at Neuilly they say he is afraid of ruffling his hair. The Duke de Nemours manifests less eagerness than the Duke de Montpensier and less negligence than the Duke d'Aumale; moreover, women say that when saluting them he looks at them in a most embarrassing way.

Donizetti's "Elixir of Love" was performed at court on February 5, 1847, by the Italian singers, the Persiani, Mario, Tagliafico. Ronconi acted (acted is the word, for he acted very well) the role of Dulcamara, usually represented by Lablache. It was in the matter of size, but not of talent, a giant in the place of a dwarf. The decoration of the theatre at the Tuileries was then still the same as it had been in the time of the Empire—designs in gold on a grey background, the ensemble being cold and pale.

There were few pretty women present. Mme. Cuvillier-Floury was the prettiest; Mme. V. H. the most handsome. The men were in uniform or full evening dress. Two officers of the Empire were conspicuous in their uniforms of that period. Count Dutaillis, a one-armed soldier of the Empire, wore the old uniform of a general of division, embroidered with oak leaves to the facings. The big straight collar reached to his occiput; his star of the Legion of Honour was all dented; his embroidery was rusty and dull. Count de Lagrange, an old beau, wore a white spangled waistcoat, black silk breeches, white, or rather pink, stockings; shoes with buckles on them, a sword at his side, a black dress coat, and a peer's hat with white plumes in it. Count Dutaillis was a greater success than Count de Lagrange. The one recalled Monaco and Trenitz; the other recalled Wagram.

M. Thiers, who the previous day had made a somewhat poor speech, carried opposition to the point of wearing a black cravat.

The Duchess de Montpensier, who had attained her fifteenth birthday eight days before, wore a large crown of diamonds and looked very pretty. M. de Joinville was absent. The three other princes were there in lieutenant-general's uniform with the star and grand cordon of the Legion of Honour. M. de Montpensier alone wore the order of the Golden Fleece.

Mme. Ronconi, a handsome person, but of a wild and savage beauty, was in a small box on the stage, in rear of the proscenium. She attracted much attention.

There was no applause, which chilled the singers and everybody else.

Five minutes before the piece terminated the King began to pack up. He folded his programme and put it in his pocket, then he wiped the glasses of his opera-glass, closed it up carefully, looked round for the case which he had laid on his chair, placed the glass in it and adjusted the hooks very scrupulously. There was a good deal of character in his methodical manner.

M. de Rambuteau was there. His latest "rambutisms" (the word was Alexis de Saint-Priest's) were recounted among the audience. It was said that on the last day of the year M. de Rambuteau wrote on his card: "M. de Rambuteau et Venus," or as a variation: "M. de Rambuteau, Venus en personne."

Wednesday, February 24, the Duke de Nemours gave a concert at the Tuileries. The singers were Mlle. Grisi, Mme. Persiani, a Mme. Corbari, Mario, Lablache and Ronconi. M. Aubert, who conducted, did not put any of his own music on the programme: Rossini, Mozart, and Donizetti, that was all.

The guests arrived at half-past eight. The Duke de Nemours lives on the first floor of the Pavilion de Marsan, over the apartments of the Duchess d'Orleans. The guests waited in a first salon until the doors of the grand salon were opened, the women seated, the men standing. As soon as the prince and princess appeared the doors were thrown wide open and everybody went in. This grand salon is a very fine room. The ceiling is evidently of the time of Louis XIV. The wails are hung with green damask striped with gold. The inner window curtains are of red damask. The furniture is in green and gold damask. The ensemble is royal.

The King and Queen of the Belgians were at this concert. The Duke de Nemours entered with the Queen, his sister, upon his arm, the King giving his arm to the Duchess de Nemours. Mmes. d'Aumale and de Montpensier followed. The Queen of the Belgians resembles the Queen of the French, save in the matter of age. She wore a sky-blue toque, Mme. d'Aumale a wreath of roses, Mme. de Montpensier a diadem of diamonds, Mme. de Nemours her golden hair. The four princesses sat in high-backed chairs opposite the piano; all the other women sat behind them; the men were in the rear, filling the doorway and the first salon. The King of the Belgians has a rather handsome and grave face, and a delicate and agreeable smile; he was seated to the left of the princesses.

The Duke de Brogue sat on his left. Next to the Duke were Count Mole and M. Dupin senior. M. de Salvandy, seeing an empty chair to the right of the King, seated himself upon it. All five wore the red sash, including M. Dupin. These four men about the King of the Belgians represented the old military nobility, the parliamentary aristocracy, the pettifogging bourgeoisie, and moonshine literature; that is to say, a little of what France possesses that is illustrious, and a little of what she possesses that is ridiculous.

MM. d'Aumale and de Montpensier were to the right in the recess of a window with the Duke of Wurtemberg, whom they called their "brother Alexander." All the princes wore the grand cordon and star of Leopold in honour of the King of the Belgians; MM. de Nemours and de Montpensier also wore the Golden Fleece. The Fleece of M. de Montpensier was of diamonds, and magnificent.

The Italian singers sang standing by the piano. When seated they occupied chairs with wooden backs.

The Prince de Joinville was absent, as was also his wife. It was said that lately he was the hero of a love affair. M. de Joinville is prodigiously strong. I heard a big lackey behind me say: "I shouldn't care to receive a slap from him." While he was strolling to his rendezvous M. de Joinville thought he noticed that he was being followed. He turned back, went up to the fellow and struck him.

After the first part of the concert MM. d'Aumale and de Montpensier came into the other salon where I had taken refuge with Théophile Gautier, and we chatted for fully an hour. The two princes spoke to me at length about literary matters, about "Les Burgraves," "Ruy Blas," "Lucrèce Borgia," Mme. Halley, Mlle. Georges, and Frédérick

Lemaitre. Also a good deal about Spain, the royal wedding, bull-fights, hand-kissings, and etiquette, that M. de Montpensier "detests." "The Spaniards love royalty," he added, "and especially etiquette. In politics as in religion they are bigots rather than believers. They were greatly shocked during the wedding fetes because the Queen one day dared to venture out afoot!"

MM. d'Aumale and de Montpensier are charming young men, bright, gay, gracious, witty, sincere, full of that ease that communicates itself to others. They have a fine air. They are princes; they are perhaps men of intellect. M. de Nemours is embarrassed and embarrassing. When he comes towards you with his blond whiskers, his blue eyes, his red sash, his white waistcoat and his melancholy air he perturbs you. He never looks you in the face. He always casts about for something to say and never knows what he does say.

November 5, 1847

Four years ago the Duke d'Aumale was in barracks at Courbevoie with the 17th, of which he was then colonel. During the summer, in the morning, after the manoeuvres which took place at Neuilly, he frequently strolled back along the river bank, alone, his hands behind his back. Nearly every day he happened upon a pretty girl named Adele Protat, who every morning went from Courbevoie to Neuilly and returned at the same hour as M. d'Aumale. The young girl noticed the young officer in undress uniform, but was not aware that he was a prince. At length they struck up an acquaintance, and walked and chatted together. Under the influence of the sun, the flowers, and the fine mornings something very much like love sprang up between them. Adele Protat thought she had to do with a captain at the most. He said to her: "Come and see me at Courbevoie." She refused. Feebly.

One evening she was passing near Neuilly in a boat. Two young men were bathing. She recognized her officer.

"There is the Duke d'Aumale," said the boatman.

"Really!" said she, and turned pale.

The next day she had ceased to love him. She had seen him naked, and knew that he was a prince.

In the Chamber of Peers. 1846

Yesterday, February 22, I went to the Chamber of Peers. The weather was fine and very cold, in spite of the noonday sun. In the Rue de Tournon I met a man in the custody of two soldiers. The man was fair, pale, thin, haggard; about thirty years old; he wore coarse linen trousers; his bare and lacerated feet were visible in his sabots, and blood-stained bandages round his ankles took the place of stockings; his short blouse was soiled with mud in the back, which indicated that he habitually slept on the ground; his head was bare, his hair dishevelled. Under his arm was a loaf. The people who surrounded him said that he had stolen the loaf, and it was for this that he had been arrested.

When they reached the gendarmerie barracks one of the soldiers entered, and the man stayed at the door guarded by the other soldier.

A carriage was standing at the door of the barracks. It was decorated with a coat of arms; on the lanterns was a ducal coronet; two grey horses were harnessed to it; behind it were two lackeys. The windows were raised, but the interior, upholstered in yellow damask, was visible. The gaze of the man fixed upon this carriage, attracted mine. In the carriage was a woman in a pink bonnet and costume of black velvet, fresh, white, beautiful, dazzling, who was laughing and playing with a charming child of sixteen months, buried in ribbons, lace and furs.

This woman did not see the terrible man who was gazing at her.

I became pensive.

This man was no longer a man for me; he was the spectre of misery, the brusque, deformed, lugubrious apparition in full daylight, in full sunlight, of a revolution that is still plunged in darkness, but which is approaching. In former times the poor jostled the rich, this spectre encountered the rich man in all his glory; but they did not look at each other, they passed on. This condition of things could thus last for some time. The moment this man perceives that this woman exists, while this woman does not see that this man is there, the catastrophe is inevitable.

General Fabvier

Fabvier had fought valiantly in the wars of the Empire; he fell out with the Restoration over the obscure affair of Grenoble. He expatriated himself about 1816. It was the period of the departure of the eagles. Lallemand went to America, Allard and Vannova to India, Fabvier to Greece.

The revolution of 1820 broke out. He took an heroic part in it. He raised a corps of four thousand palikars, to whom he was not a chief, but a god. He gave them civilization and taught them barbarity. He was rough and brave above all of them, and almost ferocious, but with that grand, Homeric ferocity. One might have thought that he had come from a tent of the camp of Achilles rather than from the camp of Napoleon. He invited the English Ambassador to dinner at his bivouac; the Ambassador found him seated by a big fire at which a whole sheep was roasting; when the animal was cooked and unskewered, Fabvier placed the heel of his bare foot upon the neck of the smoking and bleeding sheep and tore off a quarter, which he offered to the Ambassador. In bad times nothing daunted him. He was indifferent alike to cold, heat, fatigue and hunger; he never spared himself. The palikars used to say: "When the soldier eats cooked grass Fabvier eats it green."

I knew his history, but I had not seen him when, in 1846, General Fabvier was made a peer of France. One day he had a speech to make, and the Chancellor announced: "Baron Fabvier has the tribune." I expected to hear a lion, I thought an old woman was speaking.

Yet his face was a truly masculine one, heroic and formidable, that one might have fancied had been moulded by the hand of a giant and which seemed to have preserved a savage and terrible grimace. What was so strange was the gentle, slow, grave, contained, caressing voice that was allied to this magnificent ferocity. A child's voice issued from this tiger's mouth.

General Fabvier delivered from the tribune speeches learned by heart, graceful, flowery, full of allusions to the woods and country— veritable idylls. In the tribune this Ajax became a Némorin.

He spoke in low tones like a diplomat, he smiled like a courtier. He was not averse to making himself agreeable to princes. This is what the peerage had done for him. He was only a hero after all.

August 22, 1846

The Marquis de Boissy has assurance, coolness, self-possession, a voice that is peculiar to himself, facility of speech, wit occasionally, the quality of imperturbability, all the accessories of a great orator. The only thing he lacks is talent. He wearies the Chamber, wherefore the Ministers do not consider themselves bound to answer him. He talks as long as everybody keeps quiet. He fences with the Chancellor as with his particular enemy.

Yesterday, after the session which Boissy had entirely occupied with a very poor speech, M. Guizot said to me:

"It is an affliction. The Chamber of Deputies would not stand him for ten minutes after the first two times. The Chamber of Peers extends its high politeness to him, and it does wrong. Boissy will not be suppressed until the day the whole Chamber rises and walks out when he asks permission to speak."

"You cannot think of such a thing," said I. "Only he and the Chancellor would be left. It would be a duel without seconds."

It is the custom of the Chamber of Peers never to repeat in its reply to the speech from the throne the titles that the King gives to his children. It is also the custom never to give the princes the title of Royal Highness when speaking of them to the King. There is no Highness in presence of his Majesty.

Today, January 18, the address in reply to the speech from the throne was debated. Occasionally there are flashes of keen and happy wit in M. de Boissy's nonsense. He remarked today: "I am not of those who are grateful to the government for the blessings of providence."

As usual he quarrelled with the Chancellor. He was making some more than usually roving excursion from the straight path. The Chamber murmured and cried: "Confine yourself to the question." The Chancellor rose:

"Monsieur the Marquis de Boissy," he said, "the Chamber requests that you will confine yourself to the question under discussion. It has saved me the trouble of asking you to do so." ("Our colleague might as well have said 'spared me!'" I whispered to Lebrun.)

"I am delighted on your account, Monsieur the Chancellor," replied M. de Boissy, and the Chamber laughed.

A few minutes later, however, the Chancellor took his revenge. M. de Boissy had floundered into some quibble about the rules. It was late. The Chamber was becoming impatient.

"Had you not raised an unnecessary incident," observed the Chancellor, "you would have finished your speech a long time ago, to your own satisfaction and that of everybody else."

Whereat everybody laughed.

"Don't laugh!" exclaimed the Duke de Mortemart. "Laughter diminishes the prestige of a constituted body."

M. de Pontécoulant said: "M. de Boissy teases Monsieur the Chancellor, Monsieur the Chancellor torments M. de Boissy. There is a lack of dignity on both sides!"

During the session the Duke de Mortemart came to my bench and we spoke about the Emperor. M. de Mortemart went through all the great wars. He speaks nobly of him. He was one of the Emperor's orderlies in the Campaign of 1812.

"It was during that campaign that I learned to know the Emperor," he said. "I was near him night and day. I saw him shave himself in the morning, sponge his chin, pull on his boots, pinch his valet's ear, chat with the grenadier mounting guard over his tent, laugh, gossip, make trivial remarks, and amid all this issue orders, trace plans, interrogate prisoners, decree, determine, decide, in a sovereign manner, simply, unerringly, in a few minutes, without missing anything, without losing a useful detail or a second of necessary time. In this intimate and familiar life of the bivouac flashes of his intellect were seen every moment. You can believe me when I say that he belied the proverb: 'No man is great in the eyes of his valet.'"

"Monsieur the Duke," said I, "that proverb is wrong. Every great man is a great man in the eyes of his valet."

At this session the Duke d'Aumale, having attained his twenty-fifth birthday, took his seat for the first time. The Duke de Nemours and the Prince de Joinville were seated near him in their usual places behind the ministerial bench. They were not among those who laughed the least.

The Duke de Nemours, being the youngest member of his committee, fulfilled the functions of secretary, as is customary. M. de Montalembert wanted to spare him the trouble. "No," said the prince, "it is my duty." He took the urn and, as secretary, went the round of the table to collect the votes.

At the close of the session of January 21, 1847, at which the Chamber of Peers discussed Cracow and kept silent concerning the frontier of the Rhine, I descended the grand staircase of the Chamber in company with M. de Chastellux. M. Decazes stopped me and asked:

"Well, what have you been doing during the session?"

"I have been writing to Mme. Dorval." (I held the letter in my hand.)

"What a fine disdain! Why did you not speak?"

"On account of the old proverb: 'He whose opinion is not shared by anybody else should think, and say nothing.'

"Did your opinion, then, differ from that of the others?"

"Yes, from that of the whole Chamber."

"What did you want then?"

"The Rhine."

"Whew! the devil!"

"I should have protested and spoken without finding any echo to my words; I preferred to say nothing."

"Ah! the Rhine! To have the Rhine! Yes, that is a fine idea. Poetry! poetry!"

"Poetry that our fathers made with cannon and that we shall make again with ideas!"

"My dear colleague," went on M. Decazes, "we must wait. I, too, want the Rhine. Thirty years ago I said to Louis XVIII: 'Sire, I should be inconsolable if I thought I should die without seeing France mistress of the left bank of the Rhine. But before we can talk about that, before we can think of it even, we must beget children.'"

"Well," I replied, "that was thirty years ago. We have begotten the children."

April 23, 1847

The Chamber of Peers is discussing a pretty bad bill on substitutions for army service. Today the principal article of the measure was before the House.

M. de Nemours was present. There are eighty lieutenant-generals in the Chamber. The majority considered the article to be a bad one. Under the eye of the Duke de Nemours, who seemed to be counting them, all rose to vote in favour of it.

The magistrates, the members of the Institute and the ambassadors voted against it.

I remarked to President Franck-Carré, who was seated next to me: "It is a struggle between civil courage and military poltroonery."

The article was adopted.

June 22, 1847

The Girardin* affair was before the Chamber of Peers today. Acquittal. The vote was taken by means of balls, white ones for condemnation,

---

* Emile de Girardin had been prosecuted for publishing an article in a newspaper violently attacking the government.

black ones for acquittal. There were 199 votes cast, 65 white, 134 black. In placing my black ball in the urn I remarked: "In blackening him we whiten him."

I said to Mme. D—: "Why do not the Minister and Girardin provoke a trial in the Assize Court?"

She replied: "Because Girardin does not feel himself strong enough, and the Minister does not feel himself pure enough."

MM. de Montalivet and Mole and the peers of the Château voted, queerly enough, for Girardin against the Government. M. Guizot learned the result in the Chamber of Deputies and looked exceedingly wrath.

June 28, 1847

On arriving at the Chamber I found Franck-Carre greatly scandalised.

In his hand was a prospectus for champagne signed by the Count de Mareuil, and stamped with a peer's mantle and a count's coronet with the de Mareuil arms. He had shown it to the Chancellor, who had replied: "I can do nothing!"

"I could do something, though, if a mere councillor were to do a thing like that in my court," said Franck-Carré to me. "I would call the Chambers together and have him admonished in a disciplinary manner."

1848

Discussion by the committees of the Chamber of Peers of the address in reply to the speech from the throne.

I was a member of the fourth committee. Among other changes I demanded this. There was: "Our princes, your well-beloved children, are doing in Africa the duties of servants of the State." I proposed: "The princes, your well-beloved children, are doing," etc., "their duty as servants of the State." This fooling produced the effect of a fierce opposition.

January 14, 1848

The Chamber of Peers prevented Alton-Shée from pronouncing in the tribune even the name of the Convention. There was a terrific knocking upon desks with paper-knives and shouts of "Order! Order!" and he was compelled almost by force to descend from the tribune.

I was on the point of shouting to them: "You are imitating a session of the Convention, but only with wooden knives!"

I was restrained by the thought that this *mot*, uttered during their anger, would never be forgiven. For myself I care little, but it might affect the calm truths which I may have to tell them and get them to accept later on.

The Revolution of 1848

I. The Days of February

The Twenty-Third

As I arrived at the Chamber of Peers—it was 3 o'clock precisely—General Rapatel came out of the cloak-room and said: "The session is over."

I went to the Chamber of Deputies. As my cab turned into the Rue de Lille a serried and interminable column of men in shirt-sleeves, in blouses and wearing caps, and marching arm-in-arm, three by three, debouched from the Rue Bellechasse and headed for the Chamber. The other extremity of the street, I could see, was blocked by deep rows of infantry of the line, with their rifles on their arms. I drove on ahead of the men in blouses, with whom many women had mingled, and who were shouting: "Hurrah for reform!" "Hurrah for the line!" "Down with Guizot!" They stopped when they arrived within rifle-shot of the infantry. The soldiers opened their ranks to let me through. They were talking and laughing. A very young man was shrugging his shoulders.

I did not go any further than the lobby. It was filled with busy and uneasy groups. In one corner were M. Thiers, M. de Rémusat, M. Vivien and M. Merruau (of the "Constitutionnel"); in another M. Emile de Girardin, M. d'Alton-Shée and M. de Boissy, M. Franck-Carré, M. d'Houdetot, M. de Lagrenée. M. Armand Marrast was talking aside with M. d'Alton. M. de Girardin stopped me; then MM. d'Houdetot and Lagrenée. MM. Franck-Carré and Vignier joined us. We talked. I said to them:

"The Cabinet is gravely culpable. It forgot that in times like ours there are precipices right and left and that it does not do to govern too near to the edge. It says to itself: 'It is only a riot,' and it almost rejoices at the outbreak. It believes it has been strengthened by it; yesterday it fell, today it is up again! But, in the first place, who can tell what the end of a riot will be? Riots, it is true, strengthen the hands of Cabinets, but revolutions overthrow dynasties. And what an imprudent game in which the dynasty is risked to save the ministry! The tension of the situation draws the knot tighter, and now it is impossible to undo it. The hawser may break and then everything will go adrift. The Left has manoeuvred imprudently and the Cabinet wildly. Both sides are responsible. But what madness possesses the Cabinet to mix a police question with a question of liberty and oppose the spirit of chicanery to the spirit of revolution? It is like sending process-servers with stamped paper to serve upon a lion. The quibbles of M. Hébert in presence of a riot! What do they amount to!"

As I was saying this a deputy passed us and said:

"The Ministry of Marine has been taken."

"Let us go and see!" said Franc d'Houdetot to me.

We went out. We passed through a regiment of infantry that was guarding the head of the Pont de la Concorde. Another regiment barred the other end of it. On the Place Louis XV cavalry was charging sombre and immobile groups, which at the approach of the soldiers fled like swarms of bees. Nobody was on the bridge except a general in uniform and on horseback, with the cross of a commander (of the Legion of Honour) hung round his neck—General Prévot. As he galloped past us he shouted: "They are attacking!"

As we reached the troops at the other end of the bridge a battalion chief, mounted, in a bernouse with gold stripes on it, a stout man with a kind and brave face, saluted M. d'Houdetot.

"Has anything happened?" Franc asked.

"It happened that I got here just in time!" replied the major.

It was this battalion chief who cleared the Palace of the Chamber, which the rioters had invaded at six o'clock in the morning.

We walked on to the Place. Charging cavalry was whirling around us. At the angle of the bridge a dragoon raised his sword against a man in a blouse. I do not think he struck him. Besides, the Ministry of Marine had not been "taken." A crowd had thrown a stone at one of the windows, smashing it, and hurting a man who was peeping out. Nothing more.

We could see a number of vehicles lined up like a barricade in the broad avenue of the Champs-Elysées, at the rond-point.

"They are firing, yonder," said d'Houdetot. "Can you see the smoke?"

"Pooh!" I replied. "It is the mist of the fountain. That fire is water."

And we burst into a laugh.

An engagement was going on there, however. The people had constructed three barricades with chairs. The guard at the main square of the Champs-Elysées had turned out to pull the barricades down. The people had driven the soldiers back to the guard-house with volleys of stones. General Prévot had sent a squad of Municipal Guards to the relief of the soldiers. The squad had been surrounded and compelled to seek refuge in the guard-house with the others. The crowd had hemmed in the guard-house. A man had procured a ladder, mounted to the roof, pulled down the flag, torn it up and thrown it to the people. A battalion had to be sent to deliver the guard.

"Whew!" said Franc d'Houdetot to General Prévot, who had recounted this to us. "A flag taken!"

"Taken, no! Stolen, yes!" answered the general quickly.

M. Pèdre-Lacaze came up arm-in-arm with Napoleon Duchatel. Both were in high spirits. They lighted their cigars from Franc d'Houdetot's cigar and said:

"Do you know? Genoude is going to bring in an impeachment on his own account. They would not allow him to sign the Left's impeachment. He would not be beaten, and now the Ministry is between two fires. On the left, the entire Left; on the right, M. de Genoude."

Napoleon Duchâtel added: "They say that Duvergier de Hauranne has been carried about in triumph on the shoulders of the crowd."

We had returned to the bridge. M. Vivien was crossing, and came up to us. With his big, old, wide-brimmed hat and his coat buttoned up to his cravat the ex-Minister Of Justice looked like a policeman.

"Where are you going?" he said to me. "What is happening is very serious!"

Certainly at this moment one feels that the whole constitutional machine is rocking. It no longer rests squarely on the ground. It is out of plumb. One can hear it cracking.

The crisis is complicated by the disturbed condition of the whole of Europe.

The King, nevertheless, is very calm, and even cheerful. But this game must not be played too far. Every rubber won serves but to make up the total of the rubber lost.

Vivien recounted to us that the King had thrown an electoral reform bill into his drawer, saying as he did so: "That is for my successor!" "That was Louis XV's *mot*," added Vivien, "supposing reform should prove to be the deluge."

It appears to be true that the King interrupted M. Salandrouze when he was laying before him the grievances of the "Progressists," and asked him brusquely: "Are you selling many carpets?"*

At this same reception of the Progressists the King noticed M. Blanqui, and graciously going up to him asked:

"Well, Monsieur Blanqui, what do people talk about? What is going on?"

"Sire," replied M. Blanqui, "I ought to tell the King that in the departments, and especially at Bordeaux, there is a great deal of agitation."

"Ah!" interrupted the King. "More agitation!" and he turned his back upon M. Blanqui.

While we were talking Vivien exclaimed: "Listen! I fancy I can hear firing!"

A young staff officer, addressing General d'Houdetot with a smile, asked: "Are we going to stay here long?"

"Why?" said Franc d'Houdetot.

"Well, I am invited out to dinner," said the officer.

At this moment a group of women in mourning and children dressed in black passed rapidly along the other pavement of the bridge. A man held the eldest child by the hand. I looked at him and recognized the Duke de Montebello.

"Hello!" exclaimed d'Houdetot, "the Minister of Marine!" and he ran over and conversed for a moment with M. de Montebello. The Duchess had become frightened, and the whole family was taking refuge on the left bank of the river.

Vivien and I returned to the Palace of the Chamber. D'Houdetot quitted us. In an instant we were surrounded. Said Boissy to me:

"You were not at the Luxembourg? I tried to speak upon the situation in Paris. I was hooted. At the *mot*, 'the capital in danger,' I was interrupted, and the Chancellor, who had come to preside expressly

---

* M. Salandrouze was a manufacturer of carpets.

for that purpose, called me to order. And do you know what General Gourgaud said to me? 'Monsieur de Boissy, I have sixty guns with their caissons filled with grape-shot. I filled them myself.' I replied: 'General, I am delighted to know what is really thought at the Château about the situation.'"

At this moment Durvergier de Hauranne, hatless, his hair dishevelled, and looking pale but pleased, passed by and stopped to shake hands with me.

I left Duvergier and entered the Chamber. A bill relative to the privileges of the Bank of Bordeaux was being debated. A man who was talking through his nose occupied the tribune, and M. Sauzet was reading the articles of the bill with a sleepy air. M. de Belleyme, who was coming out, shook hands with me and exclaimed: "Alas!"

Several deputies came up to me, among them M. Marie, M. Roger (of Loiret), M. de Rémusat, and M. Chambolle. I related to them the incident of the tearing down of the flag, which was serious in view of the audacity of the attack.

"What is even more serious," said one of them, "is that there is something very bad behind all this. During the night the doors of more than fifteen mansions were marked with a cross, among the marked houses being those of the Princess de Liéven, in the Rue Saint Florentin, and of Mme. de Talhouët."

"Are you sure of this?" I asked.

"With my own eyes I saw the cross upon the door of Mme. de Liéven's house," he replied.

President Franck-Carré met M. Duchâtel this morning and said: "Well, how goes it?"

"All is well," answered the Minister.

"What are you going to do about the riot?"

"I am going to let the rioters alone at the rendezvous they arranged for themselves. What can they do in the Place Louis XV and the Champs-Elysées? It is raining. They will tramp about there all day. Tonight they will be tired out and will go home to bed."

M. Etienne Arago entered hastily at this juncture and said: "There are seven wounded and two killed already. Barricades have been erected in the Rue Beaubourg and in the Rue Saint Avoye."

After a suspension of the session M. Guizot arrived. He ascended the tribune and announced that the King had summoned M. Mole, to charge him with the formation of a new Cabinet.

Triumphant shouts from the Opposition, shouts of rage from the majority.

The session ended amid an indescribable uproar.

I went out with the deputies and returned by way of the quays.

In the Place de la Concorde the cavalry continued to charge. An attempt to erect two barricades had been made in the Rue Saint Honoré. The paving-stones in the Marché Saint Honoré were being torn up. The overturned omni-buses, of which the barricades had been made, had been righted by the troops. In the Rue Saint Honoré the crowd let the Municipal Guards go by, and then stoned them in the back. A multitude was swarming along the quays like irritated ants. A very pretty woman in a green velvet hat and a large cashmere shawl passed by amid a group of men wearing blouses and with bared arms. She had raised her skirt very high on account of the mud, with which she was much spattered; for it was raining every minute. The Tuileries were closed. At the Carrousel gates the crowd had stopped and was gazing through the arcades at the cavalry lined up in battle array in front of the palace.

Near the Carrousel Bridge I met M. Jules Sandeau. "What do you think of all this?" he queried.

"That the riot will be suppressed, but that the revolution will triumph."

On the Quai de la Ferraille I happened upon somebody else I knew. Coming towards me was a man covered with mud to the neck, his cravat hanging down, and his hat battered. I recognized my excellent friend Antony Thouret. Thouret is an ardent Republican. He had been walking and speech-making since early morning, going from quarter to quarter and from group to group.

"Tell me, now, what you really want?" said I. "Is it the Republic?"

"Oh! no, not this time, not yet," he answered. "What we want is reform—no half measures, oh! dear no, that won't do at all. We want complete reform, do you hear? And why not universal suffrage?"

"That's the style!" I said as we shook hands.

Patrols were marching up and down the quay, while the crowd shouted "Hurrah for the line!" The shops were closed and the windows of the houses open.

In the Place du Châtelet I heard a man say to a group:

"It is 1830 over again!"

I passed by the Hotel de Ville and along the Rue Saint Avoye. At the Hotel de Ville all was quiet. Two National Guards were walking to and fro in front of the gate, and there were no barricades in the Rue Saint Avoye. In the Rue Rambuteau a few National Guards, in uniform, and wearing their side arms, came and went. In the Temple quarter they were beating to arms.

Up to the present the powers that be have made a show of doing without the National Guard. This is perhaps prudent. A force of National Guards was to have taken a hand. This morning the guard on duty at the Chamber refused to obey orders. It is said that a National Guardsman of the 7th Legion was killed just now while interposing between the people and the troops.

The Mole Ministry assuredly is not a Reform one, but the Guizot Ministry had been for so long an obstacle to reform! Its resistance was broken; this was sufficient to pacify and content the child-like heart of the generous people. In the evening Paris gave itself up to rejoicing. The population turned out into the streets; everywhere was heard the popular refrain *Des lampioms! des larnpioms!* In the twinkling of an eye the town was illuminated as though for a fête.

In the Place Royale, in front of the Mairie, a few yards from my house, a crowd had gathered that every moment was becoming denser and noisier. The officers and National Guards in the guard-house there, in order to get them away from the Maine, shouted: "On to the Bastille!" and, marching arm-in-arm, placed themselves at the head of a column, which fell in joyously behind them and started off shouting: "On to the Bastille!" The procession marched hat in hand round the Column of July, to the shout of "Hurrah for Reform!" saluted the troops massed in the Place with the cry of "Hurrah for the line!" and went off down the Faubourg Saint Antoine. An hour later the procession returned with its ranks greatly swelled, and bearing torches and flags, and made its way to the grand boulevards with the intention of going home by way of the quays, so that the whole town might witness the celebration of its victory.

Midnight is striking. The appearance of the streets has changed. The Marais quarter is lugubrious. I have just returned from a stroll there. The street lamps are broken and extinguished on the Boulevard Bourdon, so well named the "dark boulevard." The only shops open tonight were those in the Rue Saint Antoine. The Beaumarchais Theatre was closed. The Place Royale is guarded like a place of arms. Troops are in ambush in the arcades. In the Rue Saint Louis, a battalion is leaning silently against the walls in the shadow.

Just now, as the clock struck the hour, we went on to the balcony listening and saying: "It is the tocsin!"

I could not have slept in a bed. I passed the night in my drawing-room, writing, thinking and listening. Now and then I went out on the balcony and strained my ears to listen, then I entered the room again and paced to and fro, or dropped into an arm-chair and dozed. But my slumber was agitated by feverish dreams. I dreamed that I could hear the murmur of angry crowds, and the report of distant firing; the tocsin was clanging from the church towers. I awoke. It was the tocsin.

The reality was more horrible than the dream.

This crowd that I had seen marching and singing so gaily on the boulevards had at first continued its pacific way without let or hindrance. The infantry regiments, the artillery and cuirassiers had everywhere opened their ranks to let the procession pass through. But on the Boulevard des Capucines a mass of troops, infantry and cavalry, who were guarding the Ministry of Foreign Affairs and its unpopular Minister, M. Guizot, blocked the thoroughfare. In front of this insurmountable obstacle the head of the column tried to stop and turn; but the irresistible pressure of the enormous crowd behind pushed the front ranks on. At this juncture a shot was fired, on which side is not known. A panic ensued, followed by a volley. Eighty fell dead or wounded. Then arose a general cry of horror and fury: "Vengeance!" The bodies of the victims were placed in a tumbril lighted by torches. The crowd faced about and, amid imprecations, resumed its march, which had now assumed the character of a funeral procession. In a few hours Paris was bristling with barricades.

The Twenty-Fourth

At daybreak, from my balcony, I see advancing a noisy column of people, among whom are a number of National Guards. The mob stops in front of the Mairie, which is guarded by about thirty Municipal Guards, and with loud cries demands the soldiers' arms. Flat refusal by the Municipal Guards, menacing clamours of the crowd. Two National Guard officers intervene: "What is the use of further bloodshed? Resistance will be useless." The Municipal Guards lay down their rifles and ammunition and withdraw without being molested.

The Mayor of the Eighth Arrondissement, M. Ernest Moreau, requests me to come to the Mairie. He tells me the appalling news of the massacre on the Boulevard des Capucines. And at brief intervals further news of increasing seriousness arrives. The National Guard this time has definitely turned against the Government, and is shouting: "Hurrah for Reform!" The army, frightened at what it did yesterday, appears resolved not to take any further part in the fratricidal struggle. In the Rue Sainte Croix la Bretonnerie the troops have fallen back before the National Guard. At the neighbouring Mairie of the Ninth Arrondissement, we are informed, the soldiers are fraternising and patrolling with the National Guard. Two other messengers in blouses arrive almost together: "The Reuilly Barracks has been taken." "The Minimes Barracks has surrendered."

"And from the Government I have neither instructions nor news!" says M. Ernest Moreau. "What Government, if any, is there? Is the Mole Ministry still in existence? What is to be done?"

"Go to the Prefecture of the Seine," advises M. Perret, a member of the General Council. "It isn't far to the Hotel de Ville."

"Well, then, come with me."

They go. I reconnoitre round the Place Royale. Everywhere reign agitation, anxiety and feverish expectation. Everywhere work is being actively pushed upon barricades that are already formidable. This time it is more than a riot, it is an insurrection. I return home. A soldier of the line, on sentry duty at the entrance to the Place Royale, is chatting amicably with the vedette of a barricade constructed twenty paces from him.

At a quarter past eight M. Ernest Moreau returns from the Hotel de Ville. He has seen M. de Rambuteau and brings slightly better news. The King has entrusted the formation of a Cabinet to Thiers and Odilon Barrot. Thiers is not very popular, but Odilon Barrot means reform. Unfortunately the concession is coupled with a threat: Marshal Bugeaud has been invested with the general command of the National Guard and of the army. Odilon Barrot means reform, but Bugeaud means repression. The King is holding out his right hand and clenching his left fist.

The Prefect requested M. Moreau to spread and proclaim the news in his quarter and in the Faubourg Saint Antoine.

"This is what I will do," says the Mayor.

"Very good," I observe, "but believe me, you will do well to announce the Thiers-Barrot Ministry and say nothing about Marshal Bugeaud."

"You are right."

The Mayor requisitions a squad of National Guards, takes with him his two deputies and the Municipal Councillors present, and descends into the Place Royale. The roll of drums attracts the crowd. He announces the new Cabinet. The people applaud and raise repeated shouts of "Hurrah for Reform!" The Mayor adds a few words recommending harmony and the preservation of order, and is universally applauded.

"The situation is saved!" he says, grasping my hand.

"Yes," I answer, "if Bugeaud will give up the idea of being the saviour."

M. Ernest Moreau, followed by his escort, goes off to repeat his proclamation in the Place de la Bastille and the faubourg, and I return home to reassure my family.

Half an hour later the Mayor and his cortege return greatly agitated and in disorder to the Mairie. This is what had happened:

The Place de la Bastille was occupied at its two extremities by troops, leaning on their rifles. The people moved freely and peaceably between the two lines. The Mayor, arrived at the foot of the July column, made his proclamation, and once again the crowd applauded vigorously. M. Moreau started towards the Faubourg Saint Antoine. At this moment a number of workingmen accosted the soldiers amicably and said: "Your arms, give up your arms." In obedience to the energetic orders of their captain the soldiers refused. Suddenly a shot was fired; it was followed by other shots; the terrible panic of the previous day was perhaps about to be renewed. M. Moreau and his escort were pushed about, thrown down. The firing on both sides lasted over a minute, and five or six persons were killed or wounded.

Fortunately, this time the affray occurred in broad daylight. At the sight of the blood they had shed there was a revulsion of feeling on the part of the troops, and after a moment of surprise and horror the soldiers, prompted by an irresistible impulse, raised the butts of their rifles in the air and shouted: "Long live the National Guard!" The general in command, being powerless to control his men, went off to Vincennes by way of the quays and the people remained masters of the Bastille and of the faubourg.

"It is a result that might have cost more dear, in my case especially," remarks M. Moreau and he shows us his hat which has been pierced by a bullet. "A brand new hat," he adds with a laugh.

Half past ten o'clock.—Three students from the Ecole Polytechnique have arrived at the Mairie. They report that the students have broken out of the school and have come to place themselves at the disposition of the people. A certain number have therefore distributed themselves among the mairies of Paris.

The insurrection is making progress every hour. It now demands that Marshal Bugeaud be replaced and the Chamber dissolved. The pupils of the Ecole Polytechnique go further and talk about the abdication of the King.

What is happening at the Tuileries? There is no news, either, from the Ministry, no order from the General Staff. I decide to go to the Chamber of Deputies, by way of the Hotel de Ville, and M. Ernest Moreau is kind enough to accompany me.

We find the Rue Saint Antoine bristling with barricades. We make ourselves known and the insurgents help us to clamber over the heaps of paving-stones. As we draw near to the Hotel de Ville, from which the roar of a great crowd reaches our ears, and as we cross some ground on which are buildings in course of erection, we see coming towards us with hurried steps M. de Rambuteau, the Prefect of the Seine.

"Hi! Monsieur the Prefect, what brings you here?" I cry.

"Prefect! Do I know whether I am still Prefect?" he replies with a surly air.

A crowd, which looks anything but benevolent, has already begun to gather. M. Moreau notices a house that is to let. We enter it, and M. de Rambuteau recounts his misadventure.

"I was in my office with two or three Municipal Councillors," he says, "when we heard a great noise in the corridor. The door was thrown violently open, and there entered unto me a big strapping captain of the National Guard at the head of an excited body of troops.

"'Monsieur,' said the man, 'you must get out of here.'

"'Pardon me, Monsieur, here, at the Hotel de Ville I am at home, and here I propose to stay.'

"'Yesterday you were perhaps at home in the Hotel de Ville; today the people are at home in it.'

"'Ah! But—'

"'Go to the window and look out on the square.'

"The square had been invaded by a noisy, swarming crowd in which workingmen, National Guards and soldiers were mingled pell-mell. And the rifles of the soldiers wore in the hands of the men of the people. I turned to the intruders and said:

"'You are right, messieurs, you are the masters here.'

"'Well, then,' said the captain, 'instruct your employés to recognise my authority.'

"That was too much. I replied: 'What do you take me for?' I gathered up few papers, issued a few orders, and here I am. Since you are going to the Chamber, if there is still a Chamber, tell the Minister of the Interior, if the Ministry still exists, that at the Hotel de Ville there is no longer either Prefect or Prefecture."

It is with great difficulty that we make our way through the human ocean that with a noise as of a tempest covers the Place de Hotel de Ville. At the Quai de la Mégisserie is a formidable barricade; thanks to the Mayor's sash shown by my companion we are allowed to clamber over it. Beyond this the quays are almost deserted. We reach the Chamber of Deputies by the left bank of the river.

The Palais Bourbon is encumbered by a buzzing crowd of deputies, peers and high functionaries. From a rather large group comes the sharp voice of M. Thiers: "Ah! here is Victor Hugo!" He comes to us and asks for news about the Faubourg Saint Antoine. We add that about the Hotel de Ville. He shakes his head gloomily.

"And how are things here?" I question in turn. "But first of all are you still a Minister?"

"I? Oh! I am nobody! Odilon Barrot is President of the Council and Minister of the Interior."

"And Marshal Bugeaud?"

"He has also been replaced by Marshal Gerard. But that is nothing. The Chamber has been dissolved, the King has abdicated and is on his way to Saint Cloud, and the Duchess d'Orleans is Regent. Ah! the tide is rising, rising, rising!"

M. Thiers advises us, M. Ernest Moreau and me, to come to an understanding with M. Odilon Barrot. Action by us in our quarter, which is such an important one, can be of very great utility. We therefore set out for the Ministry of the Interior.

The people have invaded the Ministry and crowded it to the very office of the Minister, where a not over respectful crowd comes and goes. At a large table in the middle of the vast room secretaries are writing. M. Odilon Barrot his face red, his lips compressed and his hands behind his back, is leaning against the mantelpiece.

"You know what is going on, do you not?" he says when he sees us; "the King has abdicated and the Duchess d'Orleans is Regent."

"If the people so wills," says a man in a blouse who is passing.

The Minister leads us to the recess of a window, looking uneasily about him as he does so.

"What are you going to do? What are you doing?" I query.

"I am sending telegrams to the departments."

"Is this very urgent?"

"France must be informed of events."

"Yes, but meanwhile Paris is making events. Alas! has it finished making them? The Regency is all very well, but it has got to be sanctioned."

"Yes, by the Chamber. The Duchess d'Orleans ought to take the Count de Paris to the Chamber."

"No, since the Chamber has been dissolved. If the Duchess ought to go anywhere, it is to the Hotel de Ville."

"How can you think of such a thing! What about the danger?"

"There is no danger. A mother, a child! I will answer for the people. They will respect the woman in the princess.

"Well, then, go to the Tuileries, see the Duchess d'Orleans, advise her, enlighten her."

"Why do you not go yourself?"

"I have just come from there. Nobody knew where the Duchess was; I could not get near her. But if you see her tell her that I am at her disposal, that I await her orders. Ah! Monsieur Victor Hugo, I would give my life for that woman and for that child!"

Odilon Barrot is the most honest and the most devoted man in the world, but he is the opposite of a man of action; one feels trouble and indecision in his words, in his look, in his whole person.

"Listen," he goes on, "what must be done, what is urgent, is that the people should be made acquainted with these grave changes, the abdication and Regency. Promise me that you will proclaim them at your mairie, in the faubourg, and wherever you possibly can."

"I promise."

I go off, with M. Moreau, towards the Tuileries.

In the Rue Bellechasse are galloping horses. A squadron of dragoons flashes by and seems to be fleeing from a man with bare arms who is running behind them and brandishing a sword.

The Tuileries are still guarded by troops. The Mayor shows his sash and they let us pass. At the gate the concierge, to whom I make myself known, apprises us that the Duchess d'Orleans, accompanied by the Duke de Nemours, has just left the château with the Count de Paris, no doubt to go to the Chamber of Deputies. We have, therefore, no other course than to continue on our way.

At the entrance to the Carrousel Bridge bullets whistle by our ears. Insurgents in the Place du Carrousel are firing upon the court carriages leaving the stables. One of the coachmen has been killed on his box.

"It would be too stupid of us to stay here looking on and get ourselves killed," says M. Ernest Moreau. "Let us cross the bridge."

We skirt the Institute and the Quai de la Monnaie. At the Pont Neuf we pass a band of men armed with pikes, axes and rifles, headed by a drummer, and led by a man brandishing a sabre and wearing a long coat of the King's livery. It is the coat of the coachman who has just been killed in the Rue Saint Thomas du Louvre.

When we arrive, M. Moreau and I, at the Place Royale we find it filled with an anxious crowd. We are immediately surrounded and questioned, and it is not without some difficulty that we reach the Mairie. The mass of people is too compact to admit of our addressing them in the Place. I ascend, with the Mayor, a few officers of the National Guard and two students of the Ecole Polytechnique, to the balcony of the Mairie. I raise my hand, the crowd becomes silent as though by magic, and I say:

"My friends, you are waiting for news. This is what we know: M. Thiers is no longer Minister and Marshal Bugeaud is no longer in command (applause). They have been replaced by Marshal Gerard and M. Odilon Barrot (applause, but less general). The Chamber has been dissolved. The King has abdicated (general cheering). The Duchess d'Orleans is Regent." (A few isolated bravos, mingled with low murmurs.)

I continue:

"The name of Odilon Barrot is a guarantee that the widest and most open appeal will be made to the nation; and that you will have in all sincerity a representative government."

My declaration is responded to with applause from several points, but it appears evident that the great bulk of the crowd is uncertain as to what view of the situation they ought to take, and are not satisfied.

We re-enter the hall of the Mairie.

"Now," I say to M. Ernest Moreau, "I must go and proclaim the news in the Place de la Bastille."

But the Mayor is discouraged.

"You can very well see that it is useless," he says sadly. "The Regency is not accepted. And you have spoken here in a quarter where you are known and loved. At the Bastille your audience will be the revolutionary people of the faubourg, who will perhaps harm you."

"I will go," I say, "I promised Odilon Barrot that I would."

"I have changed my hat," the Mayor goes on, "but remember my hat of this morning."

"This morning the army and the people were face to face, and there was danger of a conflict; now, however, the people are alone, the people are the masters."

"Masters—and hostile; have a care!"

"No matter, I have promised, and I will keep my promise."

I tell the Mayor that his place is at the Mairie and that he ought to stay there. But several National Guard officers present themselves spontaneously and offer to accompany me, among them the excellent M. Launaye, my former captain. I accept their friendly offer, and we form a little procession and proceed by the Rue du Pas de la Mule and the Boulevard Beaumarchais towards the Place de la Bastille.

Here are a restless, eager crowd in which workingmen predominate, many of them armed with rifles taken from the barracks or given up to them by the soldiers; shouts and the song of the Girondins: "Die for the fatherland!" numerous groups debating and disputing passionately. They turn round, they look at us, they interrogate us:

"What's the news? What is going on?" And they follow us. I hear my name mentioned coupled with various sentiments: "Victor Hugo! It's Victor Hugo!" A few salute me. When we reach the Column of July we are surrounded by a considerable gathering. In order that I may be heard I mount upon the base of the column.

I will only repeat the words which it was possible for me to make my turbulent audience hear. It was much less a speech than a dialogue, but the dialogue of one voice with ten, twenty, a hundred voices more or less hostile.

I began by announcing at once the abdication of Louis Philippe, and, as in the Place Royale, applause that was practically unanimous greeted the news. There were also, however, cries of "No! no abdication, deposition! deposition!" Decidedly, I was going to have my hands full.

When I announced the Regency violent protests arose:

"No! no! No Regency! Down with the Bourbons! Neither King nor Queen! No masters!"

I repeated: "No masters! I don't want them any more than you do. I have defended liberty all my life."

"Then why do you proclaim the Regency?"

"Because a Queen-Regent is not a master. Besides, I have no right whatever to proclaim the Regency; I merely announce it."

"No! no! No Regency!"

A man in a blouse shouted: "Let the peer of France be silent. Down with the peer of France!" And he levelled his rifle at me. I gazed at him steadily, and raised my voice so loudly that the crowd became silent: "Yes, I am a peer of France, and I speak as a peer of France. I swore fidelity, not to a royal personage, but to the Constitutional Monarchy. As long as no other government is established it is my duty to be faithful to this one. And I have always thought that the people approved of a man who did his duty, whatever that duty might be."

There was a murmur of approbation and here and there a few bravos. But when I endeavoured to continue: "If the Regency—" the protests redoubled. I was permitted to take up only one of these protests. A workman had shouted: "We will not be governed by a woman." I retorted quickly:

"Well, neither will I be governed by a woman, nor even by a man. It was because Louis Philippe wanted to govern that his abdication is today necessary and just. But a woman who reigns in the name of a child! Is that not a guarantee against all thought of personal government? Look at Queen Victoria in England—"

"We are French, we are!" shouted several voices. "No Regency!"

"No Regency? Then, what? Nothing is ready, nothing! It means a total upheaval, ruin, distress, civil war, perhaps; in any case, it is the unknown."

One voice, a single voice, cried: "Long live the Republic!"

No other voice echoed it. Poor, great people, irresponsible and blind! They know what they do not want, but they do not know what they do want.

From this moment the noise, the shouts, the menaces became such that I gave up the attempt to get myself heard. My brave Launaye said: "You have done what you wanted to, what you promised to do; the only thing that remains for us to do is to withdraw."

The crowd opened before us, curious and inoffensive. But twenty paces from the column the man who had threatened me with his rifle came up with us and again levelled his weapon at me, shouting: "Down with the peer of France!" "No, respect the great man!" cried a young workman, who, with a quick movement, pushed the rifle downward. I thanked this unknown friend with a wave of the hand and passed on.

At the Mairie, M. Ernest Moreau, who it appears had been very anxious about us, received us with joy and cordially congratulated me. But I knew that even when their passions are aroused the people are just; and not the slightest credit was due to me, for I had not been uneasy in the least.

While these things were happening in the Place de la Bastille, this is what was taking place at the Palais Bourbon:

There is at this moment a man whose name is in everybody's mouth and the thought of whom is in everybody's mind; that man is Lamartine. His eloquent and vivid *History of the Girondins* has for the first time taught the Revolution to France. Hitherto he had only been illustrious; he has become popular and may be said to hold Paris in his hand.

In the universal confusion his influence could be decisive. This is what they said to themselves in the offices of the National, where the possible chances of the Republic had been weighed, and where a scheme for a provisional government had been sketched, from which Lamartine had been left out. In 1842, at the time of the debate over the Regency which resulted in the choice of the Duke de Nemours, Lamartine had pleaded warmly for the Duchess d'Orleans. Was he imbued with the same ideas today? What did he want? What would he do? It was necessary that this should be ascertained. M. Armand Marrast, the editor-in-chief of the National, took with him three notorious Republicans, M. Bastide, M. Hetzel, the publisher, and M. Bocage, the eminent comedian who created the role of Didier in "Marion de Lorme." All four went to the Chamber of Deputies. They found Lamartine there and held a conference with him in one of the offices.

They all spoke in turn, and expressed their convictions and hopes. They would be happy to think that Lamartine was with them for the immediate realization of the Republic. If, however, he judged that the transition of the Regency was necessary they asked him to at least aid them in obtaining serious guarantees against any retrogression. They awaited with emotion his decision in this great matter.

Lamartine listened to their reasons in silence, then requested them to allow him a few minutes for reflection. He sat apart from them at a table, leaned his head upon his hands, and thought. His four visitors, standing and silent, gazed at him respectfully. It was a solemn moment. "We listened to history passing," said Bocage to me.

Lamartine raised his head and said: "I will oppose the Regency."

A quarter of an hour later the Duchess d'Orleans arrived at the Chamber holding by the hand her two sons, the Count de Paris and the Duke de Chartres. M. Odilon. Barrot was not with her. The Duke de Nemours accompanied her.

She was acclaimed by the deputies. But, the Chamber having been dissolved, were there any deputies?

M. Crémieux ascended the tribune and flatly proposed a provisional government. M. Odilon Barrot, who had been fetched from the Ministry of the Interior, made his appearance at last and pleaded for the Regency, but without éclat and without energy. Suddenly a mob of people and National Guards with arms and flags invaded the chamber. The Duchess d'Orleans, persuaded by her friends, withdrew with her children.

The Chamber of Deputies then vanished, submerged by a sort of revolutionary assembly. Ledru-Rollin harangued this crowd. Next came Lamartine, who was awaited and acclaimed. He opposed the Regency, as he had promised.

That settled it. The names for a provisional government were proposed to the people. And by shouts of "yes" or "no" the people elected successively: Lamartine, Dupont de l'Eure, Arago, and Ledru-Rollin unanimously, Crémieux, Gamier-Pages, and Marie by a majority.

The new ministers at once set out for the Hotel de Ville.

At the Chamber of Deputies not once was the word "Republic" uttered in any of the speeches of the orators, not even in that of Ledru-Rollin. But now, outside, in the street, the elect of the people heard this words this shout, everywhere. It flew from mouth to mouth and filled the air of Paris.

The seven men who, in these supreme and extreme days, held the destiny of France in their hands were themselves at once tools and playthings in the hands of the mob, which is not the people, and of chance, which is not providence. Under the pressure of the multitude; in the bewilderment and terror of their triumph, which overwhelmed them, they decreed the Republic without having time to think that they were doing such a great thing.

When, having been separated and dispersed by the violent pushing of the crowd, they were able to find each other again and reassemble, or rather hide, in one of the rooms of the Hotel de Ville, they took half a sheet of paper, at the head of which were printed the words: "Prefecture of the Seine. Office of the Prefect." M. de Rambuteau may that very morning have used the other half of the sheet to write a love-letter to one of his "little bourgeoises," as he called them.

Under the dictation of terrible shouts outside Lamartine traced this phrase:

"The Provisional Government declares that the Provisional Government of France is the Republican Government, and that the nation shall be immediately called upon to ratify the resolution of the Provisional Government and of the people of Paris."

I had this paper, this sheet smeared and blotted with ink, in my hands. It was still stamped, still palpitating, so to speak, with the fever of the moment. The words hurriedly scribbled were scarcely formed. *Appelée* was written *appellée*.

When these half dozen lines had been written Lamartine handed the sheet to Ledru-Rollin.

Ledru-Rollin read aloud the phrase: "The Provisional Government declares that the Provisional Government of France is the Republican Government—"

"The word 'provisional' occurs twice," he commented.

"That is so," said the others.

"One of them at least must be effaced," added Ledru-Rollin.

Lamartine understood the significance of this grammatical observation, which was simply a political revolution.

"But we must await the sanction of France," he said. "I can do without the sanction of France," cried Ledru-Rollin, "when I have the sanction of the people."

"Of the people of Paris. But who knows at present what is the will of the people of France?" observed Lamartine.

There was an interval of silence. The noise of the multitude without sounded like the murmuring of the ocean. Ledru-Rollin went on:

"What the people want is the Republic at once, the Republic without waiting."

"The Republic without any delay?" said Lamartine, covering an objection in this interpretation of Ledru-Rollin's words.

"We are provisional," returned Ledru-Rollin, "but the Republic is not!"

M. Crémieux took the pen from Lamartine's hands, scratched out the word "provisional" at the end of the third line and wrote beside it: "actual."

"The actual government? Very well!" said Ledru-Rollin, with a slight shrug of the shoulder.

The seal of the City of Paris was on the table. Since 1830 the vessel sailing beneath a sky starred with fleurs-de-lys and with the device, *Proelucent clarius astris*, had disappeared from the seal of the City. The seal was merely a circle with the words "Ville de Paris" in the centre. Crémieux took the seal and stamped the paper so hastily with it that the words appeared upside down.

But they did not sign this rough draught. Their whereabouts had been discovered; an impetuous stream was surging against the door of the office in which they had taken refuge. The people were calling, ordering, them to go to the meeting-hall of the Municipal Council.

There they were greeted by this clamour: "The Republic! Long live the Republic! Proclaim the Republic!" Lamartine, who was at first interrupted by the cries, succeeded at length with his grand voice in calming this feverish impatience.

The members of the Provisional Government were thus enabled to return and resume their session and lively discussion. The more ardent ones wanted the document to read: "The Provisional Government proclaims the Republic." The moderates proposed: "The Provisional Government desires the Republic." A compromise was reached on the proposition of M. Crémieux, and the sentence was made to read: "The Provisional Government 'is for' the Republic." To this was added: "subject to the ratification of the people, who will be immediately consulted."

The news was at once announced to the crowds in the meeting-hall and in the square outside, who would listen to nothing but the word "republic," and saluted it with tremendous cheering.

The Republic was established. *Alea jacta*, as Lamartine observed later.

The Twenty-Fifth

DURING THE MORNING EVERYTHING AT and in the neighbourhood of the Mairie of the Eighth Arrondissement was relatively calm, and the steps to maintain order taken the previous day with the approval of M. Ernest Moreau appeared to have assured the security of the quarter.*

---

* On the evening of the 24th, there had been reason to apprehend disturbances in the Eighth Arrondissement, disturbances particularly serious in that they would not have been of a political character. The prowlers and evil-doers with hang-dog mien who seem to issue from the earth in times of trouble were very much in evidence in the streets. At the Prison of La Force, in the Rue Saint Antoine, the common law criminals had begun

I thought I might leave the Place Royale and repair towards the centre of the city with my son Victor. The restlessness and agitation of a people (of the people of Paris!) on the morrow of a revolution was a spectacle that had an irresistible attraction for me.

The weather was cloudy, but mild, and the rain held off. The streets were thrilling with a noisy, joyous crowd. The people continued with incredible ardour to fortify the barricades that had already been constructed, and even to build new ones. Bands of them with flags flying and drums beating marched about shouting "Long live the Republic!" and singing the "Marseillaise and Die for the Fatherland!" The cafés were crowded to overflowing, but many of the shops were closed, as on holidays; and, indeed, the city did present a holiday appearance.

I made my way along the quays to the Pont Neuf. There, at the bottom of a proclamation I read the name of Lamartine, and having seen the people, I experienced the desire to see my great friend. I therefore turned back with Victor towards the Hotel de Ville.

As on the previous day, the square in front of the building was filled with a crowd, and the crowd was so compact that it immobilized itself. It was impossible to approach the steps of the front entrance. After several attempts to get somewhere near to them, I was about to force my way back out of the crowd when I was perceived by M. Froment-Meurice, the artist-goldsmith, brother of my young friend, Paul Meurice. He was a major of the National Guard, and on duty with his battalion at the Hotel de Ville. "Make way!" he shouted authoritatively. "Make way for Victor Hugo!" And the human wall opened, how I do not know, before his epaulettes.

The entrance once passed, M. Froment-Meurice guided us up all sorts of stairways, and through corridors and rooms encumbered with people. As we were passing a man came from a group, and planting himself in front of me, said: "Citizen Victor Hugo, shout 'Long live the Republic!'"

a revolt by locking up their keepers. To what public force could appeal be made? The Municipal Guard had been disbanded, the army was confined to barracks; as to the police, no one would have known where to find them. Victor Hugo, in a speech which this time was cheered, confided life and property to the protection and devotedness of the people. A civic guard in blouses was improvised. Empty shops that were to let were transformed into guard houses, patrols were organized and sentries posted. The rebellious prisoners at La Force, terrified by the assertion that cannon (which did not exist) had been brought to bear upon the prison and that unless they surrendered promptly and unconditionally they would be blown sky-high, submitted quietly and returned to work.

"I will shout nothing by order," said I. "Do you understand what liberty is? For my part, I practise it. I will shout today 'Long live the people!' because it pleases me to do so. The day when I shout 'Long live the Republic!' it will be because I want to."

"Hear! hear! He is right," murmured several voices.

And we passed on.

After many detours M. Froment-Meurice ushered us into a small room where he left us while he went to inform Lamartine that I wished to see him.

The glass door of the room gave on to a gallery, passing along which I saw my friend David d'Angers, the great statuary. I called to him. David, who was an old-time Republican, was beaming. "Ah! my friend, what a glorious day!" he exclaimed. He told me that the Provisional Government had appointed him Mayor of the Eleventh Arrondissement. "They have sent for you for something of the same kind, I suppose?" he said. "No," I answered, "I have not been sent for. I came of my own accord just to shake Lamartine's hand."

M. Froment-Meurice returned and announced that Lamartine awaited me. I left Victor in the room, telling him to wait there till I came back, and once more followed my obliging guide through more corridors that led to a vestibule that was crowded with people. "They are all office seekers!" explained M. Froment-Meurice. The Provisional Government was holding a session in the adjoining room. The door was guarded by two armed grenadiers of the National Guard, who were impassible, and deaf alike to entreaties and menaces. I had to force my way through this crowd. One of the grenadiers, on the lookout for me, opened the door a little way to let me in. The crowd immediately made a rush and tried to push past the sentries, who, however, aided by M. Froment-Meurice, forced them back and closed the door behind me.

I was in a spacious hall that formed the angle of one of the pavilions of the Hotel de Ville, and was lighted on two sides by long windows. I would have preferred to find Lamartine alone, but there were with him, dispersed about the room and talking to friends or writing, three or four of his colleagues in the Provisional Government, Arago, Marie, and Armand Marrast. Lamartine rose as I entered. On his frock-coat, which was buttoned up as usual, he wore an ample tri-colour sash, slung across his shoulder. He advanced to meet me, and stretching out his hand, exclaimed: "Ah! you have come over to us! Victor Hugo is a strong recruit indeed for the Republic."

"Not so fast, my friend," said I with a laugh. "I have come simply to see my friend Lamartine. Perhaps you are not aware of the fact that yesterday while you were opposing the Regency in the Chamber, I was defending it in the Place de la Bastille."

"Yesterday, that was all right; but today? There is now neither Regency nor Royalty. It is impossible that Victor Hugo is not at heart Republican."

"In principle, yes, I am. The Republic is, in my opinion, the only rational form of government, the only one worthy of the nations. The universal Republic is inevitable in the natural course of progress. But has its hour struck in France? It is because I want the Republic that I want it to be durable and definitive. You are going to consult the nation, are you not?—the whole nation?"

"The whole nation, assuredly. We of the Provisional Government are all for universal suffrage."

At this moment Arago came up to us with M. Armand Marrast, who held a folded paper in his hand.

"My dear friend," said Lamartine, "know that this morning we selected you for Mayor of your arrondissement."

"And here is the patent signed by us all," said Armand Marrast.

"I thank you," said I, "but I cannot accept it."

"Why?" continued Arago. "These are non-political and purely gratuitous functions."

"We were informed just now about the attempted revolt at La Force," added Lamartine. "You did better than suppress it, you forestalled it. You are loved and respected in your arrondissement."

"My authority is wholly moral," I rejoined; "it could but lose weight in becoming official. Besides, on no account would I dispossess M. Ernest Moreau, who has borne himself loyally and valiantly throughout this trouble."

Lamartine and Arago insisted: "Do not refuse our brevet."

"Very well," said I, "I will take it—for the sake of the autographs; but it is understood that I keep it in my pocket."

"Yes, keep it," said Armand Marrast laughingly, "so that you can say that one day you were *pair* and the next day *maire*."

Lamartine took me aside into the recess of a window.

"It is not a mairie I would like you to have, but a ministry. Victor Hugo, the Republic's Minister of Instruction! Come now, since you say that you are Republican!"

"Republican—in principle. But in fact, I was yesterday peer of France, I was yesterday for the Regency, and, believing the Republic to be premature, I should be also for the Regency today."

"Nations are above dynasties," went on Lamartine. "I, too, have been a Royalist."

"Yes, but you were a deputy, elected by the nation; I was a peer, appointed by the King."

"The King in choosing you, under the terms of the Constitution, in one of the categories from which the Upper House was recruited, but honoured the peerage and also honoured himself."

"I thank you," said I, "but you look at things from the outside; I consider them in my conscience."

We were interrupted by the noise of a prolonged fusillade which broke out suddenly on the square. A bullet smashed a window-pane above our heads.

"What is the matter now?" exclaimed Lamartine in sorrowful tones.

M. Armand Marrast and M. Marie went out to see what was going on.

"Ah! my friend," continued Lamartine, "how heavy is this revolutionary power to bear! One has to assume such weighty and such sudden responsibilities before one's conscience and in presence of history! I do not know how I have been living during the past ten days. Yesterday I had a few grey hairs; tomorrow they will be white."

"Yes, but you are doing your duty as a man of genius grandly," I commented.

In a few minutes M. Armand Marrast returned.

"It was not against us," he said. "How the lamentable affray came about could not be explained to me. There was a collision, the rifles went off, why? Was it a misunderstanding, was it a quarrel between Socialists and Republicans? No one knows."

"Are there any wounded?"

"Yes, and dead, too."

A gloomy silence followed. I rose. "You have no doubt some measures to take?" I said.

"What measures?" answered Lamartine. "This morning we resolved to decree what you have already been able to do on a small scale in your quarter: the organization of the citizen's National Guard—every Frenchman a soldier as well as a voter. But time is required, and meanwhile—" he pointed to the waves and eddies of heads surging on the square outside—"look, it is the sea!"

A boy wearing an apron entered and spoke to him in low tones.

"Ah! very good!" said Lamartine, "it is my luncheon. Will you share it with me, Hugo?"

"Thanks, I have already lunched."

"I haven't and I am dying of hunger. At least come and look on at the feast; I will let you go, afterwards."

He showed me into a room that gave on to an interior court-yard. A gentle faced young man who was writing at a table rose and was about to withdraw. He was the young workman whom Louis Blanc had had attached to the Provisional Government.

"Stay where you are, Albert," said Lamartine, "I have nothing of a private nature to say to Victor Hugo."

We saluted each other, M. Albert and I.

The little waiter showed Lamartine a table upon which were some mutton cutlets in an earthenware dish, some bread, a bottle of wine and a glass. The whole came from a wine-shop in the neighbourhood.

"Well," exclaimed Lamartine, "what about a knife and fork?"

"I thought you had knives and forks here," returned the boy. "I had trouble enough to bring the luncheon, and if I have got to go and fetch knives and forks—"

"Pshaw!" said Lamartine, "one must take things as they come!"

He broke the bread, took a cutlet by the bone and tore the meat with his teeth. When he had finished he threw the bone into the fireplace. In this manner he disposed of three cutlets, and drank two glasses of wine.

"You will agree with me that this is a primitive repast!" he said. "But it is an improvement on our supper last night. We had only bread and cheese among us, and we all drank water from the same chipped sugar-bowl. Which didn't, it appears, prevent a newspaper this morning from denouncing the great orgy of the Provisional Government!"

I did not find Victor in the room where he was to have waited for me. I supposed that, having become tired of waiting, he had returned home alone.

When I issued on to the Place de Grève the crowd was still excited and in a state of consternation at the inexplicable collision that had occurred an hour before. The body of a wounded man who had just expired was carried past me. They told me that it was the fifth. It was taken, as the other bodies had been taken, to the Salle Saint Jean, where the dead of the previous day to the number of over a hundred had been exposed.

Before returning to the Place Royale I made a tour for the purpose of visiting our guard-houses. Outside the Minimes Barracks a boy of about fifteen years, armed with the rifle of a soldier of the line, was proudly mounting guard. It seemed to me that I had seen him there in the morning or the day before.

"What!" I said, "are you doing sentry duty again?"

"No, not again; I haven't yet been relieved."

"You don't say so. Why, how long have you been here?"

"Oh, about seventeen hours!"

"What! haven't you slept? Haven't you eaten?"

"Yes, I have had something to eat."

"You went to get it, of course?"

"No, I didn't, a sentry does not quit his post! This morning I shouted to the people in the shop across the way that I was hungry, and they brought me some bread."

I hastened to have the brave child relieved from duty.

On arriving in the Place Royale I inquired for Victor. He had not returned. I was seized with a shudder of fear. I do not know why the vision of the dead who had been transported to the Salle Saint Jean should have come into my mind. What if my Victor had been caught in that bloody affray? I gave some pretext for going out again. Vacquerie was there; I told him of my anguish in a whisper, and he offered to accompany me.

First of all we called upon M. Froment-Meurice, whose establishment was in the Rue Lobau, next to the Hotel de Ville, and I asked him to have me admitted to the Salle Saint Jean. At first he sought to dissuade me from seeing the hideous sight; he had seen it the previous day and was still under the impression of the horror it inspired. I fancied his reluctance was a bad sign, that he was trying to keep something from me. This made me insist the more, and we went.

In the large Salle Saint Jean, transformed into a vast morgue, lay the long line of corpses upon camp bedsteads. For the most part they were unrecognisable. And I held the dreadful review, quaking in my shoes when one of the dead was young and slim with chestnut hair. Yes, the spectacle of the poor blood-stained dead was horrible indeed! But I could not describe it; all that I saw of each body was that it was not that of my child. At length I reached the last one, and breathed freely once more.

As I issued from the lugubrious place I saw Victor, very much alive, running towards me. When he heard the firing he had left the room where he was waiting for me, and not being able to find his way back, had been to see a friend.

II. Expulsions and Escapes

May 3, 1848

On February 24 the Duke and Duchess Decazes were literally driven from the Luxembourg. And by whom? By the very denizens of the palace, all employés of the Chamber of Peers, all appointed by the grand referendary. A rumour was circulated in the quarter that during the night the peers would commit some anti-revolutionary act, publish a proclamation, etc. The entire Faubourg Saint Jacques prepared to march against the Luxembourg. Hence, great terror. First the Duke and Duchess were begged, then pressed, then constrained to leave the palace.

"We will leave tomorrow. We do not know where to go. Let us pass the night here," they said.

They were driven out.

They slept in a lodging-house. Next day they took up their abode at 9, Rue Verneuil.

M. Decazes was very ill. A week before he had undergone an operation. Mme. Decazes bore it all with cheerfulness and courage. This is a trait of character that women often display in trying situations brought about through the stupidity of men.

The ministers escaped, but not without difficulty. M. Duchâtel, in particular, had a great fright.

M. Guizot, three days previously, had quitted the Hotel des Capucines and installed himself at the Ministry of the Interior. He lived there *en famille* with M. Duchâtel.

On February 24, MM. Duchâtel and Guizot were about to sit down to luncheon when an usher rushed in with a frightened air. The head of the column of rioters was debouching from the Rue de Bourgogne. The two ministers left the table and managed to escape just in time by way of the garden. Their families followed them: M. Duchâtel's young wife, M. Guizot's aged mother, and the children.

A notable thing about this flight was that the luncheon of M. Guizot became the supper of M. Ledru-Rollin. It was not the first time that the Republic had eaten what had been served to the Monarchy.

Meanwhile the fugitives had taken the Rue Bellechasse. M. Guizot walked first, giving his arm to Mme. Duchâtel. His fur-lined overcoat was buttoned up and his hat as usual was stuck on the back of his head. He was easily recognisable. In the Rue Hillerin-Bertin, Mme. Duchâtel noticed that some men in blouses were gazing at M. Guizot in a singular manner, She led him into a doorway. It chanced that she knew the doorkeeper. They hid M. Guizot in an empty room on the fifth floor.

Here M. Guizot passed the day, but he could not stay there. One of his friends remembered a bookseller, a great admirer of M. Guizot, who in better days had often declared that he would devote himself to and give his life for him whom he called "a great man," and that he only hoped the opportunity for doing so might present itself. This friend called upon him, reminded him of what he had said, and told him that the hour had come. The brave bookseller did not fail in what was expected of him. He placed his house at M. Guizot's disposal and hid him there for ten whole days. At the end of that time the eight places in a compartment of a carriage on the Northern Railway were hired. M. Guizot made his way to the station at nightfall. The seven persons who were aiding in his escape entered the compartment with him. They reached Lille, then Ostend, whence M. Guizot crossed over to England.

M. Duchâtel's escape was more complicated.

He managed to secure a passport as an agent of the Republic on a mission. He disguised himself, dyed his eye-brows, put on blue spectacles, and left Paris in a post-chaise. Twice he was stopped by National Guards in the towns through which he passed. With great audacity he declared that he would hold responsible before the Republic those who delayed him on his mission. The word "Republic" produced its effect. They allowed the Minister to pass. The Republic saved M. Duchâtel.

In this way he reached a seaport (Boulogne, I think), believing that he was being hotly pursued, and very nervous in consequence. A Channel steamer was going to England. He went on board at night. He was installing himself for the voyage when he was informed that the steamer would not leave that night. He thought that he had been discovered and that he was a lost man. The steamer had merely been detained by the English Consul, probably to facilitate, if necessary, the flight of Louis Philippe. M. Duchâtel landed again and spent the night and next day in the studio of a woman painter who was devoted to him.

Then he embarked on another steamer. He went below at once and concealed himself as best he could pending the departure of the vessel.

He scarcely dared to breathe, fearing that at any moment he might be recognised and seized. At last the steamer got under way. Hardly had the paddle wheels begun to revolve, however, when shouts of "Stop her! Stop her!" were raised on the quay and on the boat, which stopped short. This time the poor devil of a Minister thought it was all up with him. The hubbub was caused by an officer of the National Guard, who, in taking leave of friends, had lingered too long on deck, and did not want to be taken to England against his will. When he found that the vessel had cast off he had shouted "Stop her!" and his family on the quay had taken up the shout. The officer was put ashore and the steamer finally started.

This was how M. Duchâtel left France and reached England.

III. Louis Philippe in Exile

May 3, 1848

The Orleans family in England are literally in poverty; they are twenty-two at table and drink water. There is not the slightest exaggeration in this. Absolutely all they have to live upon is an income of about 40,000 francs made up as follows: 24,000 francs a year from Naples, which came from Queen Marie Amélie, and the interest on a sum of 340,000 francs which Louis Philippe had forgotten under the following circumstances: During his last triumphal voyage made in October, 1844, with the Prince de Joinville, he had a credit of 500,000 francs opened for him with a London banker. Of this sum he spent only 160,000 francs. He was greatly amazed and very agreeably surprised on arriving in London to find that the balance of the 500,000 francs remained at his disposal.

M. Vatout is with the Royal Family. For the whole of them there are but three servants, of whom one, and one only, accompanied them from the Tuileries. In this state of destitution they demanded of Paris the restitution of what belongs to them in France; their property is under seizure, and has remained so notwithstanding their reclamations. For different reasons. One of the motives put forward by the Provisional Government is the debt of the civil list, which amounts to thirty millions. Queer ideas about Louis Philippe were entertained. He may have been covetous, but he certainly was not miserly; he was the most prodigal, the most extravagant and least careful of men: he had debts, accounts and arrears everywhere. He owed 700,000 francs to a cabinet-maker; to his market gardener he owed 70,000 francs *for butter*.

Consequently none of the seals placed on the property could be broken and everything is held to secure the creditors—everything, even to the personal property of the Prince and Princess de Joinville, rentes, diamonds, etc., even to a sum of 198,000 francs which belongs in her own right to the Duchess d'Orleans.

All that the Royal Family was able to obtain was their clothing and personal effects, or rather what could be found of these. Three long tables were placed in the theatre of the Tuileries, and on these were laid out all that the revolutionists of February had turned over to the governor of the Tuileries, M. Durand Saint-Amand. It formed a queer medley—court costumes stained and torn, grand cordons of the Legion of Honour that had been trailed through the mud, stars of foreign orders, swords, diamond crowns, pearl necklaces, a collar of the Golden Fleece, etc. Each legal representative of the princes, an aide-de-camp or secretary, took what he recognised. It appears that on the whole little was recovered. The Duke de Nemours merely asked for some linen and in particular his heavy-soled shoes.

The Prince de Joinville, meeting the Duke de Montpensier, greeted him thus: "Ah! here you are, Monsieur; you were not killed, you have not had good luck!"

Gudin, the marine painter, who went to England, saw Louis Philippe. The King is greatly depressed. He said to Gudin: "I don't understand it. What happened in Paris? What did the Parisians get into their heads? I haven't any idea. One of these days they will recognise that I did not do one thing wrong." He did not, indeed, do one thing wrong; he did all things wrong!

He had in fact reached an incredible degree of optimism; he believed himself to be more of a king than Louis XIV and more of an emperor than Napoleon. On Tuesday the 22nd he was exuberantly gay, and was still occupied solely with his own affairs, and these of the pettiest character. At 2 o'clock when the first shots were being fired, he was conferring with his lawyers and business agents, MM. de Gérante, Scribe and Denormandie, as to what could best be done about Madame Adelaide's will. On Wednesday, at 1 o'clock, when the National Guard was declaring against the government, which meant revolution, the King sent for M. Hersent to order of him a picture of some kind.

Charles X was a lynx.

Louis Philippe in England, however, bears his misfortune worthily. The English aristocracy acted nobly; eight or ten of the wealthiest peers wrote to Louis Philippe to offer him their châteaux and their purses. The King replied: "I accept and keep only your letters."

The Duchess d'Orleans is also in straitened circumstances. She is on bad terms with the d'Orleans family and the Mecklenburg family is on bad terms with her. On the one hand she will accept nothing, and on the other she can expect nothing.

At this time of writing (May, 1848) the Tuileries have already been repaired, and M. Empis remarked to me this morning: "They are going to clean up and nothing of the damage done will be apparent." Neuilly and the Palais-Royal, however, have been devastated. The picture gallery of the Palais-Royal, a pretty poor one by the by, has practically been destroyed. Only a single picture remains perfectly intact, and that is the Portrait of Philippe Egalité. Was it purposely respected by the riot or is its preservation an irony of chance? The National Guards amused, and still amuse, themselves by cutting out of the canvases that were not entirely destroyed by fire faces to which they take a fancy.

IV. King Jerome

THERE ENTERED MY DRAWING-ROOM IN the Place Royale one morning in March, 1848, a man of medium height, about sixty-five or sixty-six years of age, dressed in black, a red and blue ribbon in his buttonhole, and wearing patent-leather boots and white gloves. He was Jerome Napoleon, King of Westphalia.

He had a very gentle voice, a charming though somewhat timid smile, straight hair turning grey, and something of the profile of the Emperor.

He came to thank me for the permission that had been accorded to him to return to France, which he attributed to me, and begged me to get him appointed Governor of the Invalides. He told me that M. Crémieux, one of the members of the Provisional Government, had said to him the previous day:

"If Victor Hugo asks Lamartine to do it, it will be done. Formerly everything depended upon an interview between two emperors; now everything depends upon an interview between two poets."

"Tell M. Crémieux that it is he who is the poet," I replied to King Jerome with a smile.

In November, 1848, the King of Westphalia lived on the first floor above the entresol at No. 3, Rue d'Alger. It was a small apartment with mahogany furniture and woollen velvet upholstering.

The wall paper of the drawing-room was grey. The room was lighted by two lamps and ornamented by a heavy clock in the Empire style and two not very authentic pictures, although the frame of one bore the name: "Titiens," and the frame of the other the name: "Rembrandt." On the mantelpiece was a bronze bust of Napoleon, one of those familiar and inevitable busts that the Empire bequeathed us.

The only vestiges of his royal existence that remained to the prince were his silverware and dinner service, which were ornamented with royal crowns richly engraved and gilded.

Jerome at that time was only sixty-four years old, and did not look his age. His eyes were bright, his smile benevolent and charming, and his hands small and still shapely. He was habitually attired in black with a gold chain in his buttonhole from which hung three crosses, the Legion of Honour, the Iron Crown, and his Order of Westphalia created by him in imitation of the Iron Crown.

Jerome talked well, with grace always and often with wit. He was full of reminiscences and spoke of the Emperor with a mingled respect and affection that was touching. A little vanity was perceptible; I would have preferred pride.

Moreover he received with bonhomie all the varied qualifications which were brought upon him by his strange position of a man who was no longer king, no longer proscribed, and yet was not a citizen. Everybody addressed him as he pleased. Louis Philippe called him "Highness," M. Boulay de la Meurthe "Sire" or "Your Majesty," Alexandre Dumas "Monseigneur," I addressed him as "Prince," and my wife called him "Monsieur." On his card he wrote "General Bonaparte." In his place I would have understood his position. King or nothing.

Related by King Jerome

IN THE EVENING OF THE day following that on which Jerome, recalled from exile, returned to Paris, he had vainly waited for his secretary, and feeling bored and lonely, went out. It was at the end of summer (1847). He was staying at the house of his daughter, Princess Demidoff, which was off the Champs-Elysées.

He crossed the Place de la Concorde, looking about him at the statues, obelisk and fountains, which were new to the exile who had not seen Paris for thirty-two years. He continued along the Quai des Tuileries. I know not what reverie took possession of his soul. Arrived at the Pavillon de Flore, he entered the gate, turned to the left, and began to walk up a flight of stairs under the arch. He had gone up two or three steps when he felt himself seized by the arm. It was the gatekeeper who had run after him.

"Hi! Monsieur, monsieur, where are you going?"

Jerome gazed at him in astonishment and replied:

"Why, to my apartments, of course!"

Hardly had he uttered the words, however, when he awoke from his dream. The past had bewitched him for a moment. In recounting the incident to me he said:

"I went away shamefacedly, and apologizing to the porter."

V. The Days of June

Miscellaneous Notes

THE INSURRECTION OF JUNE PRESENTED peculiar features from the outset.* It suddenly manifested itself to terrified society in monstrous and unknown forms.

The first barricade was erected in the morning of Friday, the 23rd, at the Porte Saint Denis. It was attacked the same day. The National Guard marched resolutely against it. The attacking force was made up of battalions of the First and Second Legions, which arrived by way of the boulevards. When the assailants got within range a formidable volley was fired from the barricade, and littered the ground with National Guards. The National Guard, more irritated than intimidated, charged the barricade.

At this juncture a woman appeared upon its crest, a woman young, handsome, dishevelled, terrible. This woman, who was a prostitute,

---

* At the end of June, four months after the proclamation of the Republic, regular work had come to a standstill and the useless workshops known as the "national workshops" had been abolished by the National Assembly. Then the widespread distress prevailing caused the outbreak of one of the most formidable insurrections recorded in history. The power at that time was in the hands of an Executive Committee of five members, Lamartine, Arago, Ledru Rollin, Garnier-Pages and Marie. General Cavaignac was Minister of War.

pulled up her clothes to her waist and screamed to the guards in that frightful language of the lupanar that one is always compelled to translate:

"Cowards! fire, if you dare, at the belly of a woman!" Here the affair became appalling. The National Guard did not hesitate. A volley brought the wretched creature down, and with a piercing shriek she toppled off the barricade. A silence of horror fell alike upon besiegers and besieged.

Suddenly another woman appeared. This one was even younger and more beautiful; she was almost a child, being barely seventeen years of age. Oh! the pity of it! She, too, was a street-walker. Like the other she lifted her skirt, disclosed her abdomen, and screamed: "Fire, brigands!" They fired, and riddled with bullets she fell upon the body of her sister in vice.

It was thus that the war commenced.

Nothing could be more chilling and more sombre. It is a hideous thing this heroism of abjection in which bursts forth all that weakness has of strength; this civilization attacked by cynicism and defending itself by barbarity. On one side the despair of the people, on the other the despair of society.

On Saturday the 24th, at 4 o'clock in the morning, I, as a Representative of the people, was at the barricade in the Place Baudoyer that was defended by the troops.

The barricade was a low one. Another, narrow and high, protected it in the street. The sun shone upon and brightened the chimney-tops. The tortuous Rue Saint Antoine wound before us in sinister solitude.

The soldiers were lying upon the barricade, which was little more than three feet high. Their rifles were stacked between the projecting paving-stones as though in a rack. Now and then bullets whistled overhead and struck the walls of the houses around us, bringing down a shower of stone and plaster. Occasionally a blouse, sometimes a cap-covered head, appeared at the corner of a street. The soldiers promptly fired at it. When they hit their mark they applauded "Good! Well aimed! Capital!"

They laughed and chatted gaily. At intervals there was a rattle and roar, and a hail of bullets rained upon the barricade from roofs and windows. A very tall captain with a grey moustache stood erect at the centre of the barrier, above which half his body towered. The bullets pattered about him as about a target. He was impassible and serene and spoke to his men in this wise:

"There, children, they are firing. Lie down. Look out, Laripaud, you are showing your head. Reload!"

All at once a woman turned the corner of a street. She came leisurely towards the barricade. The soldiers swore and shouted to her to get out of the way:

"Ah! the strumpet! Will you get out of that you w—! Shake a leg, damn you! She's coming to reconnoitre. She's a spy! Bring her down. Down with the moucharde!"

The captain restrained them:

"Don't shoot, it's a woman!"

After advancing about twenty paces the woman, who really did seem to be observing us, entered a low door which closed behind her.

This one was saved.

At 11 o'clock I returned from the barrier in the Place Baudoyer and took my usual place in the Assembly. A Representative whom I did not know, but who I have since learned was M. Belley, engineer, residing in the Rue des Tournelles, came and sat beside me and said:

"Monsieur Victor Hugo, the Place Royale has been burned. They set fire to your house. The insurgents entered by the little door in the Cul-de-sac Guéménée."

"And my family?" I inquired.

"They are safe."

"How do you know?"

"I have just come from there. Not being known I was able to get over the barricades and make my way here. Your family first took refuge in the Mairie. I was there, too. Seeing that the danger was over I advised Mme. Victor Hugo to seek some other asylum. She found shelter with her children in the home of a chimney-sweep named Martignon who lives near your house, under the arcades."

I knew that worthy Martignon family. This reassured me.

"And how about the riot?" I asked.

"It is a revolution," replied M. Belley. "The insurgents are in control of Paris at this moment."

I left M. Belley and hurriedly traversed the few rooms that separated the hall in which we held our sessions and the office occupied by the Executive Committee.

It was a small salon belonging to the presidency, and was reached through two rooms that were smaller still. In these ante-chambers was a buzzing crowd of distracted officers and National Guards. They made no attempt to prevent any one from entering.

I opened the door of the Executive Committee's office. Ledru-Rollin, very red, was half seated on the table. M. Gamier-Pages, very pale, and half reclining in an armchair, formed an antithesis to him. The contrast was complete: Garnier-Pagès thin and bushy-haired, Ledru-Rollin stout and close-cropped. Two or three colonels, among them Representative Charras, were conversing in a corner. I only recall Arago vaguely. I do not remember whether M. Marie was there. The sun was shining brightly.

Lamartine, standing in a window recess on the left, was talking to a general in full uniform, whom I saw for the first and last time, and who was Négrier. Négrier was killed that same evening in front of a barricade.

I hurried to Lamartine, who advanced to meet me. He was wan and agitated, his beard was long, his clothes were dusty.

He held out his hand: "Ah! good morning, Hugo!"

Here is the dialogue that we engaged in, every word of which is still fresh in my memory:

"What is the situation, Lamartine?"

"We are done for!"

"What do you mean by that?"

"I mean that in a quarter of an hour from now the Assembly will be invaded."

(Even at that moment a column of insurgents was coming down the Rue de Lille. A timely charge of cavalry dispersed it.)

"Nonsense! What about the troops?"

"There are no troops!"

"But you said on Wednesday, and yesterday repeated, that you had sixty thousand men at your disposal."

"So I thought."

"Well, but you musn't give up like this. It is not only you who are at stake, but the Assembly, and not only the Assembly, but France, and not only France, but the whole of civilization. Why did you not issue orders yesterday to have the garrisons of the towns for forty leagues round brought to Paris? That would have given you thirty thousand men at once."

"We gave the orders—"

"Well?"

"The troops have not come!"

Lamartine took my hand and said;

"I am not Minister of War!"

At this moment a few representatives entered noisily. The Assembly had just voted a state of siege. They told Ledru-Rollin and Garnier-Pages so in a few words.

Lamartine half turned towards them and said in an undertone:

"A state of siege! A state of siege! Well, declare it if you think it is necessary. I have nothing to say!"

He dropped into a chair, repeating:

"I have nothing to say, neither yes nor no. Do what you like!"

General Négrier came up to me.

"Monsieur Victor Hugo," he said, "I have come to reassure you; I have received news from the Place Royale."

"Well, general?"

"Your family are safe."

"Thanks! Yes, I have just been so informed."

"But your house has been burnt down."

"What does that matter?" said I.

Négrier warmly pressed my arm:

"I understand you. Let us think only of one thing. Let us save the country!"

As I was withdrawing Lamartine quitted a group and came to me.

"Adieu," he said. "But do not forget this: do not judge me too hastily; I am not the Minister of War."

The day before, as the riot was spreading, Cavaignac, after a few measures had been taken, said to Lamartine:

"That's enough for today."

It was 5 o'clock.

"What!" exclaimed Lamartine. "Why, we have still four hours of daylight before us! And the riot will profit by them while we are losing them!"

He could get nothing from Cavaignac except:

"That's enough for today!"

On the 24th, about 3 o'clock, at the most critical moment, a Representative of the people, wearing his sail across his shoulder, arrived at the Mairie of the Second Arrondissement, in the Rue Chauchat, behind the Opera. He was recognised. He was Lagrange.

The National Guards surrounded him. In a twinkling the group became menacing:

"It is Lagrange! the man of the pistol shot!* What are you doing here? You are a coward! Get behind the barricades. That is your place—your friends are there—and not with us! They will proclaim you their chief; go on! They at any rate are brave! They are giving their blood for your follies; and you, you are afraid! You have a dirty duty to do, but at least do it! Get out of here! Begone!"

Lagrange endeavoured to speak. His voice was drowned by hooting.

This is how these madmen received the honest man who after fighting for the people wanted to risk his life for society.

June 25

The insurgents were firing throughout the whole length of the Boulevard Beaumarchais from the tops of the new houses. Several had ambushed themselves in the big house in course of construction opposite the Galiote. At the windows they had stuck dummies,—bundles of straw with blouses and caps on them.

I distinctly saw a man who had entrenched himself behind a barricade of bricks in a corner of the balcony on the fourth floor of the house which faces the Rue du Pont-aux-Choux. The man took careful aim and killed a good many persons.

It was 3 o'clock. The troops and mobiles fringed the roofs of the Boulevard du Temple and returned the fire of the insurgents. A cannon had just been drawn up in front of the Gaité to demolish the house of the Galiote and sweep the whole boulevard.

I thought I ought to make an effort to put a stop to the bloodshed, if possible, and advanced to the corner of the Rue d'Angoulême. When I reached the little turret near there I was greeted with a fusillade. The bullets pattered upon the turret behind me, and ploughed up the playbills with which it was covered. I detached a strip of paper as a memento. The bill to which it belonged announced for that very Sunday a fête at the Château des Flours, "with a thousand lanterns."

FOR FOUR MONTHS WE HAVE been living in a furnace. What consoles me is that the statue of the future will issue from it. It required such a brazier to melt such a bronze.

---

* It was popularly but erroneously believed that Lagrange fired the shot that led to the massacre in the Boulevard des Capucines on February 23.

VI. Chateaubriand

July 5, 1848

Chateaubriand is dead. One of the splendours of this century has passed away.

He was seventy-nine years old according to his own reckoning; according to the calculation of his old friend M. Bertin, senior, he was eighty years of age. But he had a weakness, said M. Bertin, and that was that he insisted that he was born not in 1768, but in 1769, because that was the year of Napoleon's birth.

He died yesterday, July 4, at 8 o'clock in the morning. For five or six months he had been suffering from paralysis which had almost destroyed his brain, and for five days from inflammation of the lungs, which abruptly snuffed out his life.

M. Ampere announced the news to the Academy, which thereupon decided to adjourn.

I quitted the National Assembly, where a questor to succeed General Négrier, who was killed in June, was being nominated, and went to M. de Chateaubriand's house, No. 110, Rue du Bac.

I was received by M. de Preuille, son-in-law of his nephew. I entered Chateaubriand's chamber.

He was lying upon his bed, a little iron bedstead with white curtains round it and surmounted by an iron curtain ring of somewhat doubtful taste. The face was uncovered; the brow, the nose, the closed eyes, bore that expression of nobleness which had marked him in life, and which was enhanced by the grave majesty of death. The mouth and chin were hidden by a cambric handkerchief. On his head was a white cotton nightcap which, however, allowed the grey hair on his temples to be seen. A white cravat rose to his ears. His tawny visage appeared more severe amid all this whiteness. Beneath the sheet his narrow, hollow chest and his thin legs could be discerned.

The shutters of the windows giving on to the garden were closed. A little daylight entered through the half-opened door of the salon. The chamber and the face were illumined by four tapers which burned at the corners of a table placed near the bed. On this table were a silver crucifix, a vase filled with holy water, and an aspergillum. Beside it a priest was praying.

Behind the priest a large brown-coloured screen hid the fireplace, above which the mantel-glass and a few engravings of churches and cathedrals were visible.

At Chateaubriand's feet, in the angle formed by the bed and the wall of the room, were two wooden boxes, placed one upon the other. The largest I was told contained the complete manuscript of his Memoirs, in forty-eight copybooks. Towards the last there had been such disorder in the house that one of the copybooks had been found that very morning by M. de Preuille in a dark and dirty closet where the lamps were cleaned.

A few tables, a wardrobe, and a few blue and green armchairs in disorder encumbered more than they furnished the room.

The adjoining salon, the furniture of which was hidden under unbleached covers, contained nothing more remarkable than a marble bust of Henry V and a full-length statuette of Chateaubriand, which were on the mantelpiece, and on each side of a window plaster busts of Mme. de Berri and her infant child.

Towards the close of his life Chateaubriand was almost in his second childhood. His mind was only lucid for about two or three hours a day, at least so M. Pilorge, his former secretary, told me.

When in February he was apprised of the proclamation of the Republic he merely remarked: "Will you be any the happier for it?"

When his wife died he attended the funeral service and returned laughing heartily—which, said Pilorge, was a proof that he was of weak mind. "A proof that he was in his right mind!" affirmed Edouard Bertin.

Mme. de Chateaubriand's benevolence was official, which did not prevent her from being a shrew at home. She founded a hospice—the Marie Thérèse Infirmary—visited the poor, succoured the sick, superintended crêches, gave alms and prayed; at the same time she was harsh towards her husband, her relatives, her friends, and her servants, and was sour-tempered, stern, prudish, and a backbiter. God on high will take these things into account.

She was ugly, pitted with small-pox, had an enormous mouth, little eyes, was insignificant in appearance, and acted the *grande dame*, although she was rather the wife of a great man than of a great lord. By birth she was only the daughter of a ship-owner of Saint Malo. M. de Chateaubriand feared, detested, and cajoled her.

She took advantage of this to make herself insupportable to mere human beings. I have never known anybody less approachable or whose reception of callers was more forbidding. I was a youth when I went to M. de Chateaubriand's. She received me very badly, or rather she did not receive me at all. I entered and bowed, but Mme. de Chateaubriand did not see me. I was scared out of my wits. These terrors made my visits to M. de Chateaubriand veritable nightmares which oppressed me for fifteen days and fifteen nights in advance. Mme. de Chateaubriand hated whoever visited her husband except through the doors that she opened. She had not presented me to him, therefore she hated me. I was perfectly odious to her, and she showed it.

Only once in my life and in hers did Mme. de Chateaubriand receive me graciously. One day I entered, poor little devil, as usual most unhappy, with affrighted schoolboy air and twisting my hat about in my hands. M. de Chateaubriand at that time still lived at No. 27, Rue Saint Dominique.

I was frightened at everything there, even at the servant who opened the door. Well, I entered. Mme. de Chateaubriand was in the salon leading to her husband's study. It was a summer morning. There was a ray of sunshine on the floor, and what dazzled and astonished me much more than the ray of sunshine was a smile on Mme. de Chateaubriand's face. "Is that you, Monsieur Victor Hugo?" she said. I thought I was in the midst of a dream of the *Arabian Nights*. Mme. de Chateaubriand smiling! Mme. de Chateaubriand knowing my name, addressing me by name! It was the first time that she had deigned to notice my existence. I bowed so low that my head nearly touched the floor. She went on: "I am delighted to see you." I could not believe my ears. "I was expecting you," she continued. "It is a long time since you called." I thought then that there certainly must be something the matter either with her or myself. However, she pointed to a rather large object of some kind on a little table, and added: "I reserved this for you. I felt sure you would like to have it. You know what it is?" It was a pile of packets of chocolate made by some religious institution. She had taken the stuff under her protection and the proceeds of its sale were to be devoted to charitable works. I took it and paid for it. At that time I had to live for fifteen months on 800 francs. The Catholic chocolate and Mme. de Chateaubriand's smile cost me 15 francs; that is to say, a fortnight's board. Fifteen francs meant as much to me then as 1,500 francs does now.

It was the most costly smile of a woman that ever was sold to me.

M. de Chateaubriand, at the beginning of 1847, was a paralytic; Mme. Récamier was blind. Every day at 3 o'clock M. de Chateaubriand was carried to Mme. Recamier's bedside. It was touching and sad. The woman who could no longer see stretched forth her hands gropingly towards the man who could no longer feel; their hands met. God be praised! Life was dying, but love still lived.

VII. Debates in the National Assembly on the Days of June

Session of November 25, 1848

What had to be determined before the Assembly and the country was upon whom devolved the heavy responsibility for the painful days of June. The Executive Committee was then in power; ought it not to have foreseen and provided against the insurrection? General Cavaignac, Minister of War, and, moreover, invested with dictatorial powers by the National Assembly, had alone issued orders.

Had he issued them in time? Could he not have crushed the riot at the outset instead of permitting it to gain strength, spread and develop into an insurrection? And, finally, had not the repression which followed victory been unnecessarily bloody, if not inhuman?

As the time for rendering an account approached Cavaignac became thoughtful and his ill-humour was manifest even in the Chamber.

One day Crémieux took his seat on the ministerial bench, whence he approved with an occasional "Hear! Hear!" the remarks of the orator who occupied the tribune. The speaker chanced to belong to the Opposition.

"Monsieur Crémieux," said Cavaignac, "you are making a good deal of noise."

"What does that matter to you?" replied Crémieux.

"It matters that you are on the ministerial bench."

"Do you want me to leave it?"

"Well—"

Cremieux rose and quitted his bench, saying as he did so:

"General, you compel me to leave the Cabinet, and it was through me that you entered it."

Crémieux, in point of fact, had, as a member of the Provisional Government, had Cavaignac appointed Minister of War.

During the three days that preceded the debate, which had been fixed for the 25th, the Chamber was very nervous and uneasy. Cavaignac's friends secretly trembled and sought to make others tremble. They said: "You will see!" They affected assurance. Jules Favre having alluded in the tribune to the "great and solemn debate" which was to take place, they burst into a laugh. M. Coquerel, the Protestant pastor, happening to meet Cavaignac in the lobby, said to him: "Keep yourself in hand, General!" "In a quarter of an hour," replied Cavaignac with flashing eyes, "I shall have swept these wretches away!" These wretches were Lamartine, Gamier-Pages, and Arago. There was some doubt about Arago, however. It was said that he was rallying to Cavaignac. Meanwhile Cavaignac had conferred the cross of the Legion of Honour upon the Bishop of Quimper, the Abbé Legraverand, who had accepted it.

"A cross for a vote," was the remark made in the Chamber. And these reversed roles, a general giving a cross to a bishop, caused much amusement.

In reality we are in the midst of a quarrel over the presidency. The candidates are shaking their fists at each other. The Assembly hoots, growls, murmurs, stamps its feet, crushes one, applauds the other.

This poor Assembly is a veritable *fille a soldats*, in love with a trooper. For the time being it is Cavaignac.

Who will it be tomorrow?

General Cavaignac proved himself to be clever, and occasionally even eloquent. His defence partook more of the character of an attack. Frequently he appeared to me to be sincere because he had for so long excited my suspicion. The Assembly listened to him for nearly three hours with rapt attention. Throughout it was evident that he possessed its confidence. Its sympathy was shown every moment, and sometimes it manifested a sort of love for him.

Cavaignac, tall and supple, with his short frock-coat, his military collar, his heavy moustache, his bent brow, his brusque language, broken up by parentheses, and his rough gestures, was at times at once as fierce as a soldier and as passionate as a tribune. Towards the middle of his discourse he became an advocate, which, as far as I was concerned, spoiled the man; the harangue became a speech for the defence. But at its conclusion he roused himself again with a sort of real indignation. He pounded on the desk with his fist and overturned the glass of water, much to the consternation of the ushers, and in terminating he said:

"I have been speaking for I know not how long; I will speak again all the evening, all night, all day tomorrow, if necessary, and it will no longer be as an advocate, but as a soldier, and you will listen to me!"

The whole Assembly applauded him enthusiastically.

M. Barthélemy Saint Hilaire, who attacked Cavaignac, was an orator cold, rigid, somewhat dry and by no means equal to the task, his anger being without fierceness and his hatred without passion. He began by reading a memoir, which always displeases assemblies. The Assembly, which was secretly ill-disposed and angry, was eager to crush him. It only wanted pretexts; he furnished it with motives. The grave defect in his memoir was that serious accusations were built upon petty acts, a surcharge that caused the whole system to bend. This little pallid man who continually raised one leg behind him and leaned forward with his two hands on the edge of the tribune as though he were gazing down into a well, made those who did not hiss laugh. Amid the uproar of the Assembly he affected to write at considerable length in a copybook, to dry the ink by sprinkling powder upon it, and with great deliberation to pour the powder back into the powder-box, thus finding means to increase the tumult with his calmness. When M. Barthélemy Saint Hilaire descended from the tribune, Cavaignac had only been attacked. He had not then replied, yet was already absolved.

M. Garnier-Pagès, tried Republican and honest man, but with a substratum of vanity and an emphatic manner, succeeded M. Barthélemy Saint Hilaire. The Assembly tried to crush him, too, but he rose again amid murmurs. He reminded his hearers of his past, invoked recollections of the Salle Voisin, compared the henchmen of Cavaignac to the henchmen of Guizot, bared his breast "which had braved the poignards of the Red Republic," and ended by resolutely attacking the general, with too few facts and too many words, but fairly and squarely, taking him, so to speak, as the Bible urges that the bull be taken, by the horns.

Garnier-Pages propped up the accusation that had almost been laid low. He brought the personal pronoun much too frequently into the discussion; he acted ill-advisedly, for everybody's personality ought to have been effaced in view of the seriousness of the debate and the anxiety of the country. He turned to all sides with a sort of disconsolate fury; he summoned Arago to intervene, Ledru-Rollin to speak, Lamartine to explain. All three remained silent, thus failing in their duty and destiny.

The Assembly, however, pursued Garnier-Pages with its hooting, and when he said to Cavaignac: "You wanted to throw us down," it burst into a laugh, at the sentiment as well as at the expression. Garnier-Pages gazed at the laughing house with an air of despair.

From all sides came shouts of: "The closure!"

The Assembly had reached a state in which it would not listen and could no longer hear.

M. Ledru-Rollin appeared in the tribune.

From every bench the cry arose: "At last!"

Silence ensued.

Ledru-Rollin's speech had a physical effect as it were; it was coarse, but powerful. Garnier-Pages had pointed out the General's political shortcomings; Ledru-Rollin pointed out his military shortcomings. With the vehemence of the tribune he mingled all the skill of the advocate. He concluded with an appeal for mercy for the offender. He shook Cavaignac's position.

When he resumed his seat between Pierre Leroux and de Lamennais, a man with long grey hair, and attired in a white frock-coat, crossed the Chamber and shook Ledru-Rollin's hand. He was Lagrange.

Cavaignac for the fourth time ascended the tribune. It was half past 10 o'clock at night. The noise of the crowd and the evolutions of the cavalry on the Place de la Concorde could be heard. The aspect of the Assembly was becoming sinister.

Cavaignac, who was tired, had decided to assume a haughty attitude. He addressed the Mountain and defied it, declaring to the mountaineers, amid the cheers of the majority and of the reactionaries, that he at all times preferred "their abuse to their praise." This appeared to be violent and was clever; Cavaignac lost the Rue Taitbout, which represented the Socialists, and won the Rue de Poitiers, which represented the Conservatives.

After this apostrophe he remained a few moments motionless, then passed his hand over his brow.

The Assembly shouted to him:

"Enough! Enough!"

He turned towards Ledru-Rollin and exclaimed:

"You said that you had done with me. It is I who have done with you. You said: 'For some time.' I say to you: 'For ever!'"

It was all over. The Assembly wanted to close the debate.

Lagrange ascended the tribune and gesticulated amid hoots and hisses. Lagrange was at once a popular and chivalrous declaimer, who expressed true sentiments in a forced voice.

"Representatives," said he, "all this amuses you; well, it doesn't amuse me!"

The Assembly roared with laughter, and the roar of laughter continued throughout the remainder of his discourse. He called M. Landrin M. Flandrin, and the gaiety became delirious.

I was among those whom this gaiety made heavy at heart, for I seemed to hear the sobs of the people above these bursts of hilarity.

During this uproar a list which was being covered with signatures and which bore an order of the day proposed by M. Dupont de l'Eure, was passed round the benches.

Dupont de l'Eure, bent and tottering, read from the tribune, with the authority of his eighty years, his own order of the day, amid a deep silence that was broken at intervals by cheers.

The order of the day, which was purely and simply a reiteration of the declaration of June 28: "General Cavaignac has merited well of the fatherland," was adopted by 503 votes to 34.

Mine was among the thirty-four. While the votes were being counted, Napoleon Bonaparte, son of Jerome, came up to me and said:

"I suppose you abstained?"

"From speaking, yes; from voting, no," I replied.

"Ah!" he went on. "We ourselves abstained from voting. The Rue de Poitiers also abstained."

I took his hand and said:

"You are free to do as you like. For my part I am not abstaining. I am judging Cavaignac, and the country is judging me. I want the fullest light thrown upon my actions, and my votes are my actions."

1849

I. The Jardin d'Hiver

February, 1849

In February, 1849, in the midst of the prevailing sorrow and terror, fetes were given. People danced to help the poor. While the cannon with which the rioters were threatened on January 29, were, so to speak, still trained ready for firing, a charity ball attracted all Paris to the Jardin d'Hiver.

This is what the Jardin d'Hiver was like:

A poet had pictured it in a word: "They have put summer under a glass case!" It was an immense iron cage with two naves forming a cross, as large as four or five cathedrals and covered with glass. Entrance to it was through a gallery of wood decorated with carpets and tapestry.

On entering, the eyes were at first dazzled by a flood of light. In the light all sorts of magnificent flowers, and strange trees with the foliage and altitudes of the tropics, could be seen. Banana trees, palm trees, cedars, great leaves, enormous thorns, and queer branches twisted and mingled as in a virgin forest. The forest alone was virgin there, however. The prettiest women and the most beautiful girls of Paris whirled in this illumination *a giorno* like a swarm of bees in a ray of sunshine.

Above this gaily dressed throng was an immense resplendent chandelier of brass, or rather a great tree of gold and flame turned upside down which seemed to have its roots in the glass roof, and whose sparkling leaves hung over the crowd. A vast ring of candelabra, torch-holders and girandoles shone round the chandelier, like the constellations round the sun. A resounding orchestra perched high in a gallery made the glass panes rattle harmoniously.

But what made the Jardin d'Hiver unique was that beyond this vestibule of light and music and noise, through which one gazed as through a vague and dazzling veil, a sort of immense and tenebrous arch, a grotto of shadow and mystery, could be discerned. This grotto in which were big trees, a copse threaded with paths and clearings, and a fountain that showered its water-diamonds in sparkling spray, was simply the end of the garden. Red dots that resembled oranges of fire shone here and there amid the foliage. It was all like a dream. The lanterns in the copse, when one approached them, became great luminous tulips mingled with real camellias and roses.

One seated one's self on a garden seat with one's feet in the grass and moss, and one felt the warmth arising from a heat-grating beneath this grass and this moss; one happened upon an immense fireplace in which half the trunk of a tree was burning, in proximity to a clump of bushes shivering in the rain of a fountain. There were lamps amid the flowers and carpets in the alleys. Among the trees were satyrs, nude nymphs, hydras, all kinds of groups and statues which, like the place itself, had something impossible and living about them.

What were people doing at this ball? They danced a little, made love a little, and above all talked politics.

There were about fifty Representatives present that evening. The negro Representative Louisy Mathieu, in white gloves, was accompanied by the negrophile Representative Schoelcher in black gloves. People said: "O fraternity! they have exchanged hands!"

Politicians leaning against the mantels announced the approaching appearance of a sheet entitled the "Aristo," a reactionary paper. The Brea affair,* which was being tried at that very moment, was discussed. What particularly struck these grave men in this sinister affair was that among the witnesses was an ironmonger named "Lenclume" and a locksmith named "Laclef."

Such are the trivial things men bring into the events of God.

II. General Bréa's Murderers

March, 1849

The men condemned to death in the Bréa affair are confined in the fort at Vanves. There are five of them: Nourry, a poor child of seventeen whose father and mother died insane, type of the gamin of Paris that revolutions make a hero and riots a murderer; Daix, blind of one eye, lame, and with only one arm, a *bon pauvre* of the Bicetre Hospital, who

---

* General Bréa was assassinated on June 25, 1848, while parleying with the insurgents at the Barrière de Fontainebleau.

underwent the operation of trepanning three years ago, and who has a little daughter eight years old whom he adores; Lahr, nicknamed the Fireman, whose wife was confined the day after his condemnation, giving life at the moment she received death; Chopart, a bookseller's assistant, who has been mixed up in some rather discreditable pranks of youth; and finally Vappreaux junior, who pleaded an alibi and who, if the four others are to be believed, was not at the Barrière de Fontainebleau at all during the three days of June.

These hapless wights are confined in a big casemate of the fort. Their condemnation has crushed them and turned them towards God. In the casemate are five camp beds and five rush-bottomed chairs; to this lugubrious furniture of the dungeon an altar has been added. It was erected at the end of the casemate opposite the door and below the venthole through which daylight penetrates. On the altar is only a plaster statue of the Virgin enveloped in lace. There are no tapers, it being feared that the prisoners might set fire to the door with the straw of their mattresses. They pray and work. As Nourry has not been confirmed and wishes to be before he dies, Chopart is teaching him the catechism.

Beside the altar is a board laid upon two trestles. This board, which is full of bullet holes, was the target of the fort. It has been turned into a dining-table, a cruel, thoughtless act, for it is a continual reminder to the prisoners of their approaching death.

A few days ago an anonymous letter reached them. This letter advised them to stamp upon the flagstone in the centre of the casemate, which, it was affirmed, covered the orifice of a well communicating with old subterranean passages of the Abbey of Vanves that extended to Châtillon. All they had to do was to raise the flagstone and they could escape that very night.

They did as the letter directed. The stone, it was found, did emit a hollow sound as though it covered an opening. But either because the police had been informed of the letter, or for some other reason, a stricter watch than ever has been kept upon them from that moment and they have been unable to profit by the advice.

The gaolers and priests do not leave them for a minute either by day or by night. Guardians of the body cheek by jowl with guardians of the soul. Sorry human justice!

The execution of the condemned men in the Bréa affair was a blunder. It was the reappearance of the scaffold. The people had kicked over the guillotine. The bourgeoisie raised it again. A fatal mistake.

President Louis Bonaparte was inclined to be merciful. The revision and cassation could easily have been delayed. The Archbishop of Paris, M. Sibour, successor of a victim, had begged for their lives. But the stereotyped phrases prevailed. The country must be reassured. Order must be reconstructed, legality rebuilt, confidence re-erected! And society at that time was still reduced to employing lopped heads as building material. The Council of State, such as it then was, consulted under the terms of the Constitution, rendered an opinion in favour of the execution. M. Cresson, counsel for Daix and Lahr, waited upon the President. He was an emotional and eloquent young man. He pleaded for these men, for the wives who were not yet widows, for the children who were not yet orphans, and while speaking he wept.

Louis Bonaparte listened to him in silence, then took his hands, but merely remarked: "I am most unhappy!"

In the evening of the same day—it was on the Thursday—the Council of Ministers met. The discussion was long and animated. Only one minister opposed recourse to the scaffold. He was supported by Louis Napoleon. The discussion lasted until 10 o'clock. But the majority prevailed, and before the Cabinet separated Odilon Barrot, the Minister of Justice, signed the order for the execution of three of the condemned men, Daix, Lahr and Chopart. The sentences of Nourry and Vappreaux, junior, were commuted to penal servitude for life.

The execution was fixed for the next morning, Friday.

The Chancellor's office immediately transmitted the order to the Prefect of Police, who had to act in concert with the military authorities, the sentence having been imposed by a court-martial.

The prefect sent for the executioner. But the executioner could not be found. He had vacated his house in the Rue des Marais Saint Martin in February under the impression that, like the guillotine, he had been deposed, and no one knew what had become of him.

Considerable time was lost in tracing him to his new residence, and when they got there he was out. The executioner was at the Opera. He had gone to see "The Devil's Violin."

It was near midnight, and in the absence of the executioner the execution had to be postponed for one day.

During the interval Representative Larabit, whom Chopart had befriended at the barricade of the barriers, was notified and was able to see the President. The President signed Chopart's pardon.

The day after the execution the Prefect of Police summoned the executioner and reproved him for his absence.

"Well," said Samson, "I was passing along the street when I saw a big yellow poster announcing The Devil's Violin. 'Hello!' said I to myself, 'that must be a queer piece,' and I went to see it."

Thus a playbill saved a man's head.

There were some horrible details.

On Friday night, while those who formerly were called *les maitres des basses oeuvres** were erecting the scaffold at the Barrière de Fontainebleau, the *rapporteur* of the court-martial, accompanied by the clerk of the court, repaired to the Fort of Vanves.

Daix and Lahr, who were to die, were sleeping. They were in casemate No. 13 with Nourry and Chopart. There was a delay. It was found that there were no ropes with which to bind the condemned men. The latter were allowed to sleep on. At 5 o'clock in the morning the executioner's assistants arrived with everything that was necessary.

Then the casemate was entered. The four men awoke. To Nourry and Chopart the officials said: "Get out of here!" They understood, and, joyful and terror-stricken, fled into the adjoining casement. Daix and Lahr, however, did not understand. They sat up and gazed about them with wild, frightened eyes. The executioner and his assistants fell upon them and bound them. No one spoke a word. The condemned men began to realise what it all meant and uttered terrible cries. "If we had not bound them," said the executioner, "they would have devoured us!"

Then Lahr collapsed and began to pray while the decree for their execution was read to them.

Daix continued to struggle, sobbing, and roaring with horror. These men who had killed so freely were afraid to die.

Daix shouted: "Help! Help!" appealed to the soldiers, adjured them, cursed them, pleaded to them in the name of General Bréa.

"Shut up!" growled a sergeant. "You are a coward!"

The execution was performed with much ceremony. Let this fact be noted: the first time the guillotine dared to show itself after February an army was furnished to guard it. Twenty-five thousand men, infantry and cavalry, surrounded the scaffold. Two generals were in command. Seven guns commanded the streets which converged to the circus of the Barrière de Fontainebleau.

---

* The executioner in France is officially styled *l'executeur des hautes-oeuvres*.

Daix was executed first. When his head had fallen and his body was unstrapped, the trunk, from which a stream of blood was pouring, fell upon the scaffold between the swing-board and the basket.

The executioners were nervous and excited. A man of the people remarked: "Everybody is losing his head on that guillotine, including the executioner!"

In the faubourgs, which the last elections to the National Assembly had so excited, the names of popular candidates could still be seen chalked upon the walls. Louis Bonaparte was one of the candidates. His name appeared on these open-air bulletins, as they may be termed, in company with the names of Raspail and Barbès. The day after the execution Louis Napoleon's name wherever it was to be seen had a red smear across it. A silent protest, a reproach and a menace. The finger of the people pending the finger of God.

III. The Suicide of Antonin Moyne

April, 1849

Antonin Moyne, prior to February, 1848, was a maker of little figures and statuettes for the trade.

Little figures and statuettes! That is what we had come to. Trade had supplanted the State. How empty is history, how poor is art; inasmuch as there are no more big figures there are no more statues.

Antonin Moyne made rather a poor living out of his work. He had, however, been able to give his son Paul a good education and had got him into the Ecole Polytechnique. Towards 1847 the art-work business being already bad, he had added to his little figures portraits in pastel. With a statuette here, and a portrait there, he managed to get along.

After February the art-work business came to a complete standstill. The manufacturer who wanted a model for a candlestick or a clock, and the bourgeois who wanted a portrait, failed him. What was to be done? Antonin Moyne struggled on as best he could, used his old clothes, lived upon beans and potatoes, sold his knick-knacks to bric-à-brac dealers, pawned first his watch, then his silverware.

He lived in a little apartment in the Rue de Boursault, at No. 8, I think, at the corner of the Rue Labruyère.

The little apartment gradually became bare.

After June, Antonin Moyne solicited an order of the Government. The matter dragged along for six months. Three or four Cabinets succeeded each other and Louis Bonaparte had time to be nominated President. At length M. Leon Faucher gave Antonin Moyne an order for a bust, upon which the statuary would be able to make 600 francs. But he was informed that, the State funds being low, the bust would not be paid for until it was finished.

Distress came and hope went.

Antonin Moyne said one day to his wife, who was still young, having been married to him when she was only fifteen years old: "I will kill myself."

The next day his wife found a loaded pistol under a piece of furniture. She took it and hid it. It appears that Antonin Moyne found it again.

His reason no doubt began to give way. He always carried a bludgeon and razor about with him. One day he said to his wife: "It is easy to kill one's self with blows of a hammer."

On one occasion he rose and opened the window with such violence that his wife rushed forward and threw her arms round him.

"What are you going to do?" she demanded.

"Just get a breath of air! And you, what do you want?"

"I am only embracing you," she answered.

On March 18, 1849, a Sunday, I think it was, his wife said to him:

"I am going to church. Will you come with me?"

He was religious, and his wife, with loving watchfulness, remained with him as much as possible.

He replied: "Presently!" and went into the next room, which was his son's bedroom.

A few minutes elapsed. Suddenly Mme. Antonin Moyne heard a noise similar to that made by the slamming of a front door. But she knew what it was. She started and cried: "It is that dreadful pistol!"

She rushed into the room her husband had entered, then recoiled in horror. She had seen a body stretched upon the floor.

She ran wildly about the house screaming for help. But no one came, either because everybody was out or because owing to the noise in the street she was not heard.

Then she returned, re-entered the room and knelt beside her husband. The shot had blown nearly all his head away. The blood streamed upon the floor, and the walls and furniture were spattered with brains.

Thus, marked by fatality, like Jean Goujon, his master, died Antonin Moyne, a name which henceforward will bring to mind two things—a horrible death and a charming talent.

IV. A Visit to the Old Chamber of Peers

June, 1849

The working men who sat in the Luxembourg during the months of March and April under the presidency of M. Louis Blanc, showed a sort of respect for the Chamber of Peers they replaced. The armchairs of the peers were occupied, but not soiled. There was no insult, no affront, no abuse. Not a piece of velvet was torn, not a piece of leather was dirtied. There is a good deal of the child about the people, it is given to chalking its anger, its joy and its irony on walls; these aboring men were serious and inoffensive. In the drawers of the desks they found the pens and knives of the peers, yet made neither a cut nor a spot of ink.

A keeper of the palace remarked to me: "They have behaved themselves very well." They left their places as they had found them. One only left his mark, and he had written in the drawer of Louis Blanc on the ministerial bench:

> Royalty is abolished.
> Hurrah for Louis Blanc!

This inscription is still there.

The fauteuils of the peers were covered with green velvet embellished with gold stripes. Their desks were of mahogany, covered with morocco leather, and with drawers of oak containing writing material in plenty, but having no key. At the top of his desk each peer's name was stamped in gilt letters on a piece of green leather let into the wood. On the princes' bench, which was on the right, behind the ministerial bench, there was no name, but a gilt plate bearing the words: "The Princes' Bench." This plate and the names of the peers had been torn off, not by the working men, but by order of the Provisional Government.

A few changes were made in the rooms which served as ante-chambers to the Assembly. Puget's admirable "Milo of Crotona," which ornamented the vestibule at the top of the grand staircase, was taken to the old museum and a marble of some kind was substituted for it. The full length statue of the Duke d'Orleans, which was in the second vestibule, was taken I know not where and replaced by a statue of Pompey with gilt face, arms and legs, the statue at the foot of which, according to tradition, assassinated Caesar fell. The picture of founders of constitutions, in the third vestibule, a picture in which Napoleon,

Louis XVIII and Louis Philippe figured, was removed by order of Ledru-Rollin and replaced by a magnificent Gobelin tapestry borrowed from the Garde-Meuble.

Hard by this third vestibule is the old hall of the Chamber of Peers, which was built in 1805 for the Senate. This hall, which is small, narrow and obscure; supported by meagre Corinthian columns with mahogany-coloured bases and white capitals; furnished with flat desks and chairs in the Empire style with green velvet seats, the whole in mahogany; and paved with white marble relieved by lozenges of red Saint Anne marble,—this hall, so full of memories, had been religiously preserved, and after the new hall was built in 1840, had been used for the private conferences of the Court of Peers.

It was in this old hall of the Senate that Marshal Ney was tried. A bar had been put up to the left of the Chancellor who presided over the Chamber. The Marshal was behind this bar, with M. Berryer, senior, on his right, and M. Dupin, the elder, on his left. He stood upon one of the lozenges in the floor, in which, by a sinister hazard, the capricious tracing of the marble figured a death's head. This lozenge has since been taken up and replaced by another.

After February, in view of the riots, soldiers had to be lodged in the palace. The old Senate-hall was turned into a guard-house. The desks of the senators of Napoleon and of the peers of the Restoration were stored in the lumber rooms, and the curule chairs served as beds for the troops.

Early in June, 1849, I visited the hall of the Chamber of Peers and found it just as I had left it seventeen months before, the last time that I sat there, on February 23, 1848.

Everything was in its place. Profound calmness reigned; the fauteuils were empty and in order. One might have thought that the Chamber had adjourned ten minutes previously.

Sketches Made in the National Assembly

I. Odilon Barrot

ODILON BARROT ASCENDS THE TRIBUNE step by step and slowly; he is solemn before being eloquent. Then he places his right hand on the table of the tribune, throwing his left hand behind his back, and thus shows himself sideways to the Assembly in the attitude of an athlete. He is always in black, well brushed and well buttoned up.

His delivery, which is slow at first, gradually becomes animated, as do his thoughts. But in becoming animated his speech becomes hoarse and his thoughts cloudy. Hence a certain hesitation among his hearers, some being unable to catch what he says, the others not understanding. All at once from the cloud darts a flash of lightning and one is dazzled. The difference between men of this kind and Mirabeau is that the former have flashes of lightning, Mirabeau alone has thunder.

II. Monsieur Thiers

M. THIERS WANTS TO TREAT MEN, ideas and revolutionary events with parliamentary routine. He plays his old game of constitutional tricks in face of abysms and the dreadful upheavals of the chimerical and unexpected. He does not realise that everything has been transformed; he finds a resemblance between our own times and the time when he governed, and starts out from this. This resemblance exists in point of fact, but there is in it a something that is colossal and monstrous.

M. Thiers has no suspicion of this, and pursues the even tenour of his way. All his life he has been stroking cats, and coaxing them with all sorts of cajolling processes and feline ways. Today he is trying to play the same game, and does not see that the animals have grown beyond all measure and that it is wild beasts that he is keeping about him. A strange sight it is to see this little man trying to stroke the roaring muzzle of a revolution with his little hand.

When M. Thiers is interrupted he gets excited, folds and unfolds his arms, then raises his hands to his mouth, his nose, his spectacles, shrugs his shoulders, and ends by clasping the back of his head convulsively with both hands.

I have always entertained towards this celebrated statesman, this eminent orator, this mediocre writer, this narrow-minded man, an indefinable sentiment of admiration, aversion and disdain.

III. Dufaure

M. Dufaure is a barrister of Saintes, and was the leading lawyer in his town about 1833. This led him to aspire to legislative honours. M. Dufaure arrived in the Chamber with a provincial and cold-in-the-nose accent that was very queer. But he possessed a mind so clear that occasionally it was almost luminous, and so accurate that occasionally it was decisive.

With that his speech was deliberate and cold, but sure, solid, and calmly pushed difficulties before it.

M. Dufaure succeeded. He was a deputy, then a minister. He is not a sage. He is a grave and honest man who has held power without greatness but with probity, and who speaks from the tribune without brilliancy but with authority.

His person resembles his talent. In appearance he is dignified, simple and sober. He comes to the Chamber buttoned up in his dark grey frock-coat, and wearing a black cravat, and a shirt collar that reaches to his ears. He has a big nose, thick lips, heavy eyebrows, an intelligent and severe eye, and grey, ill-combed hair.

IV. Changarnier

Changarnier looks like an old academician, just as Soult looks like an old archbishop.

Changarnier is sixty-four or sixty-five years old, and tall and thin. He has a gentle voice, a graceful and formal air, a chestnut wig like M. Pasquier's, and a lady-killing smile like M. Brifaut's.

With that he is a curt, bold, expeditious man, resolute, but cunning and reserved.

At the Chamber he occupies the extreme end of the fourth bench of the last section on the left, exactly above M. Ledru-Rollin.

He usually sits with folded arms. The bench on which Ledru-Rollin and Lamennais sit is perhaps the most habitually irritated of the Left. While the Assembly shouts, murmurs, yells, roars, and rages, Changarnier yawns.

V. Lagrange

LAGRANGE, IT IS SAID, FIRED the pistol in the Boulevard des Capucines, fatal spark that heated the passions of the people and caused the conflagration of February. He is styled: Political prisoner and Representative of the people.

Lagrange has a grey moustache, a grey beard and long grey hair. He is overflowing with soured generosity, charitable violence and a sort of chivalrous demagogy; there is a love in his heart with which he stirs up hatred; he is tall, thin, young looking at a distance, old when seen nearer, wrinkled, bewildered, hoarse, flurried, wan, has a wild look in his eyes and gesticulates; he is the Don Quixote of the Mountain. He, also, tilts at windmills; that is to say, at credit, order, peace, commerce, industry,—all the machinery that turns out bread. With this, a lack of ideas; continual jumps from justice to insanity and from cordiality to threats. He proclaims, acclaims, reclaims and declaims. He is one of those men who are never taken seriously, but who sometimes have to be taken tragically.

VI. Prudhon

PRUDHON WAS BORN IN 1803. He has thin fair hair that is ruffled and ill-combed, with a curl on his fine high brow. He wears spectacles. His gaze is at once troubled, penetrating and steady. There is something of the house-dog in his almost flat nose and of the monkey in his chin-beard. His mouth, the nether lip of which is thick, has an habitual expression of ill-humour. He has a Franc-Comtois accent, he utters the syllables in the middle of words rapidly and drawls the final syllables; he puts a circumflex accent on every "a," and like Charles Nodier, pronounces: "*honorable, remarquable*." He speaks badly and writes well. In the tribune his gesture consists of little feverish pats upon his manuscript with the palm of his hand. Sometimes he becomes irritated, and froths; but it is cold slaver. The principal characteristic of his countenance and physiognomy is mingled embarrassment and assurance.

I write this while he is in the tribune.

Anthony Thouret met Prudhon.

"Things are going badly," said Prudhon.

"To what cause do you attribute our embarrassments?" queried Anthony Thouret.

"The Socialists are at the bottom of the trouble, of course.

"What! the Socialists? But are you not a Socialist yourself?"

"I a Socialist! Well, I never!" exclaimed Prudhon.

"Well, what in the name of goodness, are you, then?"

"I am a financier."

VII. Blanqui

BLANQUI GOT SO THAT HE no longer wore a shirt. For twelve years he had worn the same clothes—his prison clothes—rags, which he displayed with sombre pride at his club. He renewed only his boots and his gloves, which were always black.

At Vincennes during his eight months of captivity for the affair of the 15th of May, he lived only upon bread and raw potatoes, refusing all other food. His mother alone occasionally succeeded in inducing him to take a little beef-tea.

With this, frequent ablutions, cleanliness mingled with cynicism, small hands and feet, never a shirt, gloves always.

There was in this man an aristocrat crushed and trampled upon by a demagogue.

Great ability, no hypocrisy; the same in private as in public. Harsh, stern, serious, never laughing, receiving respect with irony, admiration with sarcasm, love with disdain, and inspiring extraordinary devotion.

There was in Blanqui nothing of the people, everything of the populace.

With this, a man of letters, almost erudite. At certain moments he was no longer a man, but a sort of lugubrious apparition in which all degrees of hatred born of all degrees of misery seemed to be incarnated.

VIII. Lamartine

February 23, 1850

During the session Lamartine came and sat beside me in the place usually occupied by M. Arbey. While talking, he interjected in an undertone sarcastic remarks about the orators in the tribune.

Thiers spoke. "Little scamp," murmured Lamartine.

Then Cavaignac made his appearance. "What do you think about him?" said Lamartine. "For my part, these are my sentiments: He is fortunate, he is brave, he is loyal, he is voluble—and he is stupid."

Cavaignac was followed by Emmanuel Arago. The Assembly was stormy. "This man," commented Lamartine, "has arms too small for the affairs he undertakes. He is given to joining in mêlées and does not know how to get out of them again. The tempest tempts him, and kills him."

A moment later Jules Favre ascended the tribune. "I do not know how they can see a serpent in this man," said Lamartine. "He is a provincial academician."

Laughing the while, he took a sheet of paper from my drawer, asked me for a pen, asked Savatier-Laroche for a pinch of snuff, and wrote a few lines. This done he mounted the tribune and addressed grave and haughty words to M. Thiers, who had been attacking the revolution of February. Then he returned to our bench, shook hands with me while the Left applauded and the Right waxed indignant, and calmly emptied the snuff in Savatier-Laroche's snuffbox into his own.

IX. Boulay de la Meurthe

M. Boulay de la Meurthe was a stout, kindly man, bald, pot-bellied, short, enormous, with a short nose and a not very long wit. He was a friend of Hard, whom he called *mon cher*, and of Jerome Bonaparte, whom he addressed as "your Majesty."

The Assembly, on January 20, made him Vice-President of the Republic.

It was somewhat sudden, and unexpected by everybody except himself. This latter fact was evident from the long speech learned by heart that he delivered after being sworn in. At its conclusion the Assembly applauded, then a roar of laughter succeeded the applause. Everybody laughed, including himself; the Assembly out of irony, he in good faith.

Odilon Barrot, who since the previous evening had been keenly regretting that he did not allow himself to be made Vice-President, contemplated the scene with a shrug of the shoulders and a bitter smile.

The Assembly followed Boulay de la Meurthe, congratulated and gratified, with its eyes, and in every look could be read this: "Well, I never! He takes himself seriously!"

When he was taking the oath, in a voice of thunder which made everybody smile, Boulay de la Meurthe looked as if he were dazzled by the Republic, and the Assembly did not look as if it were dazzled by Boulay de la Meurthe.

X. Dupin

DUPIN HAS A STYLE OF wit that is peculiar to himself. It is Gaulish, tinged with the wit of a limb of the law and with jovial grossness. When the vote upon the bill against universal suffrage was about to be taken some member of the majority, whose name I have forgotten, went to him and said:

"You are our president, and moreover a great legist. You know more about it than I do. Enlighten me, I am undecided. Is it true that the bill violates the Constitution?"

Dupin appeared to think for a moment and then replied:

"No, it doesn't violate it, but it lifts its clothes up as high as possible!"

This reminds me of what he said to me the day I spoke upon the Education Bill. Baudin had permitted me to take his turn to speak, and I went up to the presidential chair to notify Dupin.

"Ah! you are going to speak! So much the better!" said he; and pointing to M. Barthélemy Saint Hilaire, who was then occupying the tribune and delivering a long and minute technical speech against the measure, added:

"He is rendering you a service. He is doing the preparatory work. He is turning the bill's trousers down. This done you will be able to at once—"

He completed the phrase with the expressive gesture which consists of tapping the back of the fingers of the left hand with the fingers of the right hand.

LOUIS BONAPARTE

I. His Debuts

UPON HIS ARRIVAL IN PARIS Louis Bonaparte took up his residence in the Place Vendome. Mlle. Georges went to see him. They conversed at some length. In the course of the conversation Louis Bonaparte led Mlle. Georges to a window from which,the column with the statue of Napoleon I. upon it was visible and said:

"I gaze at that all day long."

"It's pretty high!" observed Mlle. George.

September 24, 1848

Louis Napoleon appeared at the National Assembly today. He seated himself on the seventh bench of the third section on the left, between M. Vieillard and M. Havin.

He looks young, has a black moustache and goatee, and a parting in his hair, a black cravat, a black coat buttoned up, a turned-down collar, and white gloves. Perrin and Leon Faucher, seated immediately below him, did not once turn their heads. In a few minutes the galleries began to turn their opera-glasses upon the prince, and the prince gazed at the galleries through his own glass.

September 26

Louis Bonaparte ascended the tribune (3.15 P.M.). Black frock-coat, grey trousers. He read from a crumpled paper in his hand. He was listened to with deep attention. He pronounced the word "compatriots" with a foreign accent. When he had finished a few cries of "Long live the Republic!" were raised.

He returned leisurely to his place. His cousin Napoleon, son of Jerome, who so greatly resembles the Emperor, leaned over M. Vieillard to congratulate him.

Louis Bonaparte seated himself without saying a word to his two neighbours. He is silent, but he seems to be embarrassed rather than taciturn.

October 9

While the question of the presidency was being raised Louis Bonaparte absented himself from the Assembly. When the Antony Thouret amendment, excluding members of the royal and imperial families was being debated, however, he reappeared. He seated himself at the extremity of his bench, beside his former tutor, M. Vieillard, and listened in silence, leaning his chin upon his hand, or twisting his moustache.

All at once he rose and, amid extraordinary agitation, walked slowly towards the tribune. One half of the Assembly shouted: "The vote!" The other half shouted: "Speak!"

M. Sarrans was in the tribune. The president said:

"M. Sarrans will allow M. Louis Napoleon Bonaparte to speak."

He made a few insignificant remarks and descended from the tribune amid a general laugh of stupefaction.

November 1848

On November 19 I dined at Odilon Barrot's at Bougival.

There were present MM. de Rémusat, de Tocqueville, Girardin, Leon Faucher, a member of the English Parliament and his wife, who is ugly but witty and has beautiful teeth, Mme. Odilon Barrot and her mother.

Towards the middle of the dinner Louis Bonaparte arrived with his cousin, the son of Jerome, and M. Abbatucci, Representative.

Louis Bonaparte is distinguished, cold, gentle, intelligent, with a certain measure of deference and dignity, a German air and black moustache; he bears no resemblance whatever to the Emperor.

He ate little, spoke little, and laughed little, although the party was a merry one.

Mme. Odilon Barrot seated him on her left. The Englishman was on her right.

M. de Rémusat, who was seated between the prince and myself, remarked to me loud enough for Louis Bonaparte to hear:

"I give my best wishes to Louis Bonaparte and my vote to Cavaignac."

Louis Bonaparte at the time was feeding Mme. Odilon Barrot's greyhound with fried gudgeons.

II. His Elevation to the Presidency

December 1848

The proclamation of Louis Bonaparte as President of the Republic was made on December 20.

The weather, which up to then had been admirable, and reminded one more of the approach of spring than of the beginning of winter, suddenly changed. December 20 was the first cold day of the year. Popular superstition had it that the sun of Austerlitz was becoming clouded.

This proclamation was made in a somewhat unexpected manner. It had been announced for Friday. It was made suddenly on Wednesday.

Towards 3 o'clock the approaches to the Assembly were occupied by troops. A regiment of infantry was massed in rear of the Palais d'Orsay; a regiment of dragoons was echeloned along the quay. The troopers shivered and looked moody. The population assembled in great uneasiness, not knowing what it all meant. For some days a Bonapartist movement had been vaguely spoken of. The faubourgs, it was said, were to turn out and march to the Assembly shouting: "Long live the Emperor!" The day before the Funds had dropped 3 francs. Napoleon Bonaparte, greatly alarmed, came to see me.

The Assembly resembled a public square. It was a number of groups rather than a parliament. In the tribune a very useful bill for regulating the publicity of the sessions and substituting the State Printing Office, the former Royal Printing Office, for the printing office of the "Moniteur," was being discussed, but no one listened. M. Bureau de Puzy, the questor, was speaking.

Suddenly there was a stir in the Assembly, which was being invaded by a crowd of Deputies who entered by the door on the left. It was the committee appointed to count the votes and was returning to announce the result of the election to the Presidency. It was 4 o'clock, the chandeliers were lighted, there was an immense crowd in the public galleries, all the ministers were present. Cavaignac, calm, attired in a black frock-coat, and not wearing any decoration, was in his place. He kept his right hand thrust in the breast of his buttoned frock-coat, and made no reply to M. Bastide, who now and then whispered in his ear.

M. Fayet, Bishop of Orleans, occupied a chair in front of the General. Which prompted the Bishop of Langres, the Abbé Parisis, to remark: "That is the place of a dog, not a bishop."

Lamartine was absent.

The *rapporteur* of the committee, M. Waldeck-Rousseau, read a cold discourse that was coldly listened to. When he reached the enumeration of the votes cast, and came to Lamartine's total, 17,910 votes, the Right burst into a laugh. A mean vengeance, sarcasm of the unpopular men of yesterday for the unpopular man of today.

Cavaignac took leave in a few brief and dignified words, which were applauded by the whole Assembly. He announced that the Ministry had resigned in a body, and that he, Cavaignac, laid down the power. He thanked the Assembly with emotion. A few Representatives wept.

Then President Marrast proclaimed "the citizen Louis Bonaparte" President of the Republic.

A few Representatives about the bench where Louis Bonaparte sat applauded. The remainder of the Assembly preserved a glacial silence. They were leaving the lover for the husband.

Armand Marrast called upon the elect of the nation to take the oath of office. There was a stir.

Louis Bonaparte, buttoned up in a black frock-coat, the decoration of Representative of the people and the star of the Legion of Honour on his breast, entered by the door on the right, ascended the tribune, repeated in a calm voice the words of the oath that President Marrast dictated to him, called upon God and men to bear witness, then read, with a foreign accent which was displeasing, a speech that was interrupted at rare intervals by murmurs of approval. He eulogized Cavaignac, and the eulogy was noted and applauded.

After a few minutes he descended from the tribune, not like Cavaignac, amid the acclamations of the Chamber, but amid an immense shout of "Long live the Republic!" Somebody shouted "Hurrah for the Constitution!"

Before leaving Louis Bonaparte went over to his former tutor, M. Vieillard, who was seated in the eighth section on the left, and shook hands with him. Then the President of the Assembly invited the committee to accompany the President of the Republic to his palace and have rendered to him the honours due to his rank. The word caused the Mountain to murmur. I shouted from my bench: "To his functions!"

The President of the Assembly announced that the President of the Republic had charged M. Odilon Barrot with the formation of a Cabinet, and that the names of the new Ministers would be announced to the Assembly in a Message; that, in fact, a supplement to the Moniteur would be distributed to the Representatives that very evening.

It was remarked, for everything was remarked on that day which began a decisive phase in the history of the country, that President Marrast called Louis Bonaparte "citizen" and Odilon Barrot "monsieur."

Meanwhile the ushers, their chief Deponceau at their head, the officers of the Chamber, the questors, and among them General Lebreton in full uniform, had grouped themselves below the tribune; several Representatives had joined them; there was a stir indicating that Louis Bonaparte was about to leave the enclosure. A few Deputies rose. There were shouts of "Sit down! Sit down!"

Louis Bonaparte went out. The malcontents, to manifest their indifference, wanted to continue the debate on the Printing Office Bill. But the Assembly was too agitated even to remain seated. It rose in a tumult and the Chamber was soon empty. It was half past 4. The proceedings had lasted half an hour.

As I left the Assembly, alone, and avoided as a man who had disdained the opportunity to be a Minister, I passed in the outer hall, at the foot of the stairs, a group in which I noticed Montalembert, and also Changarnier in the uniform of a lieutenant-general of the National Guard. Changarnier had just been escorting Louis Bonaparte to the Elysee. I heard him say: "All passed off well."

When I found myself in the Place de la Revolution, there were no longer either troops or crowd; all had disappeared. A few passers-by came from the Champs-Elysees. The night was dark and cold. A bitter wind blew from the river, and at the same time a heavy storm-cloud breaking in the west covered the horizon with silent flashes of lightning. A December wind with August lightning—such were the omens of that day.

III. The First Official Dinner

December 24, 1848

Louis Bonaparte gave his first dinner last evening, Saturday the 23rd, two days after his elevation to the Presidency of the Republic.

The Chamber had adjourned for the Christmas holidays. I was at home in my new lodging in the Rue de la Tour d'Auvergne, occupied with I know not what bagatelles, *totus in illis*, when a letter addressed to me and brought by a dragoon was handed to me. I opened the envelope, and this is what I read:

The orderly officer on duty has the honour to inform Monsieur the General Changarnier that he is invited to dinner at the Elysee-National on Saturday, at 7 o'clock.

I wrote below it: "Delivered by mistake to M. Victor Hugo," and sent the letter back by the dragoon who had brought it. An hour later came another letter from M. de Persigny, Prince Louis's former companion in plots, today his private secretary. This letter contained profuse apologies for the error committed and advised me that I was among those invited. My letter had been addressed by mistake to M. Conti, the Representative from Corsica.

At the head of M. de Persigny's letter, written with a pen, were the words: "Household of the President."

I remarked that the form of these invitations was exactly similar to the form employed by King Louis Philippe. As I did not wish to do anything that might resemble intentional coldness, I dressed; it was half past 6, and I set out immediately for the Elysee.

Half past 7 struck as I arrived there.

As I passed I glanced at the sinister portal of the Praslin mansion adjoining the Elysee. The large green carriage entrance, enframed between two Doric pillars of the time of the Empire, was closed, gloomy, and vaguely outlined by the light of a street lamp. One of the double doors of the entrance to the Elysee was closed; two soldiers of the line were on guard. The court-yard was scarcely lighted, and a mason in his working clothes with a ladder on his shoulder was crossing it; nearly all the windows of the outhouses on the right had been broken, and were mended with paper. I entered by the door on the perron. Three servants in black coats received me; one opened the door, another took my mantle, the third said: "Monsieur, on the first floor!" I ascended the grand staircase. There were a carpet and flowers on it, but that chilly and unsettled air about it peculiar to places into which one is moving.

On the first floor an usher asked:

"Monsieur has come to dinner?"

"Yes," I said. "Are they at table?"

"Yes, Monsieur."

"In that case, I am off."

"But, Monsieur," exclaimed the usher, "nearly everybody arrived after the dinner had begun; go in. Monsieur is expected."

I remarked this military and imperial punctuality, which used to be customary with Napoleon. With the Emperor 7 o'clock meant 7 o'clock.

I crossed the ante-chamber, then a salon, and entered the dining-room. It was a square room wainscotted in the Empire style with white wood. On the walls were engravings and pictures of very poor selection, among them "Mary Stuart listening to Rizzio," by the painter Ducis. Around the room was a sideboard. In the middle was a long table with rounded ends at which about fifteen guests were seated. One end of the table, that furthest from the entrance, was raised, and here the President of the Republic was seated between two women, the Marquise de Hallays-Coëtquen, née Princess de Chimay (Tallien) being on his right, and Mme. Conti, mother of the Representative, on his left.

The President rose when I entered. I went up to him. We grasped each other's hand.

"I have improvised this dinner," he said. "I invited only a few dear friends, and I hoped that I could comprise you among them. I thank you for coming. You have come to me, as I went to you, simply. I thank you."

He again grasped my hand. Prince de la Moskowa, who was next to General Changarnier, made room for me beside him, and I seated myself at the table. I ate quickly, for the President had interrupted the dinner to enable me to catch up with the company. The second course had been reached.

Opposite to me was General Rulhières, an ex-peer, the Representative Conti and Lucien Murat. The other guests were unknown to me. Among them was a young major of cavalry, decorated with the Legion of Honour. This major alone was in uniform; the others wore evening dress. The Prince had a rosette of the Legion of Honour in his buttonhole.

Everybody conversed with his neighbour. Louis Bonaparte appeared to prefer his neighbour on the right to his neighbour on the left. The Marquise de Hallays is thirty-six years old, and looks her age. Fine eyes, not much hair, an ugly mouth, white skin, a shapely neck, charming arms, the prettiest little hands in the world, admirable shoulders. At present she is separated from M. de Hallays. She has had eight children, the first seven by her husband. She was married fifteen years ago.

During the early period of their marriage she used to fetch her husband from the drawing-room, even in the daytime, and take him off to bed. Sometimes a servant would enter and say: "Madame the Marquise is asking for Monsieur the Marquis." The Marquis would obey the summons. This made the company who happened to be present laugh. Today the Marquis and Marquise have fallen out.

"She was the mistress of Napoleon, son of Jerome, you know," said Prince de la Moskowa to me, sotto voce, "now she is Louis's mistress."

"Well," I answered, "changing a Napoleon for a Louis is an everyday occurrence."

These bad puns did not prevent me from eating and observing.

The two women seated beside the President had square-topped chairs. The President's chair was surmounted with a little round top. As I was about to draw some inference from this I looked at the other chairs and saw that four or five guests, myself among them, had chairs similar to that of the President. The chairs were covered with red velvet with gilt headed nails. A more serious thing I noticed was that everybody addressed the President of the Republic as "Monseigneur" and "your Highness." I who had called him "Prince," had the air of a demagogue.

When we rose from table the Prince asked after my wife, and then apologized profusely for the rusticity of the service.

"I am not yet installed," he said. "The day before yesterday, when I arrived here, there was hardly a mattress for me to sleep upon."

The dinner was a very ordinary one, and the Prince did well to excuse himself. The service was of common white china and the silverware bourgeois, worn, and gross. In the middle of the table was a rather fine vase of craquelé, ornamented with ormolu in the bad taste of the time of Louis XVI.

However, we heard music in an adjoining hall.

"It is a surprise," said the President to us, "they are the musicians from the Opera."

A minute afterwards programmes written with a pen were handed round. They indicated that the following five selections were being played:

1. Priere de la "Muette."
2. Fantaisie sur des airs favoris de la "Reine Hortense."
3. Final de "Robert Bruce".
4. "Marche Republicaine."
5. "La Victoire," pas redoublé.

VICTOR HUGO

In the rather uneasy state of mind I, like the whole of France, was in at that moment, I could not help remarking this "Victory" piece coming after the "Republican March."

I rose from table still hungry.

We went into the grand salon, which was separated from the dining-room by the smaller salon that I had passed through on entering.

This grand salon was extremely ugly. It was white, with figures on panels, after the fashion of those of Pompeii, the whole of the furniture being in the Empire style with the exception of the armchairs, which were in tapestry and gold and in fairly good taste. There were three arched windows to which three large mirrors of the same shape at the other end of the salon formed pendants and one of which, the middle one, was a door. The window curtains were of fine white satin richly flowered.

While the Prince de la Moskowa and I were talking Socialism, the Mountain, Communism, etc., Louis Bonaparte came up and took me aside.

He asked me what I thought of the situation. I was reserved. I told him that a good beginning had been made; that the task was a difficult but a grand one; that what he had to do was to reassure the bourgeoisie and satisfy the people, to give tranquillity to the former, work to the latter, and life to all; that after the little governments, those of the elder Bourbons, Louis Philippe, and the Republic of February, a great one was required; that the Emperor had made a great government through war, and that he himself ought to make a great one through peace; that the French people having been illustrious for three centuries did not propose to become ignoble; that it was his failure to appreciate this high-mindedness of the people and the national pride that was the chief cause of Louis Philippe's downfall; that, in a word, he must decorate peace.

"How?" asked Louis Napoleon.

"By all the greatness of art, literature and science, by the victories of industry and progress. Popular labour can accomplish miracles. And then, France is a conquering nation; when she does not make conquests with the sword, she wants to make them with the mind. Know this and act accordingly. Ignore it and you will be lost."

He looked thoughtful and went away. Then he returned, thanked me warmly, and we continued to converse.

We spoke about the press. I advised him to respect it profoundly and at the same time to establish a State press. "The State without a newspaper, in the midst of newspapers," I observed, "restricting itself to governing while publicity and polemics are the rule, reminds one of the knights of the fifteenth century who obstinately persisted in fighting against cannon with swords; they were always beaten. I grant that it was noble; you will grant that it was foolish."

He spoke of the Emperor. "It is here," he said, "that I saw him for the last time. I could not re-enter this palace without emotion. The Emperor had me brought to him and laid his hand on my head. I was seven years old. It was in the grand salon downstairs."

Then Louis Bonaparte talked about La Malmaison. He said:

"They have respected it. I visited the place in detail about six weeks ago. This is how I came to do so. I had gone to see M. Odilon Barrot at Bougival.

"'Dine with me,' he said.

"'I will with pleasure.' It was 3 o'clock. 'What shall we do until dinner time?'

"'Let us go and see La Malmaison,' suggested M. Barrot.

"We went. Nobody else was with us. Arrived at La Malmaison we rang the bell. A porter opened the gate, M. Barrot spoke:

"'We want to see La Malmaison.'

"'Impossible!' replied the porter.

"'What do you mean, impossible?'

"'I have orders.'

"'From whom?'

"'From her Majesty Queen Christine, to whom the château belongs at present.'

"'But monsieur here is a stranger who has come expressly to visit the place.'

"'Impossible!'

"'Well,' exclaimed M. Odilon Barrot, 'it's funny that this door should be closed to the Emperor's nephew!'

"The porter started and threw his cap on the ground. He was an old soldier, to whom the post had been granted as a pension.

"'The Emperor's nephew!' he cried. 'Oh! Sire, enter!'

"He wanted to kiss my clothes.

"We visited the château. Everything is still about in its place. I recognised nearly everything, the First Consul's study, the chamber of his mother, my own. The furniture in several rooms has not been changed. I found a little armchair I had when I was a child."

I said to the Prince: "You see, thrones disappear, arm-chairs remain."

While we were talking a few persons came, among others M. Duclerc, the ex-Minister of Finance of the Executive Committee, an old woman in black velvet whom I did not know, and Lord Normanby, the English Ambassador, whom the President quickly took into an adjoining salon. I saw Lord Normanby taken aside in the same way by Louis Philippe.

The President in his salon had an air of timidity and did not appear at home. He came and went from group to group more like an embarrassed stranger than the master of the house. However, his remarks are *a propos* and sometimes witty.

He endeavoured to get my opinion anent his Ministry, but in vain. I would say nothing either good or bad about it.

Besides, the Ministry is only a mask, or, more properly speaking, a screen that hides a baboon. Thiers is behind it. This is beginning to bother Louis Bonaparte. He has to contend against eight Ministers, all of whom seek to belittle him. Each is pulling his own way. Among these Ministers some are his avowed enemies. Nominations, promotions, and lists arrive all made out from the Place Saint Georges. They have to be accepted, signed and endorsed.

Yesterday Louis Bonaparte complained about it to the Prince de la Moskowa, remarking wittily: "They want to make of me a Prince Albert of the Republic."

Odilon Barrot appeared mournful and discouraged. Today he left the council with a crushed air. M. de la Moskowa encountered him.

"Hello!" said he, "how goes it?"

"Pray for us!" replied Odilon Barrot.

"Whew!" said Moskowa, "this is tragical!"

"What are we to do?" went on Odilon Barrot. "How are we to rebuild this old society in which everything is collapsing? Efforts to prop it up only help to bring it down. If you touch it, it topples over. Ah! pray for us!"

And he raised his eyes skywards.

I quitted the Elysee about 10 o'clock. As I was going the President said to me: "Wait a minute." Then he went into an adjoining room and came out again a moment later with some papers which he placed in my hand, saying: "For Madame Victor Hugo."

They were tickets of admission to the gallery of the Garde-Meuble for the review that is to be held today.

And as I went home I thought a good deal. I thought about this abrupt moving in, this trial of etiquette, this bourgeois-republican-imperial mixture, this surface of a deep, unfathomed quantity that today is called the President of the Republic, his entourage, the whole circumstances of his position. This man who can be, and is, addressed at one and the same time and from all sides at once as: prince, highness, monsieur, monseigneur and citizen, is not one of the least curious and characteristic factors of the situation.

Everything that is happening at this moment stamps its mark upon this personage who sticks at nothing to attain his ends.

IV. The First Month

January. 1849

The first month of Louis Bonaparte's presidency is drawing to a close. This is how we stand at present:

Old-time Bonapartists are cropping up. MM. Jules Favre, Billault and Carteret are paying court—politically Speaking—to the Princess Mathilde Demidoff. The Duchess d'Orleans is residing with her two children in a little house at Ems, where she lives modestly yet royally. All the ideas of February are brought up one after the other; 1849, disappointed, is turning its back on 1848. The generals want amnesty, the wise want disarmament. The Constituent Assembly's term is expiring and the Assembly is in savage mood in consequence. M. Guizot is publishing his book *On Democracy in France*. Louis Philippe is in London, Pius IX. is at Gaete, M. Barrot is in power; the bourgeoisie has lost Paris, Catholicism has lost Rome. The sky is rainy and gloomy, with a ray of sunshine now and then. Mlle. Ozy shows herself quite naked in the role of Eve at the Porte Saint Martin; Fréderick Lemaitre is playing "L'Auberge des Adrets" there. Five per cents are at 74, potatoes cost 8 cents the bushel, at the market a pike can be bought for 20 sous. M. Ledru-Rollin is trying to force the country into war, M. Prudhon is trying to force it into bankruptcy. General Cavaignac takes part in the sessions of the Assembly in a grey waist-coat, and passes his time gazing at the women in the galleries through big ivory opera-glasses. M. de Lamartine gets 25,000 francs for his "Toussaint L'Ouverture." Louis Bonaparte gives grand dinners to M. Thiers, who had him captured, and to M. Mole, who had him condemned. Vienna, Milan, and Berlin are becoming calmer. Revolutionary fires are paling and seem to be dying out everywhere on the surface, but the peoples are still deeply stirred. The King of Prussia is getting ready to seize his sceptre again and the Emperor of Russia to draw his sword. There has been an earthquake at Havre, the cholera is at Fécamp; Arnal is leaving the Gymnase, and the Academy is nominating the Duke de Noailles as Chateaubriand's successor.

V. Feeling His Way

January, 1849

At Odilon Barrot's ball on January 28 M. Thiers went up to M. Leon Faucher and said: "Make So-and-So a prefect." M. Leon Faucher made a grimace, which is an easy thing for him to do, and said: "Monsieur Thiers, there are objections." "That's funny!" retorted Thiers, "it is precisely the answer the President of the Republic gave to me the day I said: 'Make M. Faucher a Minister!'"

At this ball it was remarked that Louis Bonaparte sought Berryer's company, attached himself to him and led him into quiet corners. The Prince looked as though he were following Berryer, and Berryer as though he were trying to avoid the Prince.

At 11 o'clock the President said to Berryer: "Come with me to the Opera."

Berryer excused himself. "Prince," said he, "it would give rise to gossip. People would believe I am engaged in a love affair!"

"Pish!" replied Louis Bonaparte laughingly, "Representatives are inviolable!"

The Prince went away alone, and the following quatrain was circulated:

> *En vain l'empire met du fard,*
> *On baisse ses yeux et sa robe.*
> *Et Berryer-Joseph so derobe*
> *A Napoléon-Putiphar.*

February, 1849

Although he is animated with the best intentions in the world and has a very visible quantity of intelligence and aptitude, I fear that Louis Bonaparte will find his task too much for him. To him, France, the century, the new spirit, the instincts peculiar to the soil and the period are so many closed books. He looks without understanding them at minds that are working, Paris, events, men, things and ideas. He belongs to that class of ignorant persons who are called princes and to that category of foreigners who are called *émigrês*. To those who examine him closely he has the air of a patient rather than of a governing man.

There is nothing of the Bonapartes about him, either in his face or manner. He probably is not a Bonaparte. The free and easy ways of Queen Hortense are remembered. "He is a memento of Holland!" said Alexis de Saint Priest to me yesterday. Louis Bonaparte certainly possesses the cold manner of the Dutch.

Louis Bonaparte knows so little about Paris that the first time I saw him he said to me:

"I have been hunting for you. I went to your former residence. What is this Place des Vosges?"

"It is the Place Royale," I said.

"Ah!" he continued, "is it an old place?"

He wanted to see Beranger. He went to Passy twice without being able to find him at home. His cousin Napoleon timed his visit more happily and found Béranger by his fireside. He asked him:

"What do you advise my cousin to do?"

"To observe the Constitution."

"And what ought he to avoid?"

"Violating the Constitution."

Béranger could not be induced to say anything else.

Yesterday, December 5, 1850, I was at the Français. Rachel played "Adrienne Lecouvreur." Jerome Bonaparte occupied a box next to mine. During an entr'acte I paid him a visit. We chatted. He said to me:

"Louis is mad. He is suspicious of his friends and delivers himself into the hands of his enemies. He is suspicious of his family and allows himself to be bound hand and foot by the old Royalist parties. On my return to France I was better received by Louis Philippe at the Tuileries than I am at the Elysee by my nephew. I said to him the other day before one of his ministers (Fould): 'Just remember a little! When you were a candidate for the presidency, Monsieur here (I pointed to Fould) called upon me in the Rue d'Alger, where I lived, and begged me in the name of MM. Thiers, Mole, Duvergier de Hauranne, Berryer, and Bugeaud to enter the lists for the presidency. He told me that never would you get the "Constitutionnel;" that in Mole's opinion you were an idiot, and that Thiers looked upon you as a blockhead; that I alone could rally everybody to me and win against Cavaignac. I refused. I told them that you represented youth and the future, that you had a quarter of a century before you, whereas I could hardly count upon eight or ten years; that I was an invalid and wanted to be let alone. That is what these people were doing and that is what I did. And you forget all this! And you make these gentlemen the masters! And you show the door to your cousin, my son, who defended you in the Assembly and devoted himself to furthering your candidacy! And you are strangling universal suffrage, which made you what you are! I' faith I shall say like Mole that you are an idiot, and like Thiers that you are a blockhead!'"

The King of Westphalia paused for a moment, then continued:

"And do you know, Monsieur Victor Hugo, what he replied to me? 'You will see!' No one knows what is at the bottom of that man!"

The Siege of Paris. Extracts
from Note-Books

Charles* leaves this morning with MM. Claretie, Proust, and Frédérix for Virton. Fighting is going on near there, at Carignan. They will see what they can of the battle. They will return tomorrow.

September 2

Charles and his friends did not return today.

September 3

Yesterday, after the decisive battle had been lost, Louis Napoleon, who was taken prisoner at Sedan, surrendered his sword to the King of Prussia. Just a month ago, on August 2, at Sarrebrück, he was playing at war.

To save France now would be to save Europe.

Shouting newsboys pass, with enormous posters on which are the words: "Napoleon III a Prisoner."

5 o'clock.—Charles and our friends have returned.

9 o'clock.—Meeting of exiles at which Charles and I are present.

Query: Tricolour flag or red flag?

September 4

The deposition of the Emperor is proclaimed in Paris.

At 1 o'clock a meeting of exiles is held at my house.

At 3 o'clock I receive a telegram from Paris couched in the following terms: "Bring the children with you." Which means "Come."

MM. Claretie and Proust dined with us.

During the dinner a telegram signed "François Hugo" arrived, announcing that a provisional government had been formed: Jules Favre, Gambetta, Thiers.

September 5

At 6 o'clock in the morning a telegram signed "Barbieux," and asking the hour of my arrival in Paris, is brought to me. I instruct Charles to

---

* Victor Hugo's son.

answer that I shall arrive at 9 o'clock at night. We shall take the children with us. We shall leave by the 2.35 o'clock train.

The Provisional Government (according to the newspapers) is made up of all the Deputies of Paris, with the exception of Thiers.

At noon, as I was about to leave Brussels for Paris, a young man, a Frenchman, accosted me in the Place de la Monnaie and said:

Monsieur, they tell me that you are Victor Hugo."

"Yes."

"Be so kind as to enlighten me. I would like to know whether it is prudent to go to Paris at present."

"Monsieur, it is very imprudent, but you should go," was my reply.

We entered France at 4 o'clock.

At Tergnier, at 6.30, we dined upon a piece of bread, a little cheese, a pear and a glass of wine. Claretie insisted upon paying, and said: "I want particularly to give you a dinner on the day of your return to France."

En route I saw in the woods a camp of French soldiers, men and horses mingled. I shouted to them: "Long live the army!" and I wept.

At frequent intervals we came across train-loads of soldiers on their way to Paris. Twenty-five of these passed during the day. As one of them went by we gave to the soldiers all the provisions we had, some bread, fruit and wine. The sun shone brightly and was succeeded by a bright moon.

We arrived in Paris at 9.35 o'clock. An immense crowd awaited me. It was an indescribable welcome. I spoke four times, once from the balcony of a café and thrice from my carriage.

When I took leave of this ever-growing crowd, which escorted me to Paul Meurice's, in the Avenue Frochot, I said to the people: "In one hour you repay me for twenty years of exile."

They sang the "Marseillaise" and the "Chant du Depart."

They shouted: "Long live Victor Hugo!"

The journey from the Northern Railway station to the Rue Laval took two hours.

We arrived at Meurice's, where I am to stay, at mid-night. I dined with my travelling companions and Victor. I went to bed at 2 o'clock.

At daybreak I was awakened by a terrible storm. Thunder and lightning.

I shall take breakfast with Paul Meurice, and we shall dine together at the Hotel Navarin, in the Rue Navarin, where my family is staying.

Innumerable visits, innumerable letters.

Rey came to ask me whether I would consent to join a triumvirate composed as follows: Victor Hugo, Ledru-Rollin, and Schoelcher. I refused. I said: "It is almost impossible to amalgamate me."

I recalled several things to his mind. He said: "Do you remember that it was I who received you when you arrived at the Baudin barricade?"* I replied: "I remember the fact so well that—. And I recited the lines at the beginning of the piece (unpublished) upon the Baudin barricade:

> *La barricade était livide dans l'aurore,*
> *Et comme j'arrivais elle fumait encore.*
> *Rey me serra la main et dit: Baudin est mort. . .*

He burst into tears.

September 7

Louis Blanc, d'Alton-Shée, Banville and others came to see me.

The women of the Markets brought me a bouquet.

September 8

I am warned that it is proposed to assassinate me. I shrug my shoulders.

This morning I wrote my "Letter to the Germans." It will be sent tomorrow.

Visit from General Cluseret.

At 10 o'clock I went to the office of the Rappel to correct the proofs of my "Letter to the Germans."

September 9

Received a visit from General Montfort. The generals are asking me for commands, I am being asked to grant audiences, office-seekers are asking me for places. I reply: "I am nobody."

I saw Captain Feval, husband of Fanny, the sister of Alice.† He was a prisoner of war, and was released on parole.

All the newspapers publish my "Appeal to the Germans."

---

* Representative Baudin was killed on the barricade in the Faubourg Saint Antoine on December 2, 1852, during Louis Bonaparte's coup d'Etat.
† Wife of Charles Hugo.

D'Alton-Shée and Louis Ulbach lunched with us. Afterwards we went to the Place de la Concorde. At the foot of the flower-crowned statue of Strasburg is a register. Everybody comes to sign the resolution of public thanks. I inscribed my name. The crowd at once surrounded me. The ovation of the other night was about to recommence. I hurried to my carriage.

Among the persons who called upon me was Cernuschi.

September 11

Received a visit from Mr. Wickham Hoffman, Secretary of the United States Legation. Mr. Washburne, the American Minister, had requested him to ask me whether I did not think that some good might result were he to intervene *officiously* and see the King of Prussia. I sent him to Jules Favre.

September 12

Among other callers was Frédérick Lemaître.

September 13

Today there is a review of the army of Paris. I am alone in my chamber. The battalions march through the streets singing the "Marseillaise" and the "Chant du Depart." I hear this immense shout:

> *For France a Frenchman should live,*
> *For France a Frenchman should die.**

I listen and I weep. On, valiant ones! I will go where you go.

Receive a visit from the United States Consul-General and Mr. Wickham Hoffman.

Julie† writes me from Guernsey that the acorn I planted on July 14 has sprouted. The oak of the United States of Europe issued from the ground on September 5, the day of my return to Paris.

---

* The "Chant du Depart."
† Victor Hugo's sister-in-law.

September 14

I received a visit from the committee of the Société des Gens de Lettres, which wants me to be its president; from M. Jules Simon, Minister of Public Instruction; from Colonel Piré, who commands a corps of volunteers, etc.

September 16

One year ago today I opened the Peace Congress at Lausanne. This morning I wrote the "Appeal to Frenchmen" for a war to the bitter end against the invasion.

On going out I perceived hovering over Montmartre the captive balloon from which a watch is to be kept upon the besiegers.

September 17

All the forests around Paris are burning. Charles made a trip to the fortifications and is perfectly satisfied with them. I deposited at the office of the Rappel 2,088 francs 30 centimes, subscribed in Guernsey for the wounded and sent by M. H. Tupper, the French Consul.

At the same time I deposited at the "Rappel" office a bracelet and earrings of gold, sent anonymously for the wounded by a woman. Accompanying the trinkets was a little golden neck medal for Jeanne.*

September 20

Charles and his little family left the Hotel Navarin yesterday and installed themselves at 174, Rue de Rivoli. Charles and his wife, as well as Victor, will continue to dine with me every day.

The attack upon Paris began yesterday.

Louis Blanc, Gambetta and Jules Ferry came to see me this morning.

I went to the Institute to sign the Declaration that it proposes to issue encouraging the capital to resist to the last.

I will not accept any limited candidacy. I would accept with devotedness the candidacy of the city of Paris. I want the voting to be not by districts, with local candidates, but by the whole city with one list to select from.

I went to the Ministry of Public Instruction to see Mme. Jules Simon, who is in mourning for her old friend Victor Bois. Georges and Jeanne were in the garden. I played with them.

---

* Victor Hugo's little granddaughter.

Nadar came to see me this evening to ask me for some letters to put in a balloon which he will send up the day after tomorrow. It will carry with it my three addresses: "To the Germans," "To Frenchmen," "To Parisians."

October 6

Nadar's balloon, which has been named the "Barbes," and which is taking my letters, etc., started this morning, but had to come down again, as there was not enough wind. It will leave tomorrow. It is said that Jules Favre and Gambetta will go in it.

Last night General John Meredith Read, United States Consul-General, called upon me. He had seen the American General Burnside, who is in the Prussian camp. The Prussians, it appears, have respected Versailles. They are afraid to attack Paris. This we are aware of, for we can see it for ourselves.

October 7

This morning, while strolling on the Boulevard de Clichy, I perceived a balloon at the end of a street leading to Montmartre. I went up to it. A small crowd bordered a large square space that was walled in by the perpendicular bluffs of Montmartre. In this space three balloons were being inflated, a large one, a medium-sized one, and a small one. The large one was yellow, the medium one white, and the small one striped yellow and red.

In the crowd it was whispered that Gambetta was going. Sure enough I saw him in a group near the yellow balloon, wearing a heavy overcoat and a sealskin cap. He seated himself upon a paving-stone and put on a pair of high fur-lined boots. A leather bag was slung over his shoulder. He took it off, entered the balloon, and a young man, the aeronaut, tied the bag to the cordage above Gambetta's head.

It was half past 10. The weather was fine and sunshiny, with a light southerly breeze. All at once the yellow balloon rose, with three men in it, one of whom was Gambetta. Then the white balloon went up with three men, one of whom waved a tricolour flag. Beneath Gambetta's balloon hung a long tricolour streamer. "Long live the Republic!" shouted the crowd.

The two balloons went up for some distance, the white one going higher than the yellow one, then they began to descend. Ballast was thrown out, but they continued their downward flight. They disappeared behind Montmartre hill. They must have landed on the Saint Denis plain. They were too heavily weighted, or else the wind was not strong enough.

THE DEPARTURE TOOK PLACE AFTER all, for the balloons went up again.

We paid a visit to Notre Dame, which has been admirably restored.

We also went to see the Tour Saint Jacques. While our carriage was standing there one of the delegates of the other day (from the Eleventh Arrondissement) came up and told me that the Eleventh Arrondissement had come round to my views, concluded that I was right in insisting upon a vote of the whole city upon a single list of candidates, begged me to accept the nomination upon the conditions I had imposed, and wanted to know what ought to be done should the Government refuse to permit an election. Ought force be resorted to? I replied that a civil war would help the foreign war that was being waged against us and deliver Paris to the Prussians.

On the way home I bought some toys for my little ones—a zouave in a sentry-box for Georges, and for Jeanne a doll that opens and shuts its eyes.

October 8

I have received a letter from M. L. Colet, of Vienna (Austria), by way of Normandy. It is the first letter that has reached me from the outside since Paris has been invested.

There has been no sugar in Paris for six days. The rationing of meat began today. We shall get three quarters of a pound per person and per day.

Incidents of the postponed Commune. Feverish unrest in Paris. Nothing to cause uneasiness, however. The deep-toned Prussian cannon thunder continuously. They recommend unity among us.

The Minister of Finance, M. Ernest Picard, through his secretary, asks me to "grant him an audience;" these are the terms he uses. I answer that I will see him on Monday morning, October 10.

October 9

Five delegates from the Ninth Arrondissement came in the name of the arrondissement to *forbid me to get myself killed*.

October 10

M. Ernest Picard came to see me. I asked him to issue immediately a decree liberating all articles pawned at the Mont de Piété for less than 15 francs (the present decree making absurd exceptions, linen, for instance). I told him that the poor could not wait. He promised to issue the decree tomorrow.

There is no news of Gambetta. We are beginning to get uneasy. The wind carried him to the north-east, which is occupied by the Prussians.

October 11

Good news of Gambetta. He descended at Epineuse, near Amiens. Last night, after the demonstrations in Paris, while passing a group that had assembled under a street lamp, I heard these words: "It appears that Victor Hugo and the others—." I continued on my way, and did not listen to the rest, as I did not wish to be recognised.

After dinner I read to my friends the verses with which the French edition of *Les Châtiments* begins ("When about to return to France," Brussels, August 31, 1870).

October 12

It is beginning to get cold. Barbieux, who commands a battalion, brought us the helmet of a Prussian soldier who was killed by his men. This helmet greatly astonished little Jeanne. These angels do not yet know anything about earth.

The decree I demanded for the indigent was published this morning in the "Journal Officiel."

M. Pallain, the Minister's secretary, whom I met as I came out of the Carrousel, told me that the decree would cost 800,000 francs.

I replied: "Eight hundred thousand francs, all right. Take from the rich. Give to the poor."

October 13

I met today Théophile Gautier, whom I I had not seen for many years. I embraced him. He was rather nervous. I told him to come and dine with me.

October 14

The Château of Saint Cloud was burned yesterday!

I went to Claye's to correct last proofs of the French edition of *Les Chatiments* which will appear on Tuesday. Dr. Emile Allix brought me a Prussian cannon-ball which he had picked up behind a barricade, near Montrouge, where it had just killed two horses. The cannon-ball weighs 25 pounds. Georges, in playing with it, pinched his fingers under it, which made him cry a good deal.

Today is the anniversary of Jena!

October 16

There is no more butter. There is no more cheese. Very little milk is left, and eggs are nearly all gone.

The report that my name has been given to the Boulevard Haussmann is confirmed. I have not been to see it for myself.

October 17

Tomorrow a postal balloon named the "Victor Hugo" is to be sent up in the Place de la Concorde. I am sending a letter to London by this balloon.

October 18

I have paid a visit to Les Feuillantines. The house and garden of my boyhood have disappeared.

A street now passes over the site.

October 19

Louis Blanc came to dine with me. He brought a declaration by ex-Representatives for me to sign. I said that I would not sign it unless it were drawn up in a different manner.

October 20

Visit from the Gens de Lettres committee. Today the first postage stamps of the Republic of 1870 were put in circulation.

Les Châtiments (French edition) appeared in Paris this morning.

The papers announce that the balloon "Victor Hugo" descended in Belgium. It is the first postal balloon to cross the frontier.

October 21

-They say that Alexandre Dumas died on October 13 at the home of his son at Havre. He was a large-hearted man of great talent. His death grieves me greatly.

Louis Blanc and Brives came to speak to me again about the Declaration of Representatives. My opinion is that it would be better to postpone it.

Nothing is more charming than the sounding of the reveille in Paris. It is dawn. One hears first, nearby, a roll of drums, followed by the blast of a bugle, exquisite melody, winged and warlike. Then all is still. In twenty seconds the drums roll again, then the bugle rings out, but further off. Then silence once more. An instant later, further off still, the same song of bugle and drum falls more faintly but still distinctly upon the ear. Then after a pause the roll and blast are repeated, very far away. Then they are heard again, at the extremity of the horizon, but indistinctly and like an echo. Day breaks and the shout "To arms!" is heard. The sun rises and Paris awakes.

October 22

The edition of 5,000 copies of *Les Châtiments* has been sold in two days. I have authorised the printing of another 3,000.

Little Jeanne has imagined a way of puffing out her cheeks and raising her arms in the air that is adorable.

The first 5,000 copies of the Parisian edition of *Les Chatiments* has brought me in 500 francs, which I am sending to the "Siècle" as a subscription to the national fund for the cannon that Paris needs.

Mathe and Gambon, the ex-Representatives, called to ask me to take part in a meeting of which former representatives are to form the nucleus. The meeting would be impossible without me, they said. But I see more disadvantages than advantages in such a meeting. I thought I ought to refuse.

We are eating horsemeat in every style. I saw the following in the window of a cook-shop: "Saucisson chevaleresque."

October 23

The 17th Battalion asked me to be the first subscriber of "one sou" to a fund for purchasing a cannon. They will collect 300,000 sous. This will make 15,000 francs, which will purchase a 24-centimetre gun, carrying 8,500 metres—equal to the Krupp guns.

Lieutenant Maréchal brought to collect my sou an Egyptian cup of onyx dating from the Pharaohs, engraved with the moon and the sun, the Great Bear and the Southern Cross (?) and having for handles two cynocephalus demons. The engraving of this cup required the life-work of a man. I gave my sou. D'Alton-Shée, who was present, gave his, as did also M. and Mme. Meurice, and the two servants, Mariette and Clémence. The 17th Battalion wanted to call the gun the "Victor Hugo." I told them to call it the "Strasburg." In this way the Prussians will still receive shots from Strasburg.

We chatted and laughed with the officers of the 17th Battalion. It was the duty of the two cynocephalus genie of the cup to bear souls to hell. I remarked: "Very well, I confide William and Bismarck to them."

Visit from M. Edouard Thierry. He came to request me to allow "Stella" to be read in aid of the wounded at the Théâtre Français. I gave him his choice of all the "Châtiments." That startled him. And I demanded that the reading be for a cannon.

Visit from M. Charles Floquet. He has a post at the Hotel de Ville. I commissioned him to tell the Government to call the Mont Valérien "Mont Strasbourg."

October 24

Visit from General Le Flo. Various deputations received.

October 25

There is to be a public reading of *Les Châtiments* for a cannon to be called "Le Châtiment." We are preparing for it.

Brave Rostan,* whom I treated harshly one day, and who likes me because I did right, has been arrested for indiscipline in the National Guard. He has a little motherless boy six years old who has nobody else to take care of him. What was to be done, the father being in prison? I told him to send the youngster to me at the Pavilion de Rohan. He sent him today.

October 26

At 6.30 o'clock Rostan, released from prison, came to fetch his little Henri. Great joy of father and son.

October 28

Edgar Quinet came to see me.

Schoelcher and Commander Farcy, who gave his name to his gunboat, dined with me. After dinner, at half past 8 I went with Schoelcher to

---

* A workingman, friend of Victor Hugo.

his home at 16, Rue de la Chaise. We found there Quinet, Ledru-Rollin, Mathé, Gambon, Lamarque, and Brives. This was my first meeting with Ledru-Rollin. We engaged in a very courteous argument over the question of founding a club, he being for and I against it. We shook hands. I returned home at midnight.

October 29

Visits from the Gens de Lettres committee, Frédérick Lemaitre, MM. Berton and Lafontaine and Mlle. Favart for a third cannon to be called the "Victor Hugo." I oppose the name.

I have authorised the fourth edition of 3,000 copies of *Les Châtiments*, which will make to date 11,000 copies for Paris alone.

October 30

I received the letter of the Société des Gens de Lettres asking me to authorise a public reading of Les Chatiments, the proceeds of which will give to Paris another cannon to be called the "Victor Hugo." I gave the authorisation. In my reply written this morning I demanded that instead of "Victor Hugo" the gun be called the "Châteaudun." The reading will take place at the Porte Saint Martin.

M. Berton came. I read to him *L'Expiation*, which he is to read. M. and Mme. Meurice and d'Alton-Shée were present at the reading.

News has arrived that Metz has capitulated and that Bazaine's army has surrendered.

Bills announcing the reading of *Les Châtiments* have been posted. M. Raphael Felix came to tell me the time at which the rehearsal is to take place tomorrow. I hired a seven-seat box for this reading, which I placed at the disposal of the ladies.

On returning home this evening I met in front of the Mairie, M. Chaudey, who was at the Lausanne Peace Conference and who is Mayor of the Sixth Arrondissement. He was with M. Philibert Audebrand. We talked sorrowfully about the taking of Metz.

October 31

Skirmish at the Hotel de Ville. Blanqui, Flourens and Delescluze want to overthrow the provisional power, Trochu and Jules Favre. I refuse to associate myself with them.

An immense crowd. My name is on the lists of members for the proposed Government. I persist in my refusal.

Flourens and Blanqui held some of the members of the Government prisoners at the Hotel de Ville all day.

At midnight some National Guards came from the Hotel de Ville to fetch me "to preside," they said, "over the new Government." I replied that I was most emphatically opposed to this attempt to seize the power and refused to go to the Hotel de Ville.

At 3 o'clock in the morning Flourens and Blanqui quitted the Hotel de Ville and Trochu entered it.

The Commune of Paris is to be elected.

November 1

We have postponed for a few days the reading of *Les Châtiments*, which was to have been given at the Porte Saint Martin today, Tuesday.

Louis Blanc came this morning to consult me as to what ought to be the conduct of the Commune.

The newspapers unanimously praise the attitude I took yesterday in rejecting the advances made to me.

November 2

The Government demands a "yes" or a "no."

Louis Blanc and my sons came to talk to me about it.

The report that Alexandre Dumas is dead is denied.

November 4

I have been requested to be Mayor of the Third, also of the Eleventh, Arrondissement. I refused.

I went to the rehearsal of *Les Châtiments* at the Porte Saint Martin. Frédérick Lemaitre and Mmes. Laurent, Lia Felix and Duguéret were present.

November 5

Today the public reading of *Les Châtiments*, the proceeds of which are to purchase a cannon for the defence of Paris, was given.

The Third, Eleventh and Fifteenth Arrondissements want me to stand for Mayor. I refuse.

Mérimée has died at Cannes. Dumas is not dead, but he is paralyzed.

November 7

The 24th Battalion waited upon me and wanted me to give them a cannon.

Last night, on returning from a visit to General Le Flo, I for the first time crossed the Pont des Tuileries, which has been built since my departure from France.

The net receipts from the reading of *Les Châtiments* at the Porte Saint Martin for the gun which I have named the "Châteaudun" amounted to 7,000 francs, the balance going to pay the attendants, firemen, and lighting, the only expenses charged.

At the Cail works mitrailleuses of a new model, called the Gatling model, are being made.

Little Jeanne is beginning to chatter.

A second reading of *Les Châtiments* for another cannon will be given at the "Théâtre Français".

Mlle. Periga called today to rehearse *Pauline Roland*, which she will read at the second reading of *Les Châtiments*, announced for tomorrow at the Porte Saint Martin. I took a carriage, dropped Mlle. Périga at her home, and then went to the rehearsal of tomorrow's reading at the theatre. Frederick Lemaitre, Berton, Maubart, Taillade, Lacressonnière, Charly, Mmes. Laurent, Lia Felix, Rousseil, M. Raphael Felix and the committee of the Société des Gens de Lettres were there.

After the rehearsal the wounded of the Porte Saint Martin ambulance asked me, through Mme. Laurent, to go and see them. I said: "With all my heart," and I went.

They are lying in several rooms, chief of which is the old green-room of the theatre with its big round mirrors, where in 1831 I read to the actors "Marion de Lorme". M. Crosnier was then director. (Mme. Dorval and Bocage were present at that reading.) On entering I said to the wounded men: "Behold one who envies you. I desire nothing more on earth but one of your wounds. I salute you, children of France, favourite sons of the Republic, elect who suffer for the Fatherland."

They seemed to be greatly moved. I shook hands with each of them. One held out his mutilated wrist. Another had lost his nose. One had that very morning undergone two painful operations. A very young man had been decorated with the military medal a few hours before. A convalescent said to me: "I am a Franc-Comtois." "Like myself," said I.

And I embraced him. The nurses, in white aprons, who are the actresses of the theatre, burst into tears.

November 13

I had M. and Mme. Paul Meurice, Vacquerie and Louis Blanc to dinner this evening. We dined at 6 o'clock, as the second reading of *Les Chatiments* was fixed to begin at the Porte Saint Martin at 7.30. I offered a box to Mme. Paul Meurice for the reading.

November 14

The receipts for *Les Chatiments* last night (without counting the collection taken up in the theatre) amounted to 8,000 francs.

Good news! General d'Aurelle de Paladine has retaken Orleans and beaten the Prussians. Schoelcher came to inform me of it.

November 15

Visit from M. Arsène Houssaye and Henri Houssaye, his son. He is going to have Stella read at his house in aid of the wounded.

M. Valois came to tell me that the two readings of *Les Châtiments* brought in 14,000 francs. For this sum not two, but three guns can be purchased. The Société des Gens de Lettres desires that, the first having been named by me the "Châteaudun" and the second "Les Châtiments", the third shall be called the "Victor Hugo." I have consented.

Pierre Veron has sent me Daumier's fine drawing representing the Empire annihilated by *Les Chatiments*.

November 16

Baroche, they say, has died at Caen.

M. Edouard Thierry refuses to allow the fifth act of "Hernani" to be played at the Porte Saint Martin for the victims of Châteaudun and for the cannon of the 24th Battalion. A queer obstacle this M. Thierry!

November 17

Visit from the Gens de Lettres committee. The committee came to ask me to authorise a reading of *Les Châtiments* at the Opera to raise funds for another cannon.

I mention here once for all that I authorise whoever desires to do so, to read or perform whatever he likes that I have written, if it be for cannon, the wounded, ambulances, workshops, orphanages, victims of the war, or the poor, and that I abandon all my royalties on these readings or performances.

I decide that the third reading of *Les Chatiments* shall be given at the Opera gratis for the people.

November 19

Mme. Marie Laurent came to recite to me *Les Pauvres Gens*, which she will recite at the Porte Saint Martin tomorrow to raise funds for a cannon.

November 20

Last evening there was an aurora borealis.

"La Grosse Josephine" is no longer my neighbour. She has just been transported to Bastion No. 41. It took twenty-six horses to draw her. I am sorry they have taken her away. At night I could hear her deep voice, and it seemed to me that she was speaking to me. I divided my love between "Grosse Joséphine" and Little Jeanne.

Little Jeanne can now say "papa" and "mamma" very well.

Today there was a review of the National Guard.

November 21

Mme. Jules Simon and Mme. Sarah Bernhardt came to see me.

After dinner many visitors called, and the drawing-room was crowded. It appears that Veuillot insulted me.

Little Jeanne begins to crawl on her hands and knees very well indeed.

November 23

Jules Simon writes me that the Opera will be given to me for the people (free reading of *Les Châtiments*) any day I fix upon. I wanted Sunday, but out of consideration for the concert that the actors and employés of the Opera give Sunday night for their own benefit I have selected Monday.

Frédérick Lemaitre called. He kissed my hands and wept.

It has been raining for two or three days. The rain has soaked the plains, the cannon-wheels would sink into the ground, and the sortie has therefore had to be deferred. For two days Paris has been living on salt meat. A rat costs 8 sous.

I authorise the Théâtre Français to play tomorrow, Friday, the 25th, on behalf of the victims of the war, the fifth act of "Hernani" by the actors of the Théâtre Français and the last act of "Lucrece Borgia" by the actors of the Porte Saint Martin, and in addition the recitation as an intermede of extracts from *Les Châtiments*, *Les Contemplations* and *La Légende des Siècles*.

Mlle. Favart came this morning to rehearse with me *Booz Endormie*. Then we went together to the Français for the rehearsal for the performance of tomorrow. She acted Doña Sol very well indeed. Mme. Laurent (Lucrèce Borgia) also played well. During the rehearsal M. de Flavigny dropped in. I said to him: "Good morning, my dear ex-colleague." He looked at me, then with some emotion exclaimed: "Hello! is that you?" And he added: "How well preserved you are!" I replied: "Banishment preserves one."

I returned the ticket for a box that the Théâtre Français sent to me for tomorrow's performance, and hired a box, which I placed at the disposal of Mme. Paul Meurice.

After dinner the new Prefect of Police, M. Cresson, paid me a visit. M. Cresson was the barrister who twenty years ago defended the murderers of General Bréa. He spoke to me about the free reading of *Les Châtiments* to be given on Monday the 28th at the Opera. It is feared that an immense crowd—all the faubourgs—will be attracted. More than 25,000 men and women. Three thousand will be able to get in. What is to be done with the rest? The Government is uneasy. Many are called but few will be chosen, and it fears that a crush, fighting and disorders will result. The Government will refuse me nothing. It wants to know whether I will accept the responsibility. It will do whatever I wish done. The Prefect of Police has been instructed to come to an understanding with me about it.

I said to M. Cresson: "Let us consult Vacquerie and Meurice and my two sons." He replied: "Willingly." The six of us held a council. We decided that three thousand tickets should be distributed on Sunday, the day before the lecture, at the mairies of the twenty arrondissements to the first persons who presented themselves after noon. Each arrondissement will receive a number of tickets in proportion to the number of its population. The next day the 3,000 holders of tickets (to all places) will wait their turn at the doors of the Opera without causing any obstruction or trouble. The "Journal Officiel" and special posters will apprise the public of the measures taken in the interest of public order.

November 25

Mlle. Lia Felix came to rehearse *Sacer Esto*, which she will recite to the people on Monday.

M. Tony Révillon, who is to make a speech, came to see me with the Gens de Lettres committee.

A deputation of Americans from the United States came to express their indignation with the Government of the American Republic and with President Grant for abandoning France—"To which the American Republic owes so much!" said I. "Owes everything," declared one of the Americans present.

A good deal of cannonading has been heard for several days. Today it redoubled.

Mme. Meurice wants some fowls and rabbits in order to provide against the coming famine. She is having a hutch made for them in my little garden. The carpenter who is constructing it entered my chamber a little while ago and said: "I would like to touch your hand." I pressed both his hands in mine.

November 27

The Academy has given a sign of life. I have received official notice that in future it will hold an extraordinary session every Tuesday.

Pâtés of rat are being made. They are said to be very good.

An onion costs a sou. A potato costs a sou.

They have given up asking my authorisation to recite my works which are being recited everywhere without my permission. They are right. What I write is not my own. I am a public thing.

November 28

Noel Parfait came to ask my help for Châteaudun. Certainly; with all my heart!

Les Châtiments was recited gratis at the Opera. An immense crowd. A gilt wreath was thrown on the stage. I gave it to Georges and Jeanne. The collection made in Prussian helmets by the actresses produced 1,521 francs 35 centimes in coppers.

Emile Allix brought us a leg of antelope from the Jardin des Plantes. It is excellent.

Tonight the sortie is to be made.

November 29

All night long I heard the cannon.

The fowls were installed in my garden today.

The sortie is being delayed. The bridge thrown across the Marne by Ducros has been carried away, the Prussians having blown open the locks.

November 30

All night long the cannon thundered. The battle continues.

At midnight last night as I was returning home through the Rue de Richelieu from the Pavilion de Rohan, I saw just beyond the National Library, the street being deserted and dark at the time, a window open on the sixth floor of a very high house and a very bright light, which appeared to be that of a petroleum lamp, appear and disappear several times; then the window closed and the street became dark again. Was it a signal?

The cannon can be heard at three points round Paris, to the east, west and south. This is because a triple attack is being made on the ring the Prussians have drawn round us. The attack is being made at Saint Denis by Laroncière, at Courbevoie by Vinoy, and on the Marne by Ducros. Laroncière is said to have swept the peninsula of Gennevilliers and compelled a Saxon regiment to lay down its arms, and Vinoy is said to have destroyed the Prussian works beyond Bougival. As to Ducros, he has crossed the Marne, taken and retaken Montédy, and almost holds Villiers-sur-Marne. What one experiences on hearing the cannon is a great desire to be there.

This evening Pelletan sent his son, Camille Pelletan, to inform me on behalf of the Government that tomorrow's operations will be decisive.

December 1

It appears that Louise Michel has been arrested. I will do all that is necessary to have her released immediately. Mme. Meurice is occupying herself about it. She went out this morning for that purpose.

D'Alton-Shée came to see me.

We ate bear for dinner.

I have written to the Prefect of Police to have Louise Michel released. There was no fighting today. The positions taken were fortified.

Louise Michel has been released. She came to thank me.

Last evening M. Coquelin called to recite several pieces from *Les Châtiments*.

It is freezing. The basin of the Pigalle fountain is frozen over.

The cannonade recommenced at daybreak.

11.30 A.M.—The cannonade increases.

Flourens wrote to me yesterday and Rochefort today. They are coming round to me again.

Dorian, Minister of Public Works, and Pelletan came to dine with me.

Excellent news tonight! The Army of the Loire is at Montargis. The Army of Paris has driven back the Prussians from the Avron plateau. The despatches announcing these successes are read aloud at the doors of the mairies.

Victory! The Second of December has been wiped out!

December 3

General Renault, who was wounded in the foot by a splinter from a shell, is dead.

I told Schoelcher that I want to go out with my sons if the batteries of the National Guard to which they belong are sent to the front. The batteries drew lots. Four are to go. One of them is the 10th Battery, of which Victor is a member. I will go out with that battery. Charles does not belong to it, which is a good job; he will stay behind, he has two children. I will order him to stay. Vacquerie and Meurice are members of the 10th Battery. We shall be together in the combat. I will have a cape with a hood made for me. What I fear is the cold at night.

I made some shadows on the wall for Georges and Jeanne. Jeanne laughed delightedly at the shadow and the grimaces of the profile; but when she saw that the shadow was me she cried and screamed. She seemed to say: "I don't want you to be a phantom!" Poor, sweet angel! Perhaps she has a presentiment of the coming battle.

Yesterday we ate some stag; the day before we partook of bear; and the two days previous we fared on antelope. These were presents from the Jardin des Plantes.

Tonight at 11 o'clock, cannonading. Violent and brief.

December 4

A notice has been posted on my door indicating the precautions to be taken "in case of bombardment." That is the title of the notice.

There is a pause in the combat. Our army has recrossed the Marne.

Little Jeanne crawls very well on her hands and knees and says "papa" very prettily.

December 5

I have just seen a magnificent hearse, draped with black velvet, embroidered with an "H" surrounded by silver stars, go by to fetch its burden. A Roman would not disdain to be borne in it.

Gautier came to dine with me. After dinner Banville and Coppée called.

Bad news. Orleans has been captured from us again. No matter. Let us persist.

December 7

I had Gautier, Banville and François Coppée to dinner. After dinner Asselineau came. I read *Floréal and L'Egout de Rome* to them.

December 8

The "Patrie en Danger" has ceased to appear. In the absence of readers, says Blanqui.

M. Maurice Lachâtre, publisher, came to make me an offer for my next book. He has sent me his *Dictionary and The History of the Revolution* by Louis Blanc. I shall present to him Napoleon the Little and *Les Châtiments*.

December 9

I woke up in the night and wrote some verses. At the same time I heard the cannon.

M. Bondes came to see me. The correspondent of the "Times," who is at Versailles, has written him that the guns for the bombardment of Paris have arrived. They are Krupp guns. They are awaiting their carriages. They have been arranged in the Prussian arsenal at Versailles side by side "like bottles in a cellar," according to this Englishman.

I copy the following from a newspaper:

M. Victor Hugo had manifested the intention to leave Paris unarmed, with the artillery battery of the National Guard to which his two sons belong.

The 144th Battalion of the National Guard went in a body to the poet's residence in the Avenue Frochot. Two delegates waited upon him.

These honourable citizens went to forbid Victor Hugo to carry out his plan, which he had announced some time ago in his "Address to the Germans."

"Everybody can fight," the deputation told him. "But everybody cannot write *Les Chatiments*. Stay at home, therefore, and take care of a life that is so precious to France."

I do not remember the number of the battalion. It was not the 144th. Here are the terms of the address which was read to me by the major of the battalion:

The National Guard of Paris forbids Victor Hugo to go to the front, inasmuch as everybody can go to the front, whereas Victor Hugo alone can do what Victor Hugo does.

"Forbids" is touching and charming.

December 11

Rostan came to see me. He has his arm in a sling. He was wounded at Créteil. It was at night. A German soldier rushed at him and pierced his arm with a bayonet. Rostan retaliated with a bayonet thrust in the German's shoulder. Both fell and rolled into a ditch. Then they became good friends. Rostan speaks a little broken German.

"Who are you?"

"I am a Wurtembergian. I am twenty-two years old. My father is a clockmaker of Leipsic."

They remained in the ditch for three hours, bleeding, numb with cold, helping each other. Rostan, wounded, brought the man who wounded him back as a prisoner. He goes to see him at the hospital. These two men adore each other. They wanted to kill each other, and now they would die for each other.

Eliminate kings from the dispute!

Visit from M. Rey. The Ledru-Rollin group is completely disorganized. No more parties; the Republic. It is well.

I presented some Dutch cheese to Mme. Paul Meurice. Sleet is falling.

I arrived in Brussels nineteen years ago today.

Since yesterday Paris has been lighted with petroleum.
    Heavy cannonade tonight.

Thaw. Cannonade.
Tonight we glanced over *Goya's Disasters of War* (brought by Burty, the art critic). It is fine and hideous.

Emmanuel Arago, Minister of Justice, came to see me and informed me that there would be fresh meat until February 15, but that in future only brown bread would be made in Paris. There will be enough of this to last for five months.

    Allix brought me a medal struck to commemorate my return to France. It bears on one side a winged genius and the words: "Liberty, Equality and Fraternity," and on the other side, round the rim: "Appeal to Universal Democracy," and in the centre: "To Victor Hugo, From His Grateful Fatherland.' September, 1870."

    This medal is sold in the streets and costs 5 centimes. There is a little ring in it by which it can be suspended to a chain.

Pelleport* came tonight. I requested him to visit Flourens, in Mazas Prison, on my behalf, and to take him a copy of *Napoleon the Little*.

The "Electeur Libre" calls upon Louis Blanc and me to enter the Government, and affirms that it is our duty to do so. My duty is dictated to me by my conscience.

    I saw the gunboat "Estoc" pass under the Pont des Arts, going up Seine. She is a fine vessel and her big gun has a terribly grand appearance.

---

* One of the editors of the "Rappel."

December 18

I worked a magic lantern for little Georges and little Jeanne.

My royalty for Mme. Favart's recitation of *Stella* at a performance given by the 14th Battalion amounted to 130 francs. My agent took my royalty in spite of my instructions. I have ordered him to turn the money over to the sick fund of the battalion.

M. Hetzel writes: "The closing of the printing office is imminent, as I can get no more coal to keep the presses going."

I authorise another issue of 3,000 copies of *Les Châtiments*, which will bring the total for Paris up to 22,000.

December 20

Captain Breton, of the Garde Mobile, who has been cashiered on the charge of being a coward, brought against him by his lieutenant-colonel, demands a court-martial, but first of all to be sent to the firing line. His company leaves tomorrow morning. He begs me to obtain for him from the Minister of War permission to go and get himself killed. I have written to General Le Flô about him. It is likely that he will take part in tomorrow's battle.

December 21

At 3 o'clock this morning I heard the bugles of the troops marching to battle. When will my turn come?

December 22

Yesterday was a good day. The action continues. The thunder of cannon can be heard to the east and west.

Little Jeanne begins to talk at length and very expressively. But it is impossible to understand a word she says. She laughs.

Leopold has sent me thirteen fresh eggs, which I will reserve for little Georges and little Jeanne.

Louis Blanc came to dine with me. He came on behalf of Edmond Adam, Louis Jourdan, Cernuschi and others to tell me that he and I must go to Trochu and summon him to save Paris or resign. I refused. I should be posing as an arbiter of the situation and at the same time hamper a battle begun and which may be a successful one. Louis Blanc was of my way of thinking, as were also Meurice, Vacquerie and my sons, who dined with us.

Henri Rochefort came to dine with me. I had not seen him since August of last year, when we were in Brussels. Georges did not recognise his godfather. I was very cordial. I like him very much. He has great talent and great courage. The dinner was a very merry one, although we are all threatened with incarceration in a Prussian fortress if Paris is captured. After Guernsey, Spandau. So be it.

I bought for 19 francs at the Magasins du Louvre a soldier's cape with hood, to wear on the ramparts.

My house continues to be crowded with visitors. Today a painter named Le Genissel called. He reminded me that I saved him from the galleys in 1848. He was one of the insurgents of June.

Heavy cannonade during the night. A battle is in preparation.

December 24

It is freezing. Ice floes are floating down the Seine.

Paris only eats brown bread now.

December 25

Heavy cannonade all night.

An item of news of present-day Paris: A basket of oysters has just reached the city. It sold for 750 francs.

At a bazar in aid of the poor at which Alice and Mme. Meurice acted as vendors, a young turkey fetched 250 francs.

The Seine is freezing over.

December 26

Louis Blanc called, then M. Floquet. They urge me to summon the Government to do something or resign. Again I refuse.

M. Louis Koch paid 25 francs for a copy of the *Rappel* at the bazar in aid of the poor. The copy of *Les Châtiments* was purchased by M. Cernuschi for 300 francs.

December 27

Violent cannonade this morning. The firing of this morning was an attack by the Prussians. A good sign. Waiting annoys them. Us, too. They threw nineteen shells, which killed nobody, into the Fort of Montrouge.

Mme. Ugalde dined with us and sang "Patria." I escorted Mme. Ugalde to her home in the Rue de Chabanais, then returned to bed.

The concierge said to me:

"Monsieur, they say that bombs will fall in this neighbourhood tonight."

"That is all right," I replied. "I am expecting one."

December 29

Heavy firing all night. The Prussians continue their attack.

Théophile Gautier has a horse. This horse was requisitioned. It was wanted for food. Gautier wrote me begging me save the animal. I asked the Minister to grant his request.

I saved the horse.

It is unfortunately true that Dumas is dead. This has been ascertained through the German newspapers. He died on December 5 at the home of his son at Puys, near Dieppe.

I am being urged more strongly than ever, to enter the Government. The Minister of Justice, M. Emmanuel Arago, called and stopped to dinner. We talked. Louis Blanc dropped in after dinner. I persist in my refusal.

Besides Emmanuel Arago and the friends who usually dine with me on Thursdays, Rochefort and Blum came. I invited them to come every Thursday if we have many more Thursdays to live. At desert I drank Rochefort's health.

The cannonade is increasing. The plateau of Avron had to be evacuated.

December 31

D'Alton-Shée paid a visit to me this morning. It appears that General Ducros wants to see me.

Within three days the Prussians have sent us 12,000 shells.

Yesterday I ate some rat, and then hiccoughed the following quatrain:

O mesdames les hétaires
Dans vos greniers, je me nourris:
Moi qui mourais de vos sourires,
Je vais vivre de vos souris.

After next week there will be no more washing done in Paris, because there is no more coal.

Lieutenant Farcy, commander of the gunboat, dined with me.

It is bitterly cold. For three days I have worn my cloak and hood whenever I have had to go out.

A doll for little Jeanne. A basketful of toys for Georges.

Shells have begun to demolish the Fort of Rosny. The first shell has fallen in the city itself. The Prussians today fired 6,000 shells at us.

In the Fort of Rosny a sailor working at the gabions was carrying a sack of earth. A shell knocked it off his shoulder. "Much obliged," commented the sailor, "but I wasn't tired."

Alexandre Dumas died on December 5. On looking over my notebook I see that it was on December 5 that a large hearse with an "H" on it passed before me in the Rue Frochot.

We have no longer even horse to eat. *Perhaps* it is dog? *Maybe* it is rat? I am beginning to suffer from pains in the stomach. We are eating the unknown!

M. Valois, representing the Société des Gens de Lettres, came to ask me what was to be done with the 3,000 francs remaining from the proceeds of the three readings of Les Châtiments, the guns having been delivered and paid for. I told him that I wanted the whole amount turned over to Mme. Jules Simon for the fund for the victims of the war.

January 1, 1871

Louis Blanc has addressed to me through the newspapers a letter upon the situation.

Stupor and amazement of little Georges and little Jeanne at their basketful of New Year presents. The toys, when unpacked from the basket, covered a large table. The children touched all of them and did not know which to take. Georges was nearly furious with joy. Charles remarked: "It is the despair of joy!"

I am hungry. I am cold. So much the better. I suffer what the people are suffering.

Decidedly horse is not good for me. Yet I ate some. It gives me the gripes. I avenged myself at dessert with the following distich:

> Mon diner m'inquiete et même me harcêle,
> J'ai mange du cheval et je songe a la selle.

The Prussians are bombarding Saint Denis.

January 2

Daumier and Louis Blanc lunched with us.

Louis Koch gave to his aunt as a New Year gift a couple of cabbages and a brace of living partridges!

This morning we lunched on wine soup. The elephant at the Jardin des Plantes has been slaughtered. He wept. He will be eaten.

The Prussians continue to send us 6,000 bombs a day.

January 3

The heating of two rooms at the Pavillon de Rohan now costs 10 francs a day.

The Mountaineers' club again demands that Louis Blanc and I be added to the Government in order to direct it. I continue to refuse.

There are at present twelve members of the French Academy in Paris, among them Ségur, Mignet, Dufaure, d'Haussonville, Legouvé, Cuvillier-Fleury, Barbier and Vitet.

Moon. Intense cold. The Prussians bombarded Saint Denis all night.

From Tuesday to Sunday the Prussians hurled 25,000 projectiles at us. It required 220 railway trucks to transport them. Each shot costs 60 francs; total, 1,500,000 francs. The damage to the forts is estimated at 1,400 francs. About ten men have been killed. Each of our dead cost the Prussians 150,000 francs.

January 5

The bombardment is becoming heavier. Issy and Vanves are being shelled.

There is no coal. Clothes cannot be washed because they cannot be dried. My washerwoman sent this message to me through Mariette:

"If M. Victor Hugo, who is so powerful, would ask the Government to give me a little coal-dust, I could wash his shirts."

Besides my usual Thursday guests I had Louis Blanc, Rochefort and Paul de Saint Victor to dinner. Mme. Jules Simon sent me a Gruyère cheese. An extraordinary luxury, this. We were thirteen at table.

January 6

At dessert yesterday I offered some bonbons to the ladies, saying as I did so:

Grace a Boissier, chêre colombes,
Heureux, a vos pieds nous tombons.
Car on prend les forts par les bombes
Et les faibles par les bonbons.

The Parisians out of curiosity visit the bombarded districts. They go to see the shells fall as they would go to a fireworks display. National Guards have to keep the people back. The Prussians are firing on the hospitals. They are bombarding Val-de-Grâce. Their shells set fire to the wooden booths in the Luxembourg, which were full of sick and wounded men, who had to be transported, undressed and wrapped up as well as they could be, to the Charité Hospital. Barbieux saw them arrive there about 1 o'clock in the morning.

Sixteen streets have already been hit by shells.

January 7

The Rue des Feuillantines, which runs through the place where the garden of my boyhood used to be, is heavily bombarded. I was nearly struck by a shell there.

My washerwoman having nothing to make a fire with, and being obliged to refuse work in consequence, addressed a demand to M. Clémenceau, Mayor of the Ninth Arrondissement, for some coal, which she said she was prepared to pay for. I endorsed it thus:

"I am resigned to everything for the defence of Paris, to die of hunger and cold, and even to forego a change of shirt. However, I commend my laundress to the Mayor of the Ninth Arrondissement."

And I signed my name. The Mayor gave her the coal.

January 8

Camille Pelletan brought us good news from the Government. Rouen and Dijon retaken, Garibaldi victorious at Nuits, and Fraidherbe at Bapaume. All goes well.

We had brown bread, now we have black bread. Everybody fares alike. It is well.

The news of yesterday was brought by two pigeons.

A shell killed five children in a school in the Rue de Vaugirard.

The performances and readings of *Les Châtiments* have had to be stopped, the theatres being without gas or coal, therefore without light or heat.

Prim is dead. He was shot and killed at Madrid the day the king after his own heart, Amedeus, Duke of Genoa, entered Spain.

The bombardment was a furious one today. A shell crashed through the chapel of the Virgin at Saint Sulpice, where my mother's funeral took place and where I was married.

January 10

Bombs on the Odéon Theatre.

Chifflard sent me a piece of a shell. This shell, which fell at Auteuil, is marked with an "H." I will have an inkstand made out of it.

January 12

The Pavilion de Rohan demands of me from today on 8 francs a head for dinner, which with wine, coffee, fire, etc., brings the cost of dinner up to 13 francs for each person.

We had elephant steak for luncheon today.

Schoelcher, Rochefort, Blum and all the usual Thursday guests dined with us. After dinner Louis Blanc and Pelletan dropped in.

January 13

An egg costs 2 francs 75 centimes. Elephant meat costs 40 francs a pound. A sack of onions costs 800 francs.

The Société des Gens de Lettres asked me to attend the presentation of the cannon to the city at the Hotel de Ville. I begged to be excused. I will not go.

We spent the day looking for another hotel. Could not find one suitable. All are closed. Expenses for the week at the Pavilion de Rohan (including the cost of a broken window-pane), 701 francs 50 centimes.

Remark by a poor woman anent some newly felled wood:

"This hapless green wood is under fire; it didn't expect that it would have to face it, and weeps all the time!"

January 15

A furious bombardment is in progress.

I have written a piece of poetry entitled "Dans le Cirque." After dinner I read it to my Sunday guests. They want me to publish it. I will give it to the newspapers.

The bombardment has been going on for three nights and three days without cessation.

Little Jeanne was cross with me because I would not let her play with the works of my watch.

All the newspapers publish my verses "Dans le Cirque." They may be useful.

Louis Blanc called this morning. He urged me to join with Quinet and himself in bringing pressure to bear upon the Government. I replied: "I see more danger in overturning the Government than in supporting it."

M. Krupp is making cannon for use specially against balloons.

There is a cock in my little garden. Yesterday Louis Blanc lunched with us. The cock crowed. Louis Blanc paused and said:

"Listen!"

"What is it?"

"A cock is crowing."

"Well, what of it?"

"Don't you hear what it says?"

"It is calling: 'Victor Hugo!'"

We listened and laughed. Louis Blanc was right It did sound as if the cock were crowing my name.

I gave some of my bread-crumbs to the fowls. They would not eat them.

This morning a sortie against Montretout was made. Montretout was taken. This evening the Prussians captured it from us again.

The attack on Montretout has interrupted the bombardment.

A child of fourteen years was suffocated in a crowd outside a baker's shop.

Louis Blanc came to see me. We held a council. The situation is becoming extreme and supreme. The Mairie of Paris asks my advice.

Louis Blanc dined with us. After dinner we held a sort of council at which Colonel Laussedat was present.

January 22

The Prussians are bombarding Saint Denis.

Tumultuous demonstrations at the Hotel de Ville. Trochu is withdrawing. Rostan comes to tell me that the Breton mobiles are firing on the people. I doubt it. I will go myself, if necessary.

I have just returned. There was a simultaneous attack by both sides. To the combatants who consulted me I said: "I recognise in the hands of Frenchmen only those rifles which are turned towards the Prussians."

Rostan said to me:

"I have come to place my battalion at your service. We are five hundred men. Where do you want us to go?"

"Where are you now?" I asked.

"We have been massed towards Saint Denis, which is being bombarded," he replied. "We are at La Villette."

"Then stay there," said I. "It is there where I should have sent you. Do not march against the Hotel de Ville, march against Prussia."

January 23

Last night there was a conference at my quarters. In addition to my Sunday guests Rochefort and his secretary, Mourot, had dined with us. Rey and Gambon came in the evening. They brought me, the former with a request that I would subscribe to it, Ledru-Rollin's poster-programme (group of 200 members), and the latter, the programme of the Republican Union (50 members). I declared that I approved of neither the one nor the other.

Chanzy has been beaten. Bourbaki has succeeded. But he is not marching on Paris. Enigma, of which I fancy I can half guess the secret.

There appears to be an interruption to the bombardment.

January 24

Flourens called this morning. He asked for my advice. I responded: "No violent pressure on the situation."

January 25

Flourens is reported to have been arrested as he was leaving the house after his visit to me.

I had a couple of fresh eggs cooked for Georges and Jeanne.

M. Dorian came to the Pavilion de Rohan this morning to see my sons. He announced that capitulation is imminent. Frightful news from outside. Chanzy defeated, Faidherbe defeated, Bourbaki driven back.

January 27

Schoelcher came to tell me that he has resigned as colonel of the artillery legion.

Again they came to ask me to head a demonstration against the Hotel de Ville. All sorts of rumours are in circulation. To everybody I counsel calmness and unity.

January 28

Bismarck in the course of the pourparlers at Versailles said to Jules Favre: "What do you think of that goose of an Empress proposing peace to me!"

It has become cold again.

Ledru-Rollin (through Brives) says he wants to come to an understanding with me.

Little Jeanne is unwell. Sweet little thing!

Leopold told me this evening that I was the subject of a dialogue between Pope Pius IX and Jules Hugo, my nephew, brother of Leopold, who died a camerico of the Pope. The Pope, on seeing Jules, said to him:

"You name is Hugo, is it not?"

"Yes, Holy Father."

"Are you a relative of Victor Hugo?"

"His nephew, Holy Father."

"How old is he?" (It was in 1857.)

"Fifty-five years."

"Alas! he is too old to return to the Church!"

Charles tells me that Jules Simon and his two sons passed the night drawing up lists of possible candidates for the National Assembly.

Cernuschi is having himself naturalized a French citizen!

January 29

The armistice was signed yesterday. It was published this morning. The National Assembly will be elected between February 5 and 18. Will meet on the 12th at Bordeaux.

Little Jeanne is a trifle better. She almost smiled at me.

No more balloons. The post. But unsealed letters. It snows. It freezes.

January 30

Little Jeanne is still poorly and does not play.

Mlle. Périga brought me a fresh egg for Jeanne.

January 31

Little Jeanne is still ill. She is suffering from a slight attack of catarrh of the stomach. Doctor Allix says it will last for another four or five days.

My nephew Leopold came to dine with us. He brought us some pickled oysters.

February 1

Little Jeanne is better. She smiled at me.

February 2

The Paris elections have been postponed to February 8.

Horsemeat continues to disagree with me. Pains in the stomach. Yesterday I said to Mme. Ernest Lefèvre, who was dining beside me:

De ces bons animaux la viande me fait mal.
J'aime tant les chevaux que je hais le cheval.

February 4

The weather is becoming milder.

A crowd of visitors this evening. Proclamation by Gambetta.

February 5

The list of candidates of the Republican journals appeared this morning. I am at the head of the list.

Bancal is dead.

Little Jeanne this evening has recovered from her cold.

I entertained my usual Sunday guests. We had fish, butter and white bread for dinner.

February 6

Bourbaki, defeated, has killed himself. A grand death.

Ledru-Rollin is drawing back from the Assembly. Louis Blanc came and read this news to me tonight.

February 7

We had three or four cans of preserves which we ate today.

February 8

Today, elections for the National Assembly. Paul Meurice and I went to vote together in the Rue Clauzel.

After the capitulation had been signed, Bismarck, on leaving Jules Favre, entered the room where his two secretaries were awaiting him and said: "The beast is dead."

I have put my papers in order in anticipation of my departure.

Little Jeanne is very merry.

February 11

The counting of the votes progresses very slowly.

Our departure for Bordeaux has been put off to Monday the 13th.

February 12

Yesterday, for the first time, I saw my boulevard. It is a rather large section of the old Boulevard Haussmann. "Boulevard Victor Hugo" is placarded on the Boulevard Haussmann at four or five street corners giving on to this boulevard.

The National Assembly opens today at Bordeaux. The result of the elections in Paris has not yet been determined and proclaimed.

While I have not yet been appointed, time presses, and I expect to leave for Bordeaux tomorrow. There will be nine of us, five masters and four servants, plus the two children. Louis Blanc wants to leave with us. We shall make the journey together.

In my hand-bag I shall take various important manuscripts and works that I have begun, among others, *Paris Besieged* and the poem "Grand Père."

February 13

Yesterday, before dinner, I read to my guests, M. and Mme. Paul Meurice, Vacquerie, Lockroy, M. and Mme. Ernest Lefevre, Louis Koch and Vilain (Rochefort and Victor did not arrive until the dinner hour), two pieces of poetry which will form part of Paris Besieged ("To Little Jeanne," and "No, You will not Take Alsace and Lorraine").

Pelleport brought me our nine passes. Not having yet been proclaimed a Representative, I wrote on mine: "Victor Hugo, proprietor," as the

Prussians require that the quality or profession of the holder of the pass be stated.

It was with a heavy heart that I quitted this morning the Avenue Frochot and the sweet hospitality that Paul Meurice had extended to me since my arrival in Paris on September 5.

The Assembly at Bordeaux.
Extracts from Note-Books

February 14

Left yesterday at 12.10 P.M. Arrived at Etampes at 3.15. Wait of two hours, and luncheon.

After lunch we returned to our drawing-room car. A crowd surrounded it, kept back by a squad of Prussian soldiers. The crowd recognised me and shouted "Long live Victor Hugo!" I waved my hand out of window, and doffing my cap, shouted: "Long live France!" Whereupon a man with a white moustache, who somebody said was the Prussian commandant of Etampes, advanced towards me with a threatening air and said something to me in German that he no doubt intended to be terrible. Gazing steadily in turn at this Prussian and the crowd, I repeated in a louder voice: "Long live France'!" Thereat all the people shouted enthusiastically: "Long live France!" The fellow looked angry but said nothing. The Prussian soldiers did not move.

The journey was a rough, long and weary one. The drawing-room car was badly lighted and not heated. One feels the dilapidation of France in this wretched railway accommodation. At Vierzon we bought a pheasant, a chicken, and two bottles of wine for supper. Then we wrapped ourselves up in our rugs and cloaks and slept on the seats.

We arrived at Bordeaux at 1.30 this afternoon. We went in search of lodgings. We took a cab and drove from hotel to hotel. No room anywhere. I went to the Hotel de Ville and asked for information. I was told that there was an apartment to let at M. A. Porte's, 13, Rue Saint Maur, near the public garden. We went there. Charles hired the apartment for 600 francs a month and paid half a month's rent in advance. Then we started out in search of a lodging for us, but could not get one. At 7 o'clock we returned to the station to fetch our trunks, and not knowing where we should pass the night. We went back to the Rue Saint Maur, where Charles is, negotiated with the landlord and his brother, who had a couple of rooms at 37, Rue de la Course, hard by, and came to an arrangement at last.

Alice made this remark:

"The number 13 clings to us. We were thirteen at table every Thursday in January. We left Paris on February 13. There were thirteen of us in the railway carriage, counting Louis Blanc, M. Béchet and the two children. We are lodging at 13, Rue Saint Maur!"

February 15

At 2 o'clock I went to the Assembly. When I came out again I found an immense crowd awaiting me in the great square. The people, and the National Guards who lined the approaches to the building, shouted: "Long live Victor Hugo!" I replied: "Long live the Republic! Long live France!" They repeated this double cry. Then the enthusiasm became delirium. It was a repetition of the ovation I met with on my arrival in Paris. I was moved to tears. I took refuge in a café at the corner of the square. I explained in a speech why I did not address the people, then I escaped—that is the word—in a carriage.

While the enthusiastic people shouted "Long live the Republic!" the members of the Assembly issued and filed past impassible, almost furious, and with their hats on, in the midst of the bare heads and the waving caps about me.

Visit from Representatives Le Flo, Rochefort, Locroy, Alfred Naquet, Emmanuel Arago, Rességuier, Floquot, Eugene Pelletan, and Noel Parfait.

I slept in my new lodging at 37, Rue de la Course.

February 16

At the Assembly today the result of the Paris elections was proclaimed. Louis Blanc was first with 216,000 votes; then came myself with 214,000 votes, then Garibaldi with 200,000.

The ovation extended to me by the people yesterday is regarded by the Majority as an insult to it. Hence a great display of troops on the square outside (army, National Guard and cavalry). There was an incident in this connection before my arrival. The men of the Right demanded that the Assembly be protected. (Against whom? Against me?) The Left replied with the shout of: "Long live the Republic!"

When I was leaving I was notified that the crowd was waiting for me in the square. To escape the ovation I went out by a side door, but the people caught sight of me, and I was immediately surrounded by an immense crowd shouting: "Long live Victor Hugo!" I replied: "Long live the Republic!" Everybody, including the National Guards and soldiers of the line, took up the shout. I drove away in a carriage, which the people followed.

The Assembly today elected its committees. Dufaure proposes Thiers as chief of the executive power.

We dined at home for the first time. I had invited Louis Blanc, Schoelcher, Rochefort and Lockroy. Rochefort was unable to come. After dinner we went to Gent's, Quay des Chartrons, to attend a meeting of the Left. My sons accompanied me. The question of the chief executive was discussed. I had the following added to the definition: appointed by the Assembly and revokable by that body.

General Cremer came this morning to enlighten us concerning the disposition of the army.

February 17

At the Assembly Gambetta came up to me and said: "Master, when can I see you? I have a good many things to explain to you."

Thiers has been named chief of the executive power. He is to leave tonight for Versailles, the headquarters of the Prussians.

February 18

Tonight there was a meeting of the Left, in the Rue Lafaurie-Monbadon. The meeting chose me as president. The speakers were Louis Blanc, Schoelcher, Colonel Langlois, Brisson, Lockroy, Millière, Clémenceau, Martin Bernard, and Joigneaux. I spoke last and summed up the debate. Weighty questions were brought up—the Bismarck-Thiers treaty, peace, war, the intolerance of the Assembly, and the case in which it would be advisable to resign in a body.

February 19

The president of the National Club of Bordeaux came to place his salons at my disposal.

My hostess, Mme. Porte, a very pretty woman, has sent me a bouquet.

Thiers has appointed his Ministers. He has assumed the equivocal and suspicious title of "head president of the executive power." The Assembly is to adjourn. We are to be notified at our residences when it is to be convened again.

February 20

Today the people again acclaimed me when I came out of the Assembly. The crowd in an instant became enormous. I was compelled to take refuge in the lodging of Martin Bernard, who lives in a street adjacent to the Assembly.

I spoke in the Eleventh Committee. The question of the magistracy (which has petitioned us not to act against it) came up unexpectedly. I spoke well. I rather terrified the committee.

Little Jeanne is more than ever adorable. She does not want to leave me at all now.

February 21

Mme. Porte, my hostess of the Rue de la Course, sends me a bouquet every morning by her little daughter.

I take little Georges and little Jeanne out whenever I have a minute to spare. I might very well be dubbed: "Victor Hugo, Representative of the People and dry nurse."

Tonight I presided at the meeting of the Radical Left.

February 25

Tonight there was a meeting of the two fractions of the Left, the Radical Left and Political Left, in the hall of the Academy, in the Rue Jacques Bell. The speakers were Louis Blanc, Emmanuel Arago, Vacherot, Jean Brunet, Bethmont, Peyrat, Brisson, Gambetta, and myself. I doubt whether my plan for fusion or even for an *entente cordiale* will succeed. Schoelcher and Edmond Adam walked home with me.

February 26

I am 69 years old today.

I presided at a meeting of the Left.

February 27

I have resigned the presidency of the Radical Left in order to afford full independence to the meeting.

February 28

Thiers read the treaty (of peace) from the tribune today. It is hideous. I shall speak tomorrow. My name is the seventh on the list, but Grévy, the president of the Assembly, said to me: "Rise and ask to be heard when you want to. The Assembly will hear you."

Tonight there was a meeting of the Assembly committees. I belong to the eleventh. I spoke.

March 1

There was a tragical session today. The Empire was executed, also France, alas! The Shylock-Bismarck treaty was adopted. I spoke.

Louis Blanc spoke after me, and spoke grandly.

I had Louis Blanc and Charles Blanc to dinner.

This evening I went to the meeting in the Rue Lafaurie-Monbadon over which I have ceased to preside. Schoelcher presided. I spoke. I am satisfied with myself.

March 2

Charles has returned. No session today. The adoption of peace has opened the Prussian net. I have received a packet of letters and newspapers from Paris. Two copies of the *Rappel*.

We dined *en famille*, all five of us. Then I went to the meeting.

Seeing that France has been mutilated, the Assembly ought to withdraw. It has caused the wound and is powerless to cure it. Let another Assembly replace it. I would like to resign. Louis Blanc does not want to. Gambetta and Rochefort are of my way of thinking. Debate.

March 3

This morning the Mayor of Strasburg, who died of grief, was buried.

Louis Blanc called in company with three Representatives, Brisson, Floquet and Cournet. They came to consult me as to what ought to be done about the resignation question. Rochefort and Pyat, with three others, are resigning. I am in favour of resigning. Louis Blanc resists. The remainder of the Left do not appear to favour resignation *en masse*.

Session.

As I ascended the stairs I heard a fellow belonging to the Right, whose back only I could see, say to another: "Louis Blanc is execrable, but Victor Hugo is worse."

We all dined with Charles, who had invited Louis Blanc and MM. Lavertujon and Alexis Bouvier.

Afterwards we went to the meeting in the Rue Lafaurie-Monbadon. The President of the Assembly having, on behalf of the Assembly, delivered a farewell address to the retiring members for Alsace and Lorraine, my motion to maintain their seats indefinitely, which was approved by the meeting, is without object, inasmuch as the question is settled. The meeting, however, appears to hold to it. We will consider the matter.

Meeting of the Left. M. Millière proposed, as did also M. Delescluze, a motion of impeachment against the Government of the National Defence. He concluded by saying that whoever failed to join him in pressing the motion was a "dupe or an accomplice."

Schoelcher rose and said:

"Neither dupe nor accomplice. You lie!"

March 5

Session of the Assembly.

Meeting in the evening. Louis Blanc, instead of a formal impeachment of the ex-Government of Paris, demands an inquiry. I subscribe to this. We sign.

Meeting of the Left. They say there is great agitation in Paris. The Government which usually never receives less than fifteen dispatches a day from Paris has not received a single one up to 10 o'clock tonight. Six telegrams sent to Jules Favre have not been answered. We decide that either Louis Blanc or I will interpellate the Government as to the situation in Paris, if the present anxiety continues and no light is thrown upon the situation.

A deputation of natives of Alsace and Lorraine came to thank us.

March 6

At noon we lunched *en famille* at Charles's. I took the two ladies to the Assembly. There is talk of transferring the Assembly to Versailles or Fontainebleau. They are afraid of Paris. I spoke at the meeting of the Eleventh Committee. I was nearly elected commissioner. I got 18 votes, but a M. Lucien Brun got 19.

Meeting in the Rue Lafaurie. I proposed that we all refuse to discuss the situation in Paris, and that a manifesto be drawn up, to be signed by all of us, declaring our intention to resign if the Assembly goes anywhere else than to Paris. The meeting did not adopt my plan, and urged me to speak tomorrow. I refused. Louis Blanc will speak.

March 8

I have handed in my resignation as a Representative.

There was a discussion about Garibaldi. He had been elected in Algeria. It was proposed that the election be annulled. I demanded to be heard. I spoke. Uproar on the Right. They shouted: "Order! Order!"

It all reads very curiously in the "Moniteur." In face of this explosion of wrath I made a gesture with my hand and said:

"Three weeks ago you refused to hear Garibaldi. Now you refuse to hear me. That is enough. I will resign."

I went to the meeting of the Left for the last time.

March 9

This morning three members of the Moderate Left, which meets in the hall of the Academy, came as delegates from that body, the 220 members of which unanimously requested me to withdraw my resignation. M. Paul Bethmon acted as spokesman. I thanked them, but declined.

Then delegates from another meeting came with the same object. The meeting of the Central Left, to which MM. d'Haussonville and de Rémusat belong, unanimously requested me to withdraw my resignation. M. Target acted as spokesman. I thanked them, but declined.

Louis Blanc ascended the tribune (in the Assembly) and bade me farewell with grandeur and nobleness.

March 10

Louis Blanc spoke yesterday and today—yesterday about my resignation, today about the question of Paris. Grandly and nobly on each occasion.

March 11

We are preparing for our departure.

March 12

Many visits. My apartment was crowded. M. Michel Levy came to ask me for a book. M. Duquesnel, associate director of the Odéon Theatre, came to ask me for *Ruy Blas*.

We shall probably leave tomorrow.

Charles, Alice and Victor went to Arcachon. They returned to dinner.

Little Georges, who has been unwell, is better.

Louis Blanc dined with me. He is going to Paris.

March 13

Last night I could not sleep. Like Pythagoras, I was thinking of numbers. I thought of all these 13's so queerly associated with our movements and actions since the first of January, and upon the fact that I was to leave this house on a 13th. Just then there was the same nocturnal knocking (three taps, as though made by a hammer on a board) that I had heard twice before in this room.

We lunched at Charles's, with Louis Blanc.

I then went to see Rochefort. He lives at 80, Rue Judaique. He is convalescent from an attack of erysipelas that at one time assumed a dangerous character. With him I found MM. Alexis Bouvier and Mourot, whom I invited to dinner today, at the same time asking them to transmit my invitation to MM. Claretie, Guillemot and Germain Casse, with whom I want to shake hands before I go.

On leaving Rochefort's I wandered a little about Bordeaux. Fine church, partly Roman. Pretty Gothic flowered tower. Superb Roman ruin (Rue du Colysée) which they call the Palais Gallien.

Victor came to embrace me. He left for Paris at 6 o'clock with Louis Blanc.

At half past 6 I went to Lanta's restaurant. MM. Bouvier, Mourot and Casse arrived. Then Alice. We waited for Charles.

Charles died at 7 o'clock.

The waiter who waits upon me at Lanta's restaurant entered and told me that somebody wanted to see me. In the ante-chamber I found M. Porte, who lets the apartment at 13, Rue Saint Maur, that Charles occupied. M. Porte whispered to me to get Alice, who had followed me, out of the way. Alice returned to the salon. M. Porte said to me:

"Monsieur be brave. Monsieur Charles—"

"Well?"

"He is dead!"

Dead! I could not believe it. Charles! I leaned against the wall for support.

M. Porte told me that Charles had taken a cab to go to Lanta's, but had told the cabman to drive first to the Café de Bordeaux. Arrived at the Café de Bordeaux, the driver on opening the door of the cab, found Charles dead. He had been stricken with apoplexy. A number of blood vessels had burst. He was covered with blood, which issued from his nose and mouth. The doctor summoned pronounced him dead.

I would not believe it. I said: "It is a lethargy." I still hoped. I returned to the salon, told Alice that I was going out, but would soon be back, and ran to the Rue Saint Maur. I had hardly reached there when they brought Charles.

Alas! my beloved Charles! He was dead.

I went to fetch Alice. What despair!

The two children were asleep.

I have read again what I wrote on the morning of the 13th about the knocking I heard during the night.

Charles has been laid out in the salon on the ground floor of the house in the Rue Saint Maur. He lies on a bed covered with a sheet which the women of the house have strewn with flowers. Two neighbours, workingmen who love me, asked permission to watch by the body all night. The coroner's physician, on uncovering the dear dead, wept.

I sent to Meurice a telegram couched in the following terms:

Meurice, 18 Rue Valois—

Appalling misfortune. Charles died this evening, 13th. Sudden stroke of apoplexy. Tell Victor to come back at once.

The Prefect sent this telegram over the official wire.

We shall take Charles with us. Meanwhile he will be placed in the depository.

MM. Alexis Bouvier and Germain Casse are helping me in these heart-rending preparations.

At 4 o'clock Charles was placed in the coffin. I prevented them from fetching Alice. I kissed the brow of my beloved, then the sheet of lead was soldered. Next they put the oaken lid of the coffin on and screwed it down; thus I shall never see him more. But the soul remains. If I did not believe in the soul I would not live another hour.

I dined with my grandchildren, little Georges and little Jeanne.

I consoled Alice. I wept with her. I said "thou" to her for the first time.

March 15

For two nights I have not slept. I could not sleep last night.

Edgar Quinet came to see me last evening. On viewing Charles's coffin in the parlor, he said:

"I bid thee adieu, great mind, great talent, great soul, beautiful of face, more beautiful of thought, son of Victor Hugo!"

We talked together of this great mind that is no more. We were calm. The night watcher wept as he listened to us.

The Prefect of the Gironde called. I could not receive him.

This morning at 10 o'clock I went to No. 13, Rue Saint Maur. The hearse was there. MM. Bouvier and Mourot awaited me. I entered the salon. I kissed the coffin. Then he was taken away. There was one carriage. These gentlemen and I entered it. Arrived at the cemetery the coffin was taken from the hearse. Six men carried it. MM. Alexis Bouvier, Mourot and I followed, bareheaded. It was raining in torrents. We walked behind the coffin.

At the end of a long alley of plane trees we found the depository, a vault lighted only by the door. You descend five or six steps to it. Several coffins were waiting there, as Charles's will wait. The bearers entered with the coffin. As I was about to follow, the keeper of the depository said to me: "No one is allowed to go in." I understood, and I respected this solitude of the dead. MM. Alexis Bouvier and Mourot took me back to No. 13, Rue Saint Maur.

Alice was in a swoon. I gave her some vinegar to smell and beat her hands. She came to, and said: "Charles, where art thou?"

I am overcome with grief.

March 16

At noon Victor arrived with Barbieux and Louis Mie. We embraced in silence and wept. He handed me a letter from Meurice and Vacquerie.

We decide that Charles shall be buried in the tomb of my father in Père Lachaise, in the place that I had reserved for myself. I write a letter to Meurice and Vacquerie in which I announce that I shall leave with the coffin tomorrow and that we shall arrive in Paris the following day. Barbieux will leave tonight and take the letter to them.

March 17

We expect to leave Bordeaux with my Charles at 6 o'clock this evening.

Victor and I, with Louis Mie, fetched Charles from the Depository, and took him to the railway station.

March 18

We left Bordeaux at 6.30 in the evening and arrived in Paris at 10.30 this morning.

At the railway station we were received in a salon where the newspapers, which had announced our arrival for noon, were handed to me. We waited. Crowd; friends.

At noon we set out for Père Lachaise. I followed the hearse bareheaded. Victor was beside me. All our friends followed, the people too. As the procession passed there were cries of: "Hats off!"

In the Place de la Bastille a spontaneous guard of honour was formed about the hearse by National Guards, who passed with arms reversed. All along the line of route to the cemetery battalions of the National Guard were drawn up. They presented arms and gave the salute to the flag. Drums rolled and bugles sounded. The people waited till I had passed, then shouted: "Long live the Republic!"

There were barricades everywhere, which compelled us to make a long detour. Crowd at the cemetery. In the crowd I recognised Rostan and Millière, who was pale and greatly moved, and who saluted me. Between a couple of tombs a big hand was stretched towards me and a voice exclaimed: "I am Courbet." At the same time I saw an energetical and cordial face which was smiling at me with tear-dimmed eyes. I shook the hand warmly. It was the first time that I had seen Courbet.

The coffin was taken from the hearse. Before it was lowered into the vault I knelt and kissed it. The vault was yawning. A stone had been raised. I gazed at the tomb of my father which I had not seen since I was exiled. The cippus has become blackened. The opening was too narrow, and the stone had to be filed. This work occupied half an hour. During that time I gazed at the tomb of my father and the coffin of my son. At last they were able to lower the coffin. Charles will be there with my father, my mother, and my brother.

Mme. Meurice brought a bunch of white lilac which she placed on Charles's coffin. Vacquerie delivered an oration that was beautiful and grand. Louis Mie also bade Charles an eloquent and touching farewell. Flowers were thrown on the tomb. The crowd surrounded me. They grasped my hands. How the people love me, and how I love them! An ardent address of sympathy from the Belleville Club, signed "Millière, president," and "Avril, secretary," was handed to me.

We went home in a carriage with Meurice and Vacquerie. I am broken with grief and weariness. Blessings on thee, my Charles!

A Note About the Author

Victor Hugo (1802–1885) was a French poet and novelist. Born in Besançon, Hugo was the son of a general who served in the Napoleonic army. Raised on the move, Hugo was taken with his family from one outpost to the next, eventually setting with his mother in Paris in 1803. In 1823, he published his first novel, launching a career that would earn him a reputation as a leading figure of French Romanticism. His Gothic novel *The Hunchback of Notre-Dame* (1831) was a bestseller throughout Europe, inspiring the French government to restore the legendary cathedral to its former glory. During the reign of King Louis-Philippe, Hugo was elected to the National Assembly of the French Second Republic, where he spoke out against the death penalty and poverty while calling for public education and universal suffrage. Exiled during the rise of Napoleon III, Hugo lived in Guernsey from 1855 to 1870. During this time, he published his literary masterpiece *Les Misérables* (1862), a historical novel which has been adapted countless times for theater, film, and television. Towards the end of his life, he advocated for republicanism around Europe and across the globe, cementing his reputation as a defender of the people and earning a place at Paris' Panthéon, where his remains were interred following his death from pneumonia. His final words, written on a note only days before his death, capture the depth of his belief in humanity: "To love is to act."

A Note from the Publisher

Spanning many genres, from non-fiction essays to literature classics to children's books and lyric poetry, Mint Edition books showcase the master works of our time in a modern new package. The text is freshly typeset, is clean and easy to read, and features a new note about the author in each volume. Many books also include exclusive new introductory material. Every book boasts a striking new cover, which makes it as appropriate for collecting as it is for gift giving. Mint Edition books are only printed when a reader orders them, so natural resources are not wasted. We're proud that our books are never manufactured in excess and exist only in the exact quantity they need to be read and enjoyed.

bookfinity™

Discover more of your favorite classics with Bookfinity™.

- Track your reading with custom book lists.
- Get great book recommendations for your personalized Reader Type.
- Add reviews for your favorite books.
- AND MUCH MORE!

Visit **bookfinity.com** and take the fun Reader Type quiz to get started.

Enjoy our classic and modern companion pairings!

Classic & Modern

Printed in the USA
CPSIA information can be obtained
at www.ICGtesting.com
JSHW022331140824
68134JS00019B/1425

9 781513 291352